JOHN FAIRFIELD DRYDEN

A STORY OF HUMAN SECURITY

The Prudential

BY

Earl Chapin May

AND

Will Oursler

ILLUSTRATIONS BY E. STANLEY TURNBULL

47531

Doubleday & Company, Inc.

GARDEN CITY, NEW YORK, 1950

Social institutions, like political institutions, can endure only if there is economic justification for their existence, and if they prove their social utility by successful adaptation and re-adaptation to the ever-changing conditions and circumstances of political and social life.

—JOHN FAIRFIELD DRYDEN

Preface

Insurance is a business of people, and this is a history primarily of people and of their quest for security with freedom and self-respect. It is a history of a company of men and women dedicated to the business of providing that kind of security to millions of homes.

On October 13, 1875, when The Prudential Friendly Society first opened for business in Newark, New Jersey, there were no celebrations—and scarcely a ripple of public notice. On October 13, 1950, three quarters of a century later, there were celebrations in many cities of the United States and Canada, birthday parties marking the seventy-fifth anniversary of this same company—The Prudential Insurance Company of America.

The biography of The Prudential is the record of the events, the growth, the expanding service to America between these two widely differing occasions.

It would not have been possible for the authors to tell this story in its basic human terms without the aid of many people. We are particularly indebted to the officials of the company, the president and vice-presidents, department heads and their assistants who provided not only the material and the information needed, but also the freedom to tell the story as we saw it.

We are also grateful for the painstaking research and checking of facts by many of the Prudential staff, and by all those who had part in gathering data and preparing charts and graphs and columns of figures for our guidance.

We are indebted also to the many retired officials of the company who gave of their time and memories and records, to those in the company who provided information through personal accounts and interviews, and to the many others who aided in the preparation of this manuscript.

THE AUTHORS

Contents

Chapter 1: MR. DRYDEN EXPOUNDS AN IDEA   1

Chapter 2: THIS FRAYED YOUNG DREAMER FROM MAINE   18

Chapter 3: A PECULIAR LITTLE COMPANY   40

Chapter 4: MEETING OF THE BOARD   61

Chapter 5: THE BATTLE FOR DEBITS   76

Chapter 6: NEW FIGURES AND HIGH WALLS   99

Chapter 7: GROWTH AND CRISIS   117

Chapter 8: DEATH AND STORM   142

Chapter 9: OF MEN AND MUTUALIZATION   158

Chapter 10: GIBRALTAR—OF MAIN STREET, AMERICA   170

Chapter 11: MR. DUFFIELD'S NEW HORIZONS   185

Chapter 12: A ROOF OVER THEIR HEADS   200

Chapter 13: GROUP GROWS UP   220

Chapter 14: MILLIONS OF CLAIMS—AND MIKE MULLOY   232

Chapter 15: D'OLIER TAKES COMMAND   246

Chapter 16: A COLONEL RETURNS TO THE FRONT   264

Chapter 17: SALESMEN OF SECURITY   276

Chapter 18: INVESTING IN AMERICA   290

Chapter 19: OPERATION NEWARK   306

Chapter 20: DECENTRALIZATION—A MID-CENTURY MILESTONE   316

Chapter 21: CARROL SHANKS TALKS ABOUT TOMORROW   332

                 APPENDIX   345

                 INDEX   357

Illustrations

John Fairfield Dryden   *Frontispiece*

                                                      FACING PAGE
Allen L. Bassett   68

Noah F. Blanchard   84

Forrest F. Dryden   180

Edward D. Duffield   196

Franklin D'Olier   260

Home Office Buildings, Newark   276

Western Home Office Building, Los Angeles   324

Carrol M. Shanks   340

CHAPTER 1

Mr. Dryden
Expounds an Idea

During the afternoon of December 14 the temperature began to drop rapidly. The Indian summer that had persisted through the long fall of 1874 in New Jersey came to an end within a few hours. In Newark the temperature stood at five degrees above zero on the morning of Tuesday the fifteenth, and though the sun shone brightly from a cloudless sky, the cold was intense all day.

It was all the worse for being so unexpected. The Newark *Daily Advertiser* made haste to comment on the change and to recall the delightful weather of the months just past. The warm October rains had broken the drought, and withering leaves on the trees in the better sections had revived in a remarkable display of rich autumn color. Nobody could remember a year when the weather had held off all through November. Two days before Thanksgiving the tail of a freak tornado lashed New Jersey. It flicked at the outskirts of Newark but did no damage. After days of drizzle and warm rain in late November apple trees were reported in bloom in several parts of the city.

The Newark *Daily Advertiser* reported the weather as it reported the other events of the city—with careful selection well flavored with opinion. As a Republican journal it was stunned that day that the new Common Council, elected in the November Democratic landslide, should be considering the expenditure of more than $500,000 to repave Market and Broad streets. Not that the *Advertiser* denied the need to replace the rutted cobbles laid twenty years before. On the contrary. "A journey from one end of Broad Street to the other," it declared briskly in its news report, "is seriously inconvenient—stunningly noisy, destructive to horses, friendly to dirt, and fatal to invalids." But was this the economy the Democrats had promised?

The discussion of the proposal had been unfortunate. For one thing the proponents of the plan pointed out that it would give employment to a "horde of laborers clamoring for work." Some of them put it more bluntly. "There are idle laborers begging for work who may soon be begging for bread without work. They may become an unrequiting expense to the city, or a nightly terror to the people. . . ."

There were a few such extremists in Newark—pessimists who felt that this second winter of recession and panic would be worse than the winter of '73–'74. They pointed at the increasing rate of crime and hinted that with the pinch of cold weather Newark might expect to see the same lawlessness that other cities had experienced. The *Advertiser* chose to share the opinions of the more conservative groups, the people of means, the old established elements that dated back to the founding families of Puritans who had settled here on the Passaic back in 1666.

The fact that Newark had risen rapidly after the war to third place among America's industrial cities was, of course, a matter of pride to the *Advertiser*. It liked to enumerate the extent and variety of Newark's products—leather goods, hats, fertilizer, jewelry, carriages, tools, thread, woolens, lumber, locks. It was a long list, and an impressive one. But as the list grew, certain problems grew with it. A tide was sweeping over the city—a tide of factories and factory hands. German and Irish immigrants were taking over the old neighborhoods, drays were pounding the streets where carriages once had rolled quietly and leisurely, lofts and warehouses were replacing the homes down by the river. Of the 115,000 people in Newark, 70,000 had crowded in within the last fifteen years; 70,000 were either immigrants or sons of immigrants. They pressed against the old conventions, broke down the old values.

There was a problem here, to be sure, but the *Advertiser* was not the journal to seek out problems. The *Advertiser* reported the news of Newark as it saw it—and by preference it saw the brighter side. The lead story that Tuesday in the middle of December was a fine one: The vile abductors of little Charley Ross of Philadelphia had been cornered and shot to death at Fort Hamilton, Long Island. The whole country had been looking for them since midsummer—detectives scouring every city, editors crying vengeance. They had been caught in the middle of the night burglarizing a house, and shot down by a handy man when they attempted to kill him. Lying in a pool of blood, one of them confessed the crime, and begged forgiveness and a decent burial. It was a good story. The *Advertiser* gave it a column with full details, and ran an editorial with a number of moral observations.

The night before, in the rink in Newark's Industrial Exposition Building, Edward Payson Weston, the celebrated pedestrian, had succeeded in walking 115 miles in twenty-four hours. Doctors certified that he had completed the grueling test in excellent physical shape and a minister had immediately announced a sermon on the event with the text "And Enoch walked with God." By telegraph came news of another disastrous fire in Boston, but it was thought the conflagration was under control. Contributions continued to pile up for the victims of the great grasshopper plague in Nebraska, and more large sums were expected in Christmas donations.

That Tuesday there were a variety of local items. There were reports of several successful temperance meetings and announcements of many more to be held soon. The season's first shipment of Florida oranges had been received by Atwater and Carter and A. Ward and Son. Diphtheria was losing ground, although some increase in smallpox was reported. Of the fifty-nine deaths in the city the previous week, fifteen were from consumption and only three from diphtheria. A certain Daniel McGill had been apprehended and accused of breaking into a store the previous Sunday and stealing six quarts of oysters, two knives, and a quart measure.

The *Advertiser* looked about hopefully for some indications of economic recovery to gladden the holiday. It reported that several mills in Manchester, New Hampshire, were planning to go back on full time. On the Chicago Exchange corn prices had risen slightly. Perhaps, after all, the financial disaster of the past months had been exaggerated. In any event, well-run businesses had now narrowed their operations to the closest and safest margin. Merchants had selected their Christmas stocks carefully. "Instead of useless trinkets and toys of a 'flush' Christmas there will be larger purchases of homey and useful articles." Shoes and dry goods, for example.

Perhaps because it was the Christmas season the *Advertiser* neglected to mention certain gloomier facts. It might have reported—but didn't—that at the year's end one half of all the steel plants in the United States were shut down. Nearly 100 railroads were in receivership. Ten thousand commercial houses had closed their doors and released their employees. Even in Newark, which had weathered the storm better than most cities, other observers noted conditions the *Advertiser* had overlooked. A few days earlier the Guild House of Prayer had announced the establishment of a relief store at 372 Broad Street with the statement that "the urgent needs of the poor, especially during the winter months, must be apparent to all." When they opened the doors that Tuesday morning 200 applicants were waiting outside. Many had been standing there for hours.

That was Tuesday, December 15. Although the sun shone brightly from a cloudless sky, it was intensely cold all day.

Dr. Ward's Pharmacy occupied the corner of a flat-roofed two-story building at the junction of Lafayette and Congress streets almost at the center of the old Fifth Ward. This was a gray sprawling section of the town backed up against the Passaic River and sliced by bands of railroad track. Because of the shape of the area it was sometimes called Down Neck, and, in later years, Ironbound.

The neighborhood was old—a middle-class one tapering off toward the north and east to the crowded ramshackle houses of the laborers and the plants along the flats by the river. There had once been some fine old houses Down Neck, and a few of them still stood stubbornly on wide plots of lawn, but down by the railroad tracks and along the river front factories were relentlessly displacing the homes. The Newark Gas Light Company had eaten up a whole block at South Market and Congress. The big sawmills, flour mills, lumberyards, and machine shops had taken almost all of the water front, and around them there was a growing ring of luggage factories, tool shops, and metal working plants. Over on the other side stood the tannery of Blanchard Brothers and Lane on Bruen Street, and on down by the tracks on Railroad Avenue there were several foundries and hat factories and a flour mill or two.

On foggy days the haze drifted in from the marshes and smoke from the mills and factories hung over the housetops. Locomotives dragging long freight trains over the tracks of the Newark and New York and the Pennsylvania scattered soot and cinders over the low wooden stoops. Down Neck was a neighborhood just beginning to go downhill. Caught in a ring of factories, it was turning at the edges respectably but inexorably to rented rooms and crowded back apartments.

Dr. Ward's Pharmacy was the only shop in the block. A weather-beaten apothecary sign—the mortar and pestle—hung obliquely from the corner and swayed a little that morning in the icy wind. The windows of the pharmacy projected out a few inches over the sidewalk and beneath them the sooty clapboard wall was covered by advertisements for the popular patented remedies of the day—the Maine Cough Curer, Duncker's Celebrated Salve, Sanford's Healing Lung Balsam. Just behind the quartered glass panes the traditional emblems of the profession, great globes of red and green liquid, glittered in the morning sun. A hand-lettered sign in the window advertised pharmaceutical items: camphor and spices, sea salt and syrup of sarsaparilla.

It was a cramped little store, scarcely 18 by 20 feet, with dark, too ornately carved shelving lining the walls to the ceiling. On a counter to the rear stood the polished brass balance scales, and on the shelves behind were rows of test tubes, beakers, wooden spatulas, a pill-coater shaped like a wooden egg cup—all the paraphernalia of the pharmacist of the time. A young clerk teetered on a ladder dusting the high shelves and setting in order the rows of gleaming bottles of liniments and emulsions and medical extracts with odd-sounding Latin names in large black letters on the labels.

Behind the pharmacy counter that morning stood the proprietor, young Dr. Leslie D. Ward, wrapping a package of pills he had himself compounded from his own prescription. It was a common practice in those days for physicians to operate their own pharmacies. Uptown, in the better sections, it is true, the custom was being dropped. But Down Neck the old doctors had all owned drugstores and had their offices in the little rooms in the rear. Young doctors coming into the area found that the patients expected them to be druggists too. It somehow gave them more confidence in the medicine.

Young Dr. Ward had carried on the tradition when he took over old Dr. O'Gorman's practice. He had tried to carry on many of the old customs with his people and they liked him for that. Not yet thirty, he was well known and well regarded in the community. A good man, people called him, a good, square, fine-looking man with reddish hair and a gleam in his eyes. They felt that he was something more than pills and medicine. He had a way of talking to you when you came in to get cured, a way of making you realize the importance of proper diet and right living.

The thing about Dr. Ward, they said, was that he cared about people. He was on call day and night, and many a man had stood in Lafayette Street in the early hours of the morning calling and throwing pebbles against the windows of the doctor's room above the drugstore. He had always been ready to come when he was needed. All over the section he had set up slates in stores and shops where people could write their names when they needed him. Early each morning he made his rounds, stopping in to read the names on the slates to know where he was wanted next.

The people Down Neck trusted Dr. Ward. Though he had been in practice only four or five years, they felt that they knew him. He had started with old Dr. Lott Southard and, after a couple of years, had taken over Dr. O'Gorman's practice when the old man died.

It was a little strange that Dr. Ward should be in practice down here. His patients sometimes wondered about it. He came from an old family in New Jersey—a family that sprang from Josiah Ward, one of the original settlers of Newark in 1666. His father owned a fine place near Madison, they said, and Dr. Leslie was sent to Newark Academy to prepare for Princeton College. He was only a boy—no more than sixteen or seventeen—when the War between the States broke out, and he had been one of the first to volunteer, but his unit was soon disbanded and he was sent home to finish his studies. He was to have been the class valedictorian, but on graduation day young Ward wasn't on hand. He was on his way with the 33d New Jersey Regiment—General Grubb's regiment—General Grubb's Game Chickens, they were called.

When he came back, Ward didn't talk much about the war or about the things he had seen, but somewhere along the line he must have found the need to be a doctor, to help others. He studied for a time with old Dr. Fisher in Morristown and later in the College of Physicians and Surgeons in New York. After graduation he had come back to Newark and hung up his shingle in an area rapidly becoming a working-class neighborhood.

It made the people wonder for a time, his coming Down Neck to set up practice, a member of one of the fine old families of the city. He was welcomed in the best homes and might easily have set up practice in one of the wealthier sections with a clientele of elderly ladies with aches and pains. It was a little strange.

But Dr. Ward was a man who loved laughter and good times too. He enjoyed the good social life of the city, and often he would steal away for a few hours to attend a fine dinner party with his bride of only a few months, the former Minnie Perry, daughter of James Perry, the prominent leather manufacturer. His neighbors and patients knew about those parties and liked them. The doctor often told them of the events of the evening before. But still they wondered a little, now that he had married Miss Perry. The newlyweds had moved into a fine home uptown. His patients wondered if the doctor would change his practice now. They thought not. Dr. Ward was a good man, they said, a good, square man.

The young physician finished wrapping the prescription, tied it with a bit of thin red twine, and handed it to his customer, an aging German woman with a shawl over her head. She took it from him silently. "There you are!" He had a hearty, robust voice, full of friendliness and warmth. "Now you're to make Julius take these just as I ordered, once every three hours by the clock. You understand?"

She nodded, her tired eyes looking up into his. "Doctor, like I have told you, we have no—no way right at this moment to——"

Beneath the golden-red curving mustaches the doctor's lips broke into a smile. "Money? Who has money these days? When he's on his feet again and has work, that'll be soon enough. I want him to have plenty of rest and no worry. And be careful with his diet. Make him take liquids. Hot broths. There's plenty of health in good hot broth."

The woman smiled and shook her head. "Julius says broth is for old women and young girls."

The tall young doctor laughed. "If he starts getting ram-

bunctious about it, you let me know." He reached for the
prescription ledger behind him.

As the old lady turned away, the tinkling bell above the
door signaled the arrival of a new customer. A blast of wintry
wind swept in, and the old woman drew her shawl around
her more tightly. Intent on her own worries, she hardly

noticed the man who came in, a tall, austere-looking figure
with a dark brown, square-clipped beard with prematurely
graying sideburns. He wore a long black frock coat and carried a brown envelope bulging with papers.

Dr. Ward closed the ledger in which all prescriptions had
to be posted and placed it on top of other ledgers and the
dog-eared copy of the *United States Dispensatory* on the
shelf immediately behind him. He turned and faced the newcomer—a lean, spare, unsmiling man. In spite of the bitter
day outside, his thin face was exceedingly pale, the physician
noted. He had the appearance of a man who had been working too hard and eating too little. The frock coat, Dr. Ward
also observed, was a little shiny and somewhat worn at the
cuffs.

Yet the man carried himself with an unusual air of dignity.
There was nothing of the ingratiating manner of the hopeful
salesman about him. On the mat just inside the door he
paused and deliberately stamped the dirt from his boots. He

carefully removed his black flat-topped hat and walked slowly to the counter.

His steady blue eyes met those of the young physician. "I am looking," he said, "for Dr. Ward—Dr. Leslie Ward—who is, I believe, the proprietor."

This formal manner of approach was unusual here, and the physician smiled. Most of his patients and customers he called by their first names. "I am Dr. Ward, sir," he said. "At your service."

The stranger seemed momentarily startled. "I had expected an older man, Dr. Ward," he said slowly. "You do not know me, sir, but I have come here to discuss with you a matter of some importance. Allow me to introduce myself. My name is John F. Dryden."

"Delighted to know you, Mr. Dryden—if you're not selling cough drops. I'm pretty well stocked up——"

"I share an office," the unruffled Mr. Dryden continued, "with a friend of yours on Broad Street, Mr. Allen Bassett. It is at his urgent suggestion——"

Dr. Ward's palm slapped the counter. "Oh, Bassett! Of course. Real estate. Or used to be, at least. Last I heard he was trying to raise money for some wild insurance scheme."

The spare figure of Mr. Dryden seemed to grow even taller. "It happens that insurance is what I came here to talk to you about. But it is no wild scheme. It is a very solid business proposition."

The doctor laughed. "Mr. Dryden, I've been married scarcely six months and, do you know, you're the sixth man who's come in here trying to sell me insurance. As I tried to explain to the others——"

"I'm not here to sell you an insurance policy," the thin-faced caller persisted. "I'm offering you an opportunity to participate in establishing a new kind of insurance in this country—insurance for the poor."

Dr. Ward raised a protesting hand. "I'm afraid I'm going to have to disappoint you. I'm not in a position either to buy insurance or to establish any new company. I'm not a wealthy man, and after all——"

After all, he might have finished, insurance firms were failing on all sides nowadays, except for the few solid old companies like Newark's Mutual Benefit. Thousands had lost their money in fly-by-night schemes, and insurance had fallen on lean days.

"Dr. Ward," said Mr. Dryden firmly, "I propose to sell insurance to the working people of Newark—to some of your own patients, sir—at a cost of three cents a week."

The physician leaned forward, incredulous. "How much did you say it would cost?"

"I repeat—as little as three cents a week."

Dr. Ward looked at him a moment and then let out a peal of rich laughter. "Three cents!" he echoed. "What will you people dream up next! How in tarnation for three pennies a week could a policy——" He turned away and began straightening the bottles behind him. "Sorry, Mr. Dryden, I'd like to help these people too. But this sounds like a wild, useless scheme. Three cents a week!"

"For as little as that—yes—we can provide these people with at least enough money to bury their dead decently." For a moment Mr. Dryden seemed to lose his studied manner. His voice took on a new excitement. "Industrial insurance—that's what they call it in England, where it's been sold since 1854. It's insurance for the industrial classes, men and women who work in the factories and mills, and for their families. Why should insurance be only for the wealthier classes, as it is today, when it is the poor who need it most?"

Dr. Ward made no reply. But the question struck a responsive chord. In these months of depression he had learned a great deal about the privations and suffering of the poor, the grim story of destitution, of pauper funerals and nameless graves.

Nervously his fingers tapped on the counter. "What made you come to me, sir? What made Bassett or you imagine I'd be interested in this fantastic scheme of yours?"

For the first time Mr. Dryden allowed himself the faintest hint of a smile. He measured Dr. Ward with his eyes. "I know a great deal about you, Dr. Ward," he declared. "Your family, your background, your service in the war. I know that with your aid we could convince others of the great need these people have——"

"Of course there is need," the other broke in heatedly. "All of us know it—doctors, businessmen, storekeepers. Hardly a day passes but some poor soul is in here collecting for someone's funeral expenses. You don't have to tell *me* anything about that. But charity is one thing——"

"I'm not talking of charity," Dryden insisted calmly. "This is a sound business—a business of providing help for others in time of need. A business which will provide profit for those who invest and at the same time personal security—with decency and self-respect—for the industrial classes."

"Insurance for the laboring man!" Dr. Ward murmured. Insurance, as he knew it, was the special prerogative of the well-to-do. There had been a few attempts to sell policies to the poor, but they had failed or proved fraudulent.

Dr. Ward leaned against the shelves of liniments and stared at Mr. Dryden. "I'm a busy man. All doctors are at this season. But I suppose I *could* spare a few more moments to hear your plan. Not that I have much faith in it, mind you. But if you will just step inside, Mr. Dryden."

For the better part of an hour, seated by the desk in the doctor's small office, the two men talked. At first the physician was troubled by the man's somewhat shabby appearance and his obvious financial distress. He wondered how this man, who looked as though he could hardly pay his own debts, could be thinking of launching a costly adventure of this sort —and an unproved scheme, at that. But while he wondered the man talked—talked with such evident sincerity and conviction that Dr. Ward hesitated to interrupt. One fact was clear: This Mr. Dryden did nothing by guesswork. Out of a bulging envelope he drew a sheaf of papers which he placed beside him on the desk. From these papers he drew the figures, the evidence, to support his every point.

One by one, carefully and thoroughly, he presented the facts. The death rate had risen to 29.9 per thousand population, and during the last two depression years was climbing at an even more alarming rate. Newark workers earned an average of $513 a year and spent an average of $521. Benevolent societies were overwhelmed by demands for assistance. In New York City pauper burials had risen to a shameful height, and in Newark conditions rivaled or were worse than those in New York. The mortality of children under fifteen had increased to 43.7 per thousand. Cholera, smallpox, and yellow fever were claiming an increasing toll as people's resistance was lowered. These were facts—facts that would never yield to the charitable ministrations of the wealthy and well-disposed. These were the facts that made this new insurance system necessary, that made it inevitable.

Dryden's lean fingers moved from chart to chart, punctuating his points as he drove them home. Industrial insurance, he pointed out, was not just for the breadwinner but for the whole family. It was designed basically as burial insurance, to take care of final expenses which could wreck a home. It was very different from ordinary life insurance. Instead of annual or quarterly payments, an agent would collect the premiums weekly—in the home. That was a new method of collection. It had never been tried here, but in England it had already proved a success. The Prudential Assurance Company of London had grown enormously and was now issuing more than 300,000 policies each year. If it could be done in England, it could be done here.

The physician listened as the caller outlined his plans for the new company. Much of the grim picture Dryden painted

Dr. Ward could verify from his own knowledge. Perhaps the scheme *would* work. Newark, the new Newark with its growing industries, was not unlike the factory areas of England.

Dr. Ward rose from the desk and began to pace the office. They made a remarkable contrast, these two, the man pacing and the visitor in the chair examining his documents and explaining their import. An austere, serious, almost evangelical figure he was, far different from the robust redheaded doctor with the gleam of warmth and humor in his eye.

Dryden began to assemble the papers in a neat pile on the desk. Carefully he returned them to the envelope and fixed the clasp. Then he leaned back in his chair and touched the tips of his fingers together before him. "Dr. Ward," he said coolly, "we need $30,000 to launch this venture. I am asking you to contribute—as an investor—the first one thousand."

Dr. Ward stopped pacing and stood in the center of the room, looking down at his caller. "I rather wish I *could* be of help," he declared. "Your plan may well have real merit. But I'm not a man of business. Why not try some of our business leaders? Men much more qualified——"

Mr. Dryden rose slowly to his feet. It seemed to Dr. Ward that his blue eyes almost glowed in the shadows of the office. "We have already approached a number of businessmen, men that Mr. Bassett knows—men who could easily afford a venture of this sort. They are conservative men. They do not like the new and untried."

Mr. Dryden paused a moment, then continued, "Frankly, I've come to you now because I believe you are the one person in Newark who can appreciate the need. With your help we could find others."

"So what you want is not only my thousand dollars," the physician said, laughing, "but also my influence."

Mr. Dryden nodded. "But if you were an investor, would it not be to your interest——"

There was a knock at the door, the side entrance to the doctor's office. The two men turned. The doctor called out, "Come in, please."

A dark-haired young woman entered. Her coat was thrown over her shoulders and drawn around her, only partially covering the long-skirted black dress with the wide, leg-of-mutton sleeves of the day. "He's worse, Doctor. You said if he got worse—— Can you come now?"

The doctor was already putting on his coat. "Your father— is he delirious yet?" he asked in a calm professional tone. The girl nodded. Dr. Ward opened the door leading into the drugstore. "Joseph," he called in to the clerk, "I'll be at the Thomas's if anyone wants me. I'll probably be late."

Mr. Dryden gathered up his envelope and followed the physician and the young woman to the windy street. Dr. Ward and the girl had gone several paces before the physician seemed aware of his sudden leavetaking. He turned quickly.

"Mr. Dryden, you'll forgive me, of course. It's pneumonia. I must go immediately." He paused. "I'd like a little time to think about your plan. It's——" He seemed about to express some opinion but instead abruptly thrust out a hand and shook Dryden's hand warmly. "Come back and see me—tomorrow morning." He turned and took the girl by the arm.

Dryden stood by the curb watching the doctor and the girl hurry along the street until they turned the corner. Then he buttoned his coat, set his hat against the wind, and walked briskly back toward town. Perhaps, he thought, as he picked his way carefully across the broken old cobblestones, perhaps this would be the turning point for which he had waited so long. Perhaps. More likely another refusal. Would he ever find men with the vision to back this plan of his?

After all, Bassett had tried—had tried the best men in Newark—and had failed. If solid, conservative Bassett couldn't interest men who had known him all their lives, what could Dryden—a shabby newcomer to Newark—hope to achieve by talking to strangers? Still, he had caught Dr. Ward's interest. There was a chance. The doctor had asked him to come back again in the morning. Well, there was nothing to do but wait.

He turned into Broad Street, stepped carefully over a patch of ice at the curb, and headed back toward his office—the basement office where Mr. Bassett kindly furnished him desk space free of charge.

CHAPTER 2

This Frayed Young
Dreamer from Maine

IN THE SUMMER of 1839 the town of Temple Mills, Maine, not far from Farmington, was scarcely more than a general store and a few scattered houses clustered on the edge of a wilderness. The countryside was a harsh, unyielding tangle of pine and scrub oak spotting the rocky hills. Years before the Massachusetts Bay Colony had distributed thousands of handbills describing the rich farming land to be had in Maine for the clearing, and offering settlers generous homestead grants. But most of those who had trekked there with their families had found the going hard. Many of them were never able to open up more than an acre or two of land or to build more than rough cabins for shelter.

All across this rocky timberland of central Maine the settlers had drawn together into scattered little villages. Temple Mills was such a town. John and Elizabeth Dryden had come there in the early thirties and set up housekeeping in a sagging old house against the side of a hill, just down the way from the crossroads and the general store. It was here that John Fairfield Dryden was born on the blistering day of August 7, 1839.

The elder Dryden was something of a dreamer. He had started life as a mechanic down in Holden, Massachusetts. He was the kind of man who was never quite satisfied with what he had and was always on the lookout for new opportunities and a way to better his lot. When he and Elizabeth moved to Maine in the early thirties, it seemed to Dryden that a whole new life was opening up for them. Hopefully the mechanic-turned-farmer had cleared a few acres and had begun to till the soil. He soon found that the soil was thin over the rocks and that the pine stumps clung tenaciously to the hillsides. The crops were sparse and gave no signs of increasing. Solitary life on a farm didn't go too well with a mechanic used to working and living with shopmates. In time

he abandoned the plan to clear a farm and began to assume an assortment of odd jobs around Temple Mills. If the jobs paid little, they at least gave him the opportunity of spending his time with people instead of alone in the fields. He became tax assessor and collector, constable, clerk of the school, and highway surveyor. The stipends he received were at least enough to pay for the necessaries in the crossroads store.

John Fairfield Dryden was the fourth child and the first boy born to the family. Hannah, the eldest girl, was born in 1830, and now, almost ten, was able to help look after the younger ones—wide-eyed Mary Elizabeth who was seven and curly-haired Caroline who was five. When John Fairfield was born his father was pleased to have a son. He bought cigars and went calling on the neighbors in town. He worried some when the infant appeared to be croupy and subject to chills. On nights when it grew cold John Dryden would hang quilts across the board walls to keep the wind off the cradle.

For a few years John Dryden continued to work his scanty fields and to carry on his several odd jobs. The family got along about as well as their neighbors. Elizabeth made many of their clothes and they grew most of the food they needed in the garden. On Sunday mornings they rode together in the family buggy down to the white one-room church in town.

But as time went on John Dryden began to feel discontented in Temple Mills. The opportunities he had foreseen there had never crystallized, and now he knew that they never would. Visitors to Temple Mills were few and news was scarce, but stories drifted in occasionally about the great mills and factories springing up to the south in Massachusetts, Pennsylvania, and New Jersey. Dryden was a machinist, and the stories he heard about this new growth in industry set his mind all the more against Maine. Life grew no easier in Temple Mills, and the fields never yielded the hoped-for harvest. The farm began to be a millstone about Dryden's neck. In the fall of 1848 he decided that he had taken enough of drought and cold and rocks. "There's a new wind stirring in Massachusetts," he told Elizabeth. "Factories are going up all along the rivers in Lowell and Lawrence. Mechanics are coming in from the old country, thousands of them, and they are all finding good jobs down there. Here there is only cold and emptiness and . . ."

Elizabeth had nodded. She had never been happy up here in Maine. She had come only because of John's enthusiasm, and now that he had grown restless and tired of it all she was glad to go back. It had been a hard, unfriendly country. Still fresh in her mind was the memory of her second son, Albion. They had lost him in 1845, when he was four years old. Several of the family had been down with scarlet fever that winter, but only he had died. Now the time had come to leave Maine. "You're a good mechanic, John," she said. "There will always be a place down there for a good mechanic."

In the winter of 1848 they packed their belongings, sold their acres of pines and rocks to a neighbor, and went back to the bustling civilization of Worcester, Massachusetts. Dryden soon found a job in a machine shop, and the family settled down in a house all their own. Here John Dryden felt that he was back in the stream of life, he was back in the trade where he belonged. It wasn't a fine job, but it supplied their needs. There were plenty of other places, and in time he would move on to something better.

No one would have called them rich, but there was enough to eat, and Elizabeth kept the small home tidy and the children went to school. For a while young John seemed unhappy in the town. He was the new boy in the neighborhood and he made friends slowly. His evenings he spent at home studying, and at school they said he was quite a scholar. He read too much, his father would say, he was too much with books for a lad of ten.

After a while young John began to get used to the town. At school he made a good friend—Freddie Bernard, a boy from one of the old and comfortable families in town. Freddie was a little older than John and he taught him the ways of a city boy. Sometimes in the fall they would play hookey and hike out along the rutted winding highway toward the Berkshires.

In 1850 the world was still the exciting kind of place that a boy could enjoy. Conestoga wagons were lumbering westward on the frontier. Indian bands were still on the prowl. Wells, Fargo and the pony express rolled between the boom towns and across the mountains. There was gold in California to be had for the panning. Those were exciting days for boys, and sometimes on their walks Freddie and John would talk about what they could do in the Gold Rush. Perhaps someday they would run off, heading west with one of those wagon trains, helping to fight off the murderous attacks of the Sioux and the Apaches.

They talked about these things, and even as they talked they knew they were dreams. But they talked, too, of the real future. Freddie already had a solid New England career planned for himself. When he had finished high school in Worcester he would go on to Yale and study law. John Dryden listened and nodded. That was a fine plan. He hoped that someday he, too, would be going to Yale.

But for John the future seemed to end abruptly in the fall of 1852. One day his father came home early from work. The doctor came the following afternoon and stayed a long time, and went away looking very solemn. That night John's mother woke him to tell him that his father was dead.

The neighbors began to gather as soon as they heard the news. They helped to make arrangements for the funeral, cleaned the house and prepared the meals, took care of John and the girls, and in the evening, after the children had gone to sleep upstairs, sat late talking with Mrs. Dryden. The next morning neighbor women stayed behind while John and his mother and sister followed the hearse to the church. When they came silently home the shades were up and the smell of flowers was gone from the parlor. Lunch was waiting for them on the table.

That evening, when they were alone again, they held a family conference and talked about the future. There was little money left after the funeral expenses had been paid. Hannah was already married and would be away from home, but Mary Elizabeth and Caroline, almost grown up now, could find work somewhere. There were always families that needed help, and Mrs. Dryden had raised her girls to be good housekeepers. Perhaps, Mrs. Dryden said, she could take in a boarder or two. That would be all right. It was a good way, a respectable way for a widow woman to meet the responsibility of keeping a home together.

The boy fought back his tears. After all, the man of the family couldn't cry like a girl. He was grateful for his mother's gentle help when she asked him to share in the decisions. "We'll be able to get along, don't you think, John?" she said. "You'll go on with your schooling, of course, and we will all help as much as we can. The boarders will give us a few extra dollars. We'll have to watch every single penny, but we'll manage."

Always his mother had been the practical one, the planner who could make the most of what little they had. Spindle-legged John felt himself a man. "I could help, Mom. I could get a job in the mornings before school and maybe in the afternoons when school is over."

Young Dryden got his job. He was out each morning before daybreak delivering bread. At seven he was back for breakfast and on his way to school. After school he trudged down to a machine shop off Main Street, where he worked till dinnertime as a machinist's apprentice. In the evening he did his algebra and Latin by an oil lamp on the kitchen table.

Those were long, draining years—those of growing up. When he was fifteen John Dryden suddenly became a tall young man—tall and very thin. He was working too hard and studying too much. His mother worried about his frequent colds and the long hours in school and at the shop. Young John brushed aside her fears. He was earning more money now, and after his graduation from high school he worked full time in the machine shop. He was able not only to help out at home, but he also began saving money. Another year or two—a fellow could make something of himself at Yale.

Boarders came and went in his mother's home. They were drummers, many of them—expansive traveling men who liked to sit in the parlor in the evening and talk about life in New York and Philadelphia and the way things were growing up west of the Alleghenies.

John already knew a good deal about the West. His sister Hannah, who had moved out to Ohio with her husband, wrote exciting letters about the young state and the lush farm land where the corn grew higher than a man could reach. It was a big country out there—big and growing.

The West was beginning to be an important part of the nation. In the congressional elections of 1858 Abe Lincoln, the politician from Illinois, had begun to attract attention with a series of debates with Stephen Douglas on the slavery issue. A lot of people in New England had strong convictions about slavery and there was a good deal of dispute about Lincoln—whether he was actually sincere or just another loud-talking politician. Many people still weren't convinced, when in 1860, under the banner of the new party called the Republicans, "Honest Abe" had been elected to the highest office.

After Fort Sumter, when the first call came for volunteers in Massachusetts, the young men of Worcester made up a company and marched off to the strains of "Glory, glory, hallelujah." But John Dryden wasn't to have any chance to take part in that fight. The strain of the years of work and

study was all too evident. He was a thin, spindling youth,
unfit for active service in combat.

But he had at least won a personal victory. In the Worcester bank he had saved sufficient funds to pay his first year's
tuition at college. Late in the summer of 1861 he learned that
he had passed his entrance examinations and had been admitted as a freshman to Yale.

In those days Yale wasn't a comfortable place for a youth
of limited means. Most of the boys were from the old upper-
class and professional families of New England. They came
to Yale as a leisurely preparation for careers in law, medicine,
or the ministry. Dryden found it difficult to enter into the
life of his classmates and share their interests. He had never
been far from Worcester. His friends were the neighbors he'd
grown up with, the fellows who worked in the shop. Here at
Yale he became overconscious of the fact that his family had
always been poor; that most of his life he had worked at
rough menial jobs. Dryden wasn't much of a mixer, and in
time he was accepted by his classmates as a quiet, studious
fellow who kept pretty much to himself and his books. When
the boys put on their bowlers of an evening to go uptown
for dinner at Hoadley's, a show at Smith's Concert Hall, and
a glass of beer in Mory's, Dryden wasn't among them. His
evenings were spent in the dormitory or the library with his
textbooks.

Dryden took his meals across the campus, at a private
student dining room operated by Mrs. Abigail Fairchild who
had come to New Haven from Newtown, Connecticut, to
support herself and her daughters by serving meals to the
Yale boys. Mrs. Fairchild had taken over an old house on
Chapel Street and set up long oaken tables and straight-
backed chairs for the eighteen or twenty youths who dined
there regularly. Mrs. Fairchild and her daughters, the tall,

dark-haired Cynthia and Eliza, the younger girl, did the cooking and the serving.

There was always plenty of talk around the tables, especially in the evening when the boys were all there. Sometimes they raised such a rumpus that Mrs. Fairchild would have to quiet them with stern admonitions. Sometimes, too, they would tease the lovely Cynthia, offering her bribes for extra desserts or demanding to know which one of them she intended to marry.

Young Dryden participated little in the loud talk and the pranks. It seemed to Cynthia that he was shy and ill at ease in the crowd and she tried sometimes to draw him into the fun, called him "Old Sobersides," and teased him about his seriousness. "You'll dry up like an old crust of bread," she once told him in disgust when she found him poring over a book while the soup grew cold.

Somehow Cynthia's interest was caught by this long-legged youth with the intense blue eyes who seemed forever buried in his thoughts or in his books. The shy, lonely Dryden began to notice the extra little attentions she paid to him. He was pleased and proud that the vivacious and attractive girl should have noticed him. He began to find reasons to linger in the dining hall to talk to her after the others had gone.

Sometimes, after the dining rooms had been cleared and tidied up, they would sit out on the stoop on Chapel Street. After he knew her better and was more at ease, John began to talk to Cynthia about himself, about his ideas and his plans. He had thought of being a lawyer when he first came to college. It was doubtful now if his health—or his finances— would allow him to launch upon this profession.

He told her how his life, the life of his whole family had suddenly been changed by the death of his father. If it hadn't been for that, everything would have been different. There wouldn't have been the fear of poverty, the endless hours of work for him or his mother or his sisters, the uncertainty and worry.

"People need some protection against such disasters," he told her. "Especially the working people. It's easy to say they should be more provident. But how can they? They never get a chance to save up any money. How can people expect a workingman to provide against sickness and accident and death, Cynthia, when he can hardly earn enough to live on from day to day?" His voice rose, and he pounded his fist on his knee to emphasize his words.

Cynthia was a little frightened at the sudden excitement in his words. "It isn't just me or my family," he was saying. "It's a big problem, Cynthia, a problem that affects nearly everybody. And in some places they are doing something about it!"

Over in England, he told her, there was a new company. It wrote insurance policies for poor people, so that they'd have a little money to pay expenses if death struck. It was a new kind of company, but already, he explained, in only a few years, it had become a tremendous success. They called it The Prudential Assurance Company of London.

Cynthia listened to him sympathetically. She didn't try to understand much about this insurance business he was talking about. She knew only that he was lonely and wanted someone who would listen. Whenever they could be together in the weeks that followed John would tell her about the articles he was reading in the newspapers and journals of the day. There was a bitter battle going on between Gladstone, the British Prime Minister, and The Prudential Company of England. "Gladstone thinks the government ought to handle industrial insurance through its post offices." He would slap his fist against his palm. "But it wouldn't work, Cynthia!

Poor people just won't bother going each week to pay out their premiums."

Cynthia would frown, and smile, and shake her head, and cup her hands under her chin and let him talk. His eyes always seemed a deeper blue when he was excited, she thought.

Sometimes on warm spring evenings they would go riding on the horsecars all the way to the end of the line and back. And often he would talk about these ideas of his. He had studied the whole history of insurance and spun it out for her, how it began back in the days of the cave man and the primitive tribes. "Savages, we call them. But when death or sickness struck, each member of the tribe would give up some small part of his wealth to help the widow and the children."

In every period of history, John told her, the people tried to find some means of protecting themselves and their dependents against death and the poverty that it brought to a family. The old craft guilds of England had once provided funeral and sickness payments for their members. And after them had come the "friendly" societies and secret societies formed to help care for the sick and the bereaved who had nowhere else to turn. These old associations were poorly organized and in time most of them failed. But out of them had grown this new scheme—this industrial insurance—which hadn't failed because it was based on sound, mathematical calculations. There were exact mortality tables. For every thousand people alive . . . And John would plunge into a description of actuarial methods.

As he talked, Cynthia would listen and ask questions. Walking with her arm through his in the evening, she would smile to herself. It was funny that she should be strolling along here talking about industrial insurance—something she had never heard of until a few months before. And yet—

Cynthia knew that nowhere else in the world was there anyone she'd rather hear talk about anything than big, long-legged, shy John Dryden.

Hers was the strangest courtship that Cynthia had ever heard of, so strange that it had taken her months to realize that it was a courtship. She looked up at John and smiled again, and wondered when he would find out.

John and Cynthia were married in the spring of 1864. Not quite sure how Cynthia's mother felt about the romance, they had eloped to Massachusetts. When they returned, Mrs. Fairchild forgave them, but only after they had agreed to a second wedding ceremony in Cynthia's own church, the First Baptist Church of New Haven with the Reverend S. D. Phelps officiating.

They had planned to stay in New Haven during the coming winter, while Dryden finished his senior year at Yale and took his degree. That degree, he knew, would mean a great deal to him in business, whether he decided on insurance or any other field.

But the plan was not fulfilled. In June 1864, largely from the strain of overwork in his courses, Dryden's health broke. The doctors informed him that he could not continue. He would have to give up his academic studies entirely.

"Try to find work that gives you exercise and keeps you out of doors," they told him. "You've been cooped up too many years with your books."

Somehow he was going to have to find a way to earn a living, a decent living to support them. He remembered his sister Hannah, out in Ohio, and the letters he had had occasionally from her, letters talking of the fields, the clear air, the new businesses springing up. He wrote a letter to Hannah and had her answer quickly: Come on out and bring your bride!

John and Cynthia packed their belongings in valises and

carpetbags and set out on what was to them a great adventure, the long trip west to the town of Bedford, Ohio.

And so they began—those years of apprenticeship, those
years of training and learning.

Out in Bedford, Ohio, his brother-in-law scoffed at his
notions on industrial insurance. The people out there would
never trust a scheme like that, he said, but if Dryden knew
anything about the regular, standard insurance, they might
be able to do something about that. "There's a man named
Judd," the brother-in-law recalled. "Insurance man, down in
Cleveland. Has the agency for the Aetna Insurance Company. Now you just drop those crazy notions of yours,
Dryden, and get down to business. I'll put you in touch with
this Judd. Give you a letter to him."

So John Dryden went to work for Mr. Samuel E. Judd, the
resident agent assigned by the Aetna people to develop the
territory of Ohio. Mr. Judd was a solid citizen of the community, with a good reliable business in Cleveland and the
surrounding area. He trained Dryden in his office for a time,
and then assigned him as a roving agent in the outlying farm
area all the way down to Cincinnati, where Mr. Judd had
opened a sub-office for his company.

"You're working for a great company," Judd told Dryden.
"A tremendous concern with millions behind it. The income
of the Aetna Life is almost $1,000 a day. Just think what that
means, young man."

That figure of $1,000 a day, which Mr. Judd always in-
toned with a certain awesome air for the benefit of new
agents, made a tremendous impression on the mind of young
Dryden. This was an enormous sum, a staggering figure to a
youth who, from his youngest days, had been forced to eke
out an existence on a few dollars a week at best. Under the
tutelage of Judd, Dryden learned the practical side of the in-

surance business in the field, selling to businessmen and well-to-do farmers and traveling much of the time through the wide agricultural areas of the state.

While John was learning his trade in the villages and farms of Ohio, Cynthia, expecting their first child, stayed with his sister and brother-in-law back in Bedford. On Christmas Day John was back and they all had dinner together. The day after Christmas their son was born. Forrest Fairchild Dryden they called him. After New Year's John spoke to Mr. Judd about his new responsibilities, and a month later he and his wife and the baby moved to Columbus and set up housekeeping.

It was harder to get established in Columbus than John thought it would be. Sales were few and commissions slim, and Dryden was forced to find new ways to better his showing. Somehow he had to organize his business to bring in sales. He was new in town, working against men who had lived there all their lives and knew everybody who could afford a policy. Dryden knew that if he was to get anywhere he had to tell people who he was and what he was doing. He had to advertise. In spite of his thin purse, he managed to launch a small-scale advertising campaign in the winter of 1865. One of these early advertisements ran:

THE AETNA LIFE INSURANCE COMPANY OF HARTFORD, CONNECTICUT, offers among *many other* advantages the following: A *paid up and well secured capital* and large surplus annual dividends which are *paid the same year.* Its dividends once declared are *not forfeitable.* It is *economical* in the management of its business. It is *prompt* in the payment of its losses. It accommodates the insured by giving a *credit for life for one half the premium,* when desired. Get your life insured in the AETNA.

JOHN F. DRYDEN, Agent
107 South High Street, Columbus

However little the advertisements produced in cash business, they were useful in making Dryden's name known in the community. Having thus established himself in the business he was able, later that year, to join forces with a Mr. Huston, also an agent in the area. Together they managed to bring in enough business to keep their heads above water for a year or so. But whatever they were able to accomplish wasn't good enough, and in 1867 the firm of Dryden and Huston, agents for the Travelers and Aetna insurance companies, quietly closed its doors.

John Dryden and his family packed up once more and went back East, this time to New York City. It wasn't a happy trip. Almost thirty now, Dryden was plainly floundering, unable to settle down as other men did. In Ohio he had been forced to leave some unpaid debts and a record of failure. The few men to whom he had broached his ideas about industrial insurance had laughed and gone about their business.

In New York the Drydens found quarters out in Belmont Heights in Brooklyn. It was an inexpensive, lower-middle-class neighborhood, proper and respectable, where a man could live frugally without being ashamed. He continued as an insurance agent. For a time he worked for the Home Life Insurance Company and later for the Globe Mutual.

But Dryden had not given up the dream—the great idea—of industrial insurance here in America, even though the top minds of insurance said it wouldn't work. He had read every word he could obtain about the subject. He had studied the history of the friendly societies and followed the controversy between Elizur Wright and Prime Minister Gladstone in *The Spectator, The Insurance Monitor,* and *The Insurance Times.* Sometimes at night he and Cynthia, as they had in the days before their marriage, would talk over the possibilities.

"What do people need?" he demanded. "If you know that, you know what the future will bring. People need a burial fund to take care of funeral expenses and a little something to help them through the hard days that follow. Industrial insurance provides both! Cynthia, an insurance system that supplies these two needs couldn't fail!"

That was in 1868, a boom year in insurance. A score or more of new companies had been launched in New York and a compact little insurance community had grown up around them. Along Wall Street and William some of the insurance men had heard about Dryden's plan. "Poor-man's insurance," they called it, and joked about it in some of the eating places where people from the Mutual of New York and the Manhattan Life and the new New York Life used to gather for lunch.

After a time, however, Dryden was able to find at least one person who was interested in his theories—an old-line insurance man and lawyer named H. H. Goodman. They talked about the plan, and then over a period of several weeks set down in detail the program of a projected company.

The proposal embraced all of the fundamental concepts of "poor-man's insurance." The company was designed to provide death benefits and sickness insurance for small weekly premiums to be collected by agents calling at the homes of policyholders. Goodman, the older man, was to be the president, and Dryden, who had worked out all of the details, was entered as secretary. The firm was to be called The United States Mutual Benefit Company. It was a fine, high-sounding name for a company with an empty till.

There was, of course, the problem of obtaining a charter. Before they could set up in business the charter had to be approved in a bill passed by the State Legislature. Dryden went to Albany to buttonhole representatives in the Legislature and discuss his plans with them. In two days he succeeded in getting the necessary support, and along with numerous similar "private" bills connected with the formation of new enterprises, the charter for his company was passed.

Dryden returned to New York cheered with the first tangible signs of success. They were finally on the road. He began at once to speed up his plans of organization and with Goodman set about mapping out the program for raising the funds they would need to start actual operations.

But the period of elation was short-lived. A week or so after Dryden returned from Albany word came that Governor Hoffman had vetoed the charter bill, with the explanation that it gave the company too much power in the handling of funds. The firm proposed to provide both sickness benefits and death benefits and thus to be both "friendly society" and insurance company. In the eyes of Governor Hoffman such an arrangement violated the principles of sound business practice.

The next three years were grim ones, culminating, in 1873, in the great financial panic touched off by the failure of the firm of Jay Cooke and Company, backers of the Northern Pacific Railroad. Other businesses soon began closing their doors, insurance firms were beginning to waver, and hundreds of workers were being "laid off." Even the few dollars Dryden had been earning as an agent dwindled to practically nothing; no one was buying insurance and many were starting to let their policies lapse.

Out in Brooklyn, in the tiny rented apartment, Dryden and Cynthia once more sat down to take inventory. They had two children to think of now: Susan, their little girl, born in Brooklyn, and Forrest, now nearly nine years old. But there was still no thought of quitting. Not even with the crash, or with the governor's veto. It was still only a question of where to turn.

"Ohio was wrong for me and my ideas," Dryden told Cynthia. "Now New York has shut us out. The place to begin is where they need us most. It ought to be a thriving, growing industrial area. I think I know where that is—right across the river, in the city of Newark."

The year before he had attended Newark's Industrial Exhibit, had seen the displays of cutlery and iron work and steel, padlocks and shears, carriages and gleaming harness, beaver hats and fine jewelry, leatherwork and other products which had made Newark the third largest industrial center in America. Even now, with many factories beginning to close their doors, hundreds of immigrant workers continued to pour into the city daily.

Cynthia Dryden must have smiled as they talked. In spite of this New York failure, John Dryden was still going on. If you took away this dream of his, she knew, there would be nothing left for him. It was as though he had now become dedicated to this one consuming purpose.

Once again, as they had done so many times before, they drew out valises and trunks and made ready to move, this time to Newark, New Jersey.

David Maclure, who served as an office boy when The Prudential Insurance Company of America was started, remembered those early days of the Drydens in Newark and years afterward was to describe them in a letter:

> I think I was the first person in Newark [he wrote], to know Mr. John F. Dryden. . . . My acquaintance began the day he and his family moved next door to my father's house on Lincoln Avenue. I infer that Mr. Dryden was not in opulent circumstances for I remember that it was his habit to walk to his office . . . which I am sure was a matter of economy and not of health. . . .

The office to which he walked was that of Allen Bassett, in the old State Bank at the corner of Broad and Mechanic. It was the older Maclure who had introduced Dryden to Bassett. An officer in the Civil War, Captain Bassett, as he was known to many, was a genial, friendly man, with a civic-minded interest in local politics. He had a certain literary flair and had once edited a magazine. Now he was a real estate broker. Bassett was one of the first persons in Newark to listen to Dryden and to see possibilities in this industrial insurance idea if properly handled.

"You listen to me now," he told the younger man. "This plan of yours has promise. I'll give you desk space and help you along. I know everybody in town, you understand, almost everybody. But with men like these you have to move slow. You have to show them that you're cautious and not given to taking rash chances."

So Dryden had taken desk space, and he and Bassett began the job of organizing The Widows and Orphans Friendly Society. Another who was deeply interested in this project was John Whitehead, a public-spirited lawyer of that day who had been appalled at the number of widows and orphans thrown on public charity. Whitehead was a friend of Bassett, and the two men had often discussed the increasing economic distress.

The three men had worked closely together in the organization of the new Friendly Society. It is probable that it was Whitehead who actually drew up the charter in legal form. They moved slowly. Over the ensuing months, operating only within Newark city limits, they managed to sell a few policies. It was strictly a "friendly" society and no more: a collection agency whose few policies were reinsured in one of the substantial old firms to cover the death and sickness claims of the members.

Dryden was wise enough to know there would be no profit in The Widows and Orphans Friendly Society. It was merely the start he wanted, the solid foundation on which he could build. John Whitehead became president and George D. G. Moore, well known in Newark legal and political circles, served as treasurer. Dryden himself once more took over the minor role of secretary. Whitehead's law partner was a member of the State Legislature and was able to be of assistance to them in Trenton in winning legislative approval for the charter.

None of the officers drew any salary. Dryden, with an occasional sale for one of the New York companies, managed to earn enough to support his family modestly. Whitehead and Moore, both well to do, were serving primarily because they saw in the society a way of helping the poor in this time of trouble.

During the long months of struggle to keep the Friendly Society from foundering, Dryden and Bassett had many talks about Dryden's insurance ideas. The time had come, Dryden insisted, to make the next move—to convert The Widows and Orphans Friendly Society into an actual industrial insurance company, writing its own policies based on its own actuarial tables, sending out its own agents to collect premiums, paying its own claims.

"People know the Prudential of England," Dryden told Bassett. "They'd recognize the type of insurance by the name. Call it—The Prudential Friendly Society."

He leaned back in his chair behind the desk and brought his fingertips together in a characteristic gesture of thoughtfulness. Bassett watched him from across the office. This Dryden was learning. He was taking hold. He might be able to make the thing work.

"There's the matter of raising funds, of course," Bassett declared. "And I think I can do it. I'm acquainted with the important people in Newark—I could go to Blanchard or Robotham and get cash from them as quick as that."

The snap of his fingers echoed in the basement office. It sounded easy enough as Bassett talked that day, but as the weeks dragged on it became clear to Dryden that Bassett's approach was never going to succeed. Businessmen of the city were wary. They distrusted most new insurance schemes, and this one in particular sounded bad. Newark's Mutual Benefit now, that was different—a sound old business run by people of solid standing in the community. They didn't question Bassett's standing, of course. But the idea was new, and they held back.

Bassett continued to try to promote the idea for a time but was finally forced to admit failure. He just hadn't been able to convince the others, he said frankly. Maybe Dryden himself ought to take over. It was his scheme, after all. Maybe he was the one to put it across.

They were alone in the basement office one evening. Outside on Broad Street it was already growing dark and the lamplighters were turning on the gas lamps. Dryden was standing gazing out into the dusk. Bassett was putting on his coat, making ready to go home. "I haven't talked to everybody in town yet, John," Bassett declared. "Now I'd planned to see that Dr. Ward over on Lafayette Street. You know about him, of course. He's a man might help you. From what I hear, he's got a good head—and a heart as big as an onion patch. Why not go to see him for a start?"

John Dryden nodded silently, watching the other button his coat tightly against the chill of the night outside.

At eight o'clock on the morning of December 16, the day after his first visit to Dr. Ward, Mr. Dryden returned to the pharmacy. The doctor was out on calls and Joseph, the assistant, was running the shop. The young man seemed curious about just what business this caller had with the doctor. Mr. Dryden said he would wait until Dr. Ward returned.

It was almost an hour later when the horse and buggy drew up in front of the store and the physician climbed out. He greeted Dryden with a hearty handshake. "Well, Mr. Dryden, so you did come back!"

Dryden nodded. With only a hint of excitement he inquired, "Did you—did you consider my suggestion, Dr. Ward?"

Dr. Ward drew off his coat. "Come on inside, Mr. Dryden. I think I ought to explain——"

In the privacy of his office the young doctor threw himself down in the chair. "Mr. Dryden, I talked over your idea last night with my brother, Elias. We went into the proposition pretty thoroughly, as much as I could remember from those mountains of figures you quoted yesterday."

He hesitated a moment as his caller waited. "My brother thinks it's a pretty good idea, Mr. Dryden. And, since it's my money, he says, well, go ahead and plunge if I want. As he points out, a thousand dollars wouldn't ruin me. Although, on the other hand——"

Dryden started to speak, but Ward hurried on, "You know, as soon as he made up my mind for me, I tried to hook him, too, with an eye to business, you understand. Tried to convince him to come in for another thousand. But it didn't work. I have an idea Elias feels it's all right for me to be partially unbalanced if I will, but one in the family is enough."

Dr. Ward stood up. "Mr. Dryden," he said slowly, "I wonder if we may not be at the start of something much more important than even you imagine." He paused a moment, and the gleam of humor flashed in his eyes. "Well, sir, your company has been launched. Where do we go from here?"

CHAPTER 3

A Peculiar Little Company

IN THE snowy winter of 1874–75 officers of the respected and conservative banking and security houses of Newark began to receive inquiries from clients about a new company which was being formed for the sale of "cheap" insurance for the poor—"industrial insurance," the organizers were calling it.

These conservative banking officials were somewhat at a loss as to what to advise their clients about investing in this nebulous concern, still in the process of formation. On the surface, certainly, it sounded like a highly doubtful scheme. Insurance in general, with the exception of the old-line companies, was highly risky. And this five-and-ten-cent insurance idea, from what they could learn, had the hollow ring of a street-corner flim-flam game.

What made these bankers hesitate, however, were reports that some of the leading businessmen of the city had already begun to invest in the concern and to lend it their name and prestige.

Horace Alling was in it, for instance. Alling was a member

of one of the finest families in Newark, a partner in the jewelry concern of Alling Brothers, a prominent citizen in the community. Benjamin Atha, owner of the great Atha Steel Company, was in it, too, the stories had it. And Henry Yates, the hat manufacturer, who was also a member of the Newark Common Council. Yates was one of the most prominent Republicans in the city and might very well be Newark's next mayor. Other names, too, began cropping up. They said Aaron Carter, Jr., was in it, and Alfred Lister, both of them leading manufacturers, and George Richards, the railroad man and mine owner.

There were some among the staid and cautious groups in the city who shook their heads. Had the best business minds in Newark suddenly lost their sense of balance? These men were risking not only their pledged investments—said to average around $1,000 each—but also their business reputations, on an untried and very likely unsound scheme put forward by young Dr. Ward, who certainly knew little enough about business matters, and a tall, bearded newcomer named John F. Dryden, an erstwhile insurance agent whom no one knew much about.

It was young Dr. Ward, of course, who had opened the doors for Dryden, Dr. Ward whose name carried weight in Newark's better circles. It was he who had gone to his father-in-law, James Perry, and talked him into investing. Through Perry he had reached Noah Blanchard, leading leather manufacturer of the city, a round massive man with large hands and a gleaming black beard. Blanchard had slapped his knee. "There's an idea!" he'd exclaimed. "A godsend to these working people, sir. Wouldn't I know? Didn't I work my way up through the mills myself?"

It was true that Dr. Ward had opened the doors, but it was the newcomer Dryden who did most of the talking and whose mass of figures and statistics did most of the persuading. Dryden coolly and carefully explained his points: the value to the employer constantly besieged by appeals whenever they passed the hat for some worker's family, the respect given to the workers themselves, the teaching of the idea of thrift to the poor.

Dryden, through long years of trial and error and failure, had by now learned the need for care and exacting preparation. It was he who sometimes had to rein in the galloping optimism of young Dr. Ward. "We must have the best men available on our board, Leslie. If it takes all winter and into the summer, we want the finest names in Newark—names the people cannot fail to trust."

On February 18, 1875, the charter of The Widows and Orphans Friendly Society was amended. The supplementary covenants gave it new powers to issue insurance policies on the lives of men and married women under the new name of The Prudential Friendly Society. With the approval of that amended charter, industrial insurance had actually begun in America.

But the founder—the man behind this new concept of insurance and the role it should play in the lives of America's working people—still held back. The financing was still not complete. Pledges had come in, with one fifth of the money pledged put up in cash, as provided by law, but more was needed. Organizational plans were not ready. The board of directors still had to be formed.

For almost a year—since March of 1874—Dryden had been in correspondence with Professor John E. Clark, who taught mathematics at the Sheffield Scientific School of Yale and was something of an expert on actuarial matters. In February Dryden had engaged Clark to prepare life-expectancy tables and to help in fixing the rates to be charged.

Professor Clark was a scholarly, conscientious man. He diligently applied himself to the task at hand. But clearly he was moving into uncharted territory with this industrial insurance —and clearly there were moments when the professor had his doubts.

Soon after he began working on the problem he wrote soberly, "You are aware of the important precautions which this writer suggests should be taken in the administration of such societies. I may, however, recall them briefly.

"1. Care should be taken to secure a sufficient number of members, so that the law of averages upon which the Tables of Contribution and Benefit are based may be applicable.

"2. Proper precautions should be taken to prevent deception on the part of members by appropriate Medical Supervision where necessary. . . .

"3. The present sickness rates should not be applied to such extra-hazardous occupations as sailors, painters, mining and railway employees.

"4. Care should be taken in all cases in the admission of members.

"5. A distinct account should of course be kept of the receipts and disbursements in each branch of your business. . . .

"6. You should, not very long after you get fairly started, have a proper evaluation made of your liabilities in each Department. . . ."

A little further on in the same letter the professor added another note of caution: "Meanwhile, as at all times, your Directors should be impressed with the importance of keeping sacredly the proper reserve on all your policies, so that if your business is successful, as I most sincerely hope it may be, you may secure constantly increasing confidence; and if, in the worst event . . . it should chance to be unsuccessful it may at least not end in dishonor."

Professor Clark's doubts about the future of the company were not allayed by Dryden's slowness in paying the professor's bills for services rendered. The harassed Dryden, faced with mounting expenses during that summer, was forced to put off payment several times, and a rising note of acrimony and insistence crept into the professor's letters as the summer lengthened.

In June he declared, "Touching upon the payment of $300, I shall be very sorry to put you to serious inconvenience, but I have been depending upon it to meet an obligation that I must attend to promptly July 1st. . . ."

And a few days later, "The payment of $300 can remain until such reasonable time as you can make it without undue inconvenience. . . . I will frankly add, however, without fear of being misunderstood, that I do need it as soon as you can reasonably call upon your friends for their subscriptions. . . ."

By late August, however, the tone of Professor Clark's demands had completely changed. He stated in his letter that he found himself "seriously embarrassed" by Dryden's "protracted postponement" of payment. And on September 17 he declared bluntly, "I have strained my credit thus far to oblige you but I cannot reasonably do it further. . . . While I feel sympathy for you and would not say aught unnecessary to annoy you, it does seem to me that you ought to demand of your immediate associates to come to your rescue in this matter. . . ."

The bills owed the good professor were only one more harassment in that hot summer of 1875. Promised investments came in slowly, and those that were received could not be touched until the board of directors was actually organized and voted payment. There were a thousand details to take care of. Bassett and Dr. Ward and a few others were helping. But the main organization burden was Dryden's alone.

Nights would find the secretary at the kitchen table, working on the actuarial figures, the rates and costs and commissions. Sometimes Dr. Ward would come in and smoke a cigar in the hot night. He urged Dryden to slow up. "You're using up your strength before we're fairly started," he'd declare. "We can't afford to lose you now, John."

But Dryden would brush these pleas aside and go back to his charts.

They were almost ready, he knew, to begin. Nothing must be wrong this time. This was Dryden's greatest gamble. If he failed this time, there would be no more chances.

By the end of September he had the actual pledges required: Approximately $30,000, of which 20 per cent had been deposited in cash. The bank account of The Prudential Friendly Society stood at what must have seemed to John F. Dryden a stupendous sum—$5,900.

At a meeting of stockholders on October 3 Dryden explained to those present—eleven men, including himself—the purposes, aims, and plans. It was a careful and thorough explanation of the details of the business to be undertaken.

On October 13, 1875, in a board room of the Republic Life Assurance and Trust Company, the stockholders elected the first board of directors of The Prudential Friendly Society. Among the directors elected at that meeting were some of the impressive names of the city: Isaac Gaston, cashier of the National State Bank and former treasurer of the Newark Board of Trade; Allen Bassett and George DeGraw Moore, Noah Blanchard, William Whitty, and David Hayes, the lawyer; Dr. Leslie Ward, Elias Wilkinson of the produce concern of Wilkinson, Gaddis and Company; and John F. Dryden.

Other directors were added at a later meeting that month: Charles Campbell, in the mirror and picture business; and Marcus Ward, Jr., son of the former governor of New Jersey; William R. Drake and Horace Alling, Charles Romer, and the Reverend Andrew Hopper, the retired Baptist minister; George Richards, Walter Conger, and Edgar B. Ward, Dr. Ward's lawyer brother.

There were other names on the list too: James Durand, Alfred Lister, and William Murphy, the boot manufacturer whose son was one day to be governor of the state; Aaron Carter, Jr., and Albert Headley, trunk manufacturer; Mayor-elect Henry Yates, and William Robotham, who manufactured harness ornaments.

Immediately after the stockholders' meeting on October 13, the first meeting of the board of directors of The Prudential Friendly Society was held. At that meeting the company's first officers were elected. Genial Allen Bassett—who had done so much to aid Dryden over the rough road since 1873—was named the first president. Isaac Gaston, the banker, took over the post of treasurer. Once again John Dryden accepted the minor role of secretary.

But Prudential was on its way. The big dream—industrial insurance for America's workers—had become a business at last. The first office of the new firm was located at 812 Broad Street—the same cramped basement office of Allen Bassett in the bank building, where Dryden had occupied a desk in the corner.

Shortly after the directors had assumed office Secretary John Dryden presented to a meeting of the board the details of a minor crisis which had arisen. "Our company, gentlemen," he declared, "can succeed only if it has the confidence of the public, and it will gain that confidence only by paying all claims and all other just debts promptly."

The secretary paused and looked around at these men of commerce. "Gentlemen, we also need our charts, our actuarial rate sheets, life expectancies, claim rates, and commission percentages. These have been prepared for us by Professor Clark, as you know, and Professor Clark is now demanding payment as due."

The secretary then read to the directors the latest missive from Professor Clark. Declared the professor brusquely: "Dear Sir: I have just drawn on you three days after sight for $600, the amount of my account for services. Please honor the draft and oblige. Very truly yours, John E. Clark."

The board of directors solemnly considered the matter, their first sizable venture, and after brief discussion voted unanimously to honor the draft forthwith. The tone of Professor Clark's letters changed perceptibly after he received notification that the draft for $600 had been accepted. Sometime previously Dryden had requested permission to list Clark as actuary. The professor now hastened to reply:

"There is no objection to your speaking of me . . . as your 'Actuary.' But if you wish to enroll my name in your list of officers I think I should prefer to have you do so as 'Consulting Actuary.' This title will express cordially my willingness to have my name appear in connection with so honorable and influential a body of gentlemen as your officers must be. . . ."

When a New Jersey state actuary was sent a little later to make a routine report on the activities of the new company, he was instructed by his superiors to call on "a peculiar little company, which is doing a novel kind of insurance business in Newark."

Most of the residents of Newark would have accepted that description. Certainly there was nothing pretentious about this society which had opened for business in the gaslighted basement offices of the bank, next door to the colonial First Presbyterian Church.

But even though the company was located in modest basement quarters, it had invested in certain new fixtures and some secondhand office furniture, to the somewhat reckless total of $52.40. A further item was a new desk for John Dryden, his old one having fallen into a sad and battered state of disrepair.

The caller coming down the few steps from the street level and through the double doors into the new establishment would hardly have been overwhelmed by any sense of luxury. The plaster walls were stained and tinged with soot from the iron coal stove in the corner. On the left was the bookkeeper's high desk where entries were made in the large new ledger purchased for that purpose.

Behind the bookkeeper was the desk where President Bassett worked, and over to the right, in the corner, directly under the gaslight on the wall, was the desk of Secretary

Dryden. For the remaining office help there was another "homemade" desk against the wall—two planks resting on two wooden horses and covered over with brown wrapping paper neatly tacked in place.

Though limited, the office space was adequate for their needs. Actually, it included a little more than was necessary, and Dryden frugally decided to reduce the rent of $116.67 per month by subletting the small back room to the Penn Mutual Life Insurance Company for $20 per month and, shortly thereafter, by leasing desk space in Prudential's room to J. M. Bradstreet and Sons for $15 per month. By retrenching at the very start the secretary was able to show a saving of nearly one third in rent charges.

Even so, expenses that first month ran a trifle high. The office was still costing $81.67 a month. There were the monthly salaries to pay, of course: $150 for President Bassett; $100 for Secretary Dryden; and $40 for the bookkeeper, the precise and correct Colonel Samuel L. Buck, veteran of several Civil War campaigns. The office boy, George H. R. Gaston, Isaac Gaston's son, was paid $3.00 a week. In addition to these fixed expenses and the outlay for the furniture and office fixtures, there were certain other minor items listed in the records:

Cleaning and laying of secondhand rug	$3.59
Gas bill	1.69
Matches	.25
Key for the front door	.30
Ruler	.50
Mr. Dryden's expenses to and from New York	.52

There were no filing cabinets, of course. Records during that whole first year of operation were kept in cardboard boxes arranged alphabetically on wooden shelves in the rear of the office. They could not afford a safe, either. During the first months, when business began to come in, the mail boy often took the day's receipts home in his pocket for safekeeping.

Additional employees were hired only as the volume of work warranted. In the course of the next few months, however, it became necessary to add a few more to the staff: Christopher Blake, clerk, at $10 a week; David Maclure, junior clerk, $5.00, and George Babbitt, office boy, at $2.00.

The weeks following the October 13 meeting were spent in organizing the office and obtaining the printed policy forms, application blanks, ledgers, and office stationery. Not until the first days of November was the company actually ready to do business. On November 10, 1875, the first Prudential policy was written by Mr. Dryden on the life of William R. Drake, one of the directors, for the sum of $500.

What public reaction there was in those opening days was mixed. The public was still highly suspicious of insurance schemes. Many of the clergy in Newark and elsewhere opposed the whole concept of insurance on the ground that it was an attempt to thwart the will of God. Some Newark ministers, as they began to learn of this new enterprise, openly warned their congregations to stay clear of the tempting promises of the society.

There is the story—perhaps apocryphal—of one minister who inveighed so violently against The Prudential in his Sunday sermon that Dryden himself, hearing of it, called upon the preacher at the rectory the next morning. For more than an hour he sat in the minister's study explaining with all his accustomed patience and clarity the purposes, the methods, the lofty aims of his organization. When he walked out, he had in his pocket an application for $500 on the minister's own life.

The press had been slow to react to this "novel" experiment

in insurance. Notices had been sent out announcing the election of the board of directors, but none of the editors of Newark's newspapers thought the matter of any news interest. Dryden knew well the importance of advertising and publicity in this business of insurance, and he was anxious to get his plan and his company known to the public. Soon after its organization he had the printing house of Drake and Cook run off a large quantity of leaflets. These were distributed on the streets and in stores as well as among newspaper editors and other opinion makers of the city. Declared this brochure:

> The Prudential Friendly Society pays Cash each week (from $3 to $25) when incapacitated for labor by sickness or accident.
> $100 a year (in monthly installments), sick or well, at 65 years of age—at that age the stated premium ceases.
> At death, from $50 to $500.
> For a child's burial (from one to ten years of age) for $1.25 yearly from $10 to $50.

At the end, in bold type, were listed the officers and the impressive board of directors. Dryden's idea of sending this leaflet out to the papers as straight publicity proved highly valuable. On November 13 stories appeared in the Newark papers describing this new company. All of the comments were highly favorable. The conservative Newark *Register,* after praising the aims of the organization, noted with some surprise the distinguished board of directors. "It is not too much to say," declared the paper, "that no institution in Newark . . . has a board of directors that can more strongly claim the confidence of our people. The gentlemen are unexceptionable as to ability, wealth, and character." A little farther along in the story the writer added a curiously prophetic sentence: "The society may be said to be founded upon a rock."

Flushed with this first favorable reaction, Dryden prepared to flood the city with his new sales literature. Unfortunately such an intensive campaign required tens of thousands of copies of the leaflet, and the secretary's plans were circumscribed by a non-existent budget and a highly conservative board of directors. In an effort to carry out his plan Dryden approached the printers with an unusual offer: Would they prepare for him large quantities of pamphlets and other material in exchange for stock in The Prudential Society? Messrs. Drake and Cook shook their heads dubiously. "Who knows how much Prudential stock will be worth a year from now?" they queried. "We do a cash business, Mr. Dryden. Sorry."

But if he could not reach the people by one road, there were other roads open. Through the directors he could now get to almost every important businessman and factory owner in town. Once he had persuaded these employers of the value of Prudential insurance and indicated how it would relieve them of the necessity of meeting many of the expenses of sickness and death among their employees, Dryden was confident that they would help him reach their workers. He could talk to them at lunch-hour meetings or at other hours when it wouldn't interfere with the day's production. Dryden briskly set about developing this approach.

There was also in those hectic days of beginning the unique job of selecting and training agents capable of selling this startling new kind of insurance. Some of the directors were in favor of sending to England, to bring over men who had already sold industrial for England's Prudential Assurance. "After all, there's not an agent in America who knows what industrial insurance is all about or how to sell it," one of the directors declared.

It was Dryden who opposed the plan and won the others

to his views. The business they were launching was no carbon copy of what was being done in England. It was a strictly American enterprise, with its own special problems. "Let's try to get our men here," he declared. "In the long run we'll be better off with agents who know how Americans think and act, even if they don't know as much about industrial insurance. This is a slower way, but a better and safer one. I say pick our men and train them ourselves."

In December want "ads" began to appear in the Newark papers. A typical insert ran:

> Wanted! Canvassers for The Prudential Friendly Society. This first effort in this country to establish a Friendly Society worthy of the patronage of all classes is meeting with a generous response. People in these hard times are more than usually thoughtful in making provisions for sickness, accident, old age, and a burial fund, beyond the reach of the exigencies of business. Intelligent ladies and gentlemen can secure good districts by applying to the principal office, 812 Broad Street, State Bank Building.

There was, of course, no question of experience. Dryden was looking for men and women who knew how to talk to the people he was trying to reach. Education and past employment were less important than the common touch. Dryden could take care of the rest. Leaning back in the swivel chair at his desk, he would explain to them how industrial insurance operated and make sure that they understood the commissions involved: Three times the first weekly premium for all "new business" and 10 per cent on all weekly collections. He would stress the importance of building up the weekly collections as the agent's way of assuring himself a good basic weekly income. The actual techniques of selling could only be learned in the field. Dryden found that the best way to start their training was to take them along with him when he

went to address one of the lunchtime meetings of Newark
workers.

The secretary was spending many of his lunch hours at
these meetings now. More than anything else he got from
them an insight into what people thought about insurance
and what they expected of it. At the Blanchard Tannery, for
instance, a hundred or more workers would gather in the
great yard of the plant at the noon hour with their lunch
boxes and their pails of coffee or beer. Rugged, hard men,
with the soot and stain of the day's work on their face and
their hands, they would listen as this lean, bewhiskered man,
standing on a box, explained the protection that could be
bought for a few cents a week.

His tone and approach were a little different now from those
he had used with the employers upstairs. Here he was telling
the direct story of what industrial insurance could do for
them and for their families. A man sitting there in the yard
would munch the sandwich his wife had prepared for him
that morning before he left home, and wonder: Is he talking
about me? Is this thing he's trying to sell something I ought
to have for my wife and my kids?

There were few sales made at those lunchtime rallies.
But the men would ask questions and often, in the evening,
when their day's stint at the plant was finished, they would

show up at 812 Broad Street, asking for information and literature on the subject. "Like to talk it over with the wife, Mr. Dryden. Want to get this thing straight in my mind."

So many of these late-hour workers showed up that the new company was finally forced to stay open in the evenings to handle inquiries. Nights would find gaslights burning high at 812 Broad Street. Across the street, hazy through the steamed windows, were the lights of Stoutenburgh and Company, Marshall and Company, Colyer and Company, and Watson's—clothiers' row, open every evening to accommodate workers seeking bargains in the new checkered suits of the day.

Some of the old-line families in Newark regarded this bustling newcomer in the insurance business with a little surprise. Lunchtime rallies in the factories. An odd assortment of individuals trekking into the basement office until heaven knows how late. And this tall Mr. Dryden conferring with these unemployed workers and mechanics they were taking on as agents. The old-timers were inclined to question the whole enterprise.

Meanwhile the agents were having their troubles too. Nobody had ever heard of industrial insurance, few knew of the existence of the new Prudential Friendly Society, and most of those who had heard of it were wary. The whole scheme sounded like a swindle to them. "How do we know this won't be a fake like others I hear about?" a prospect would demand, and a door would slam in the agent's face. Or the prospect had been warned against this thing, this industrial insurance, by his minister. "So you're selling that peanut insurance? And how many babies did you insure today?" Prospects seemed to enjoy these delicately sarcastic rejoinders. The agents either learned to endure them or moved on to easier employment.

The going in these first months was cruelly disappointing. Only the merest trickle of applications came into the office. The agents struggled along on commissions hardly large enough to pay carfare. One of the earliest agents, who spent many years with the company, recalled long afterward that the first week with Prudential the commissions totaled ten cents—and forty-five cents for the entire first month. This was not, of course, a typical experience, but there were weeks when even the best agent wondered if either he or this new-fangled scheme of Dryden's would survive.

But during the fall and winter the number of applications slowly began to increase. Most of them were for small amounts—$100 or $150; many were the three-cent-a-week infant burial policies. A few, a very few, were for as much as $500. But to Secretary Dryden and the always optimistic Dr. Ward every new policy was one more sign of the success ahead. Many years later Carl August Giese, a one-time office boy, wrote:

> At that time applications came in very slowly. . . . I can remember the pleasure of Dr. Ward in keeping tab on the number, when I brought the applications on odd days to his office on Walnut Street for his O. K. as medical director, after reading the physician's report. He always used a blue pencil in affixing his initials, L. D. W. So also was Mr. Dryden pleased when I laid the finished policies on his desk for signature—the policies then were signed in longhand by the president and the secretary, but the writing of his name proved irksome to him. It was his custom to have me stand at his side to blot his signature as he finished it in his cramped handwriting, and often the perspiration stood out on his forehead before the tenth policy was signed. . . .

At the end of 1875, as the bells of Newark's churches rang out the old year, Secretary Dryden added up the figures. To that date they had written only 279 policies, and expenses for rent and light and salaries far exceeded the money they were taking in.

There were claims in those first months, of course, and fortunately the company was able to honor them. More than once, however, it seemed that they would be unable to meet their obligations. Dryden was several times forced to send out young Gaston or Giese to try to collect quarterly premiums due on the Widows and Orphans Society policies which Prudential had taken over. By the end of the business day they would round up sufficient cash to meet a sickness insurance claim.

It wasn't all an unremitting struggle to keep the company alive. Sometimes after the officers had managed to raise the money to pay one of these embarrassing claims the agent would drop in at the office to tell them what had happened when he delivered the check. Occasionally Dryden would receive a scrawled, almost illegible letter of thanks. He read them again and again, and passed them on to the other officers. In time someone realized that these simple letters were the most convincing proof of the value of industrial insurance and the reliability of The Prudential. They were then circulated among the agents and soon thereafter began to appear in the columns of the local newspapers.

One, in cramped, old-fashioned writing, was from a Mrs. Hannah Izon who had received $441 when her husband died. "O sirs," she wrote, "I cannot tell you from the depth of my sorrow how much I have lost which your money cannot restore. But I can say that the little sum paid each week to your agent cost us very little in comparison with the priceless value, just at this time, of the money."

Fifteen-year-old William H. Digannard, described by a newswriter of that time as "of good character and dutiful to his parents," was killed under the wheels of a Newark and

New York railroad train while running an errand for his
mother, a laundress. The parents had carried a small policy
on the youth's life and the claim was paid within twenty-
four hours. "What my poor desolate household would have
done without this policy," wrote the boy's father, "I do
not know. God bless and prosper The Prudential Company. . . ."

The flow of such letters into the Prudential office increased
through the winter and early summer of 1876, as the number
of policies sold—all within the limits of the Newark area—
steadily mounted. But as the number of policies increased,
so also did the claims and the problem of meeting them
promptly.

There are always certain moments and incidents which
seem to stand out as symbols of difficult periods and storms
weathered in the past. One such moment of high peril in the
annals of Prudential was often recalled in later years by
Dr. Ward and Mr. Dryden.

The story involved a certain Mrs. Grover who shortly
before had been insured by the company for $500. Late one
February afternoon in 1876, as Dr. Ward told the story, Mr.
Dryden called the doctor to his desk and told him that he had
just learned that Mrs. Grover was ill with pneumonia and
was not expected to survive the night. "Mr. Dryden and I
both realized that a claim of $500 at that particular time
would very likely wreck the company. The only way to
save the company was to save Mrs. Grover. And this I endeavored to do."

After securing the permission of the woman's physician,
Dr. Ward hurried to the house in Court Street. He found the
patient in delirium, tossing on a bed in a cold, sparsely furnished house heated only by a smoking coal stove. Dr. Ward
set quickly about the task of treating the woman. He raised

her in the bed so that she could breathe more easily, applied poultices to her chest, and administered stimulants. All night long he sat by the woman's bed waiting for the moment of crisis.

"As consulting physician," he used to say, "I found that it was not only a case of keeping the policyholder alive—which I am delighted to say that I succeeded in doing—it was also a case of keeping the balance of the Grover family and myself from freezing to death. The fire in the stove kept going out. I found I had to 'treat' that fire almost as regularly as I treated the patient. It was a long, cold night. Now whether in helping to save the life of the policyholder I also saved the life of the company I leave to others."

In spite of the fact that during 1876 policies continued to be sold at an increasing rate, the balance sheet showed a discouraging tendency. By mid-November more than 7,000 policies had been written, but expenses were such that the company would finish its first full year of operation with a deficit of at least $1,500. On November 23 the directors met to consider this problem.

"We have been surprisingly successful in selling our policies," said one of the directors. "I am afraid, however, that we are likely to be swamped by this expensive kind of success."

The directors debated the problem heatedly throughout the evening. It was a complicated one involving rates, commissions to agents, sickness and death benefits, and the accuracy of their mortality tables. They had used the best information available, but clearly it was not sufficiently reliable. The only place in the world where it was possible to check their procedures against continued practical experience was in London, the home of The Prudential Assurance Company. Late that night it was agreed that rather than risk disaster because of inadequate information one of the directors should be sent to London to obtain a firsthand report.

The question then was whom to send. The meeting leaned toward sending one of their more substantial members, a person who could meet with executives in the large London offices on terms of equality—smooth-talking Bassett, perhaps, or George Moore with his legal training. But before a vote could be taken, Dr. Ward was on his feet.

"Gentlemen," said the doctor, "I am amazed that this meeting should be frittering away its time on such childish nonsense. You know—every one of you knows—that there is only one man here who understands enough about the business to know what questions to ask or what information to bring back. We would be inviting disaster to send anyone else. Gentlemen, we have no choice." He paused, then added slowly, "We must send John Dryden."

There was an embarrassed silence. None of them chose to dispute Dr. Ward's decision. Dr. Ward waited a moment. "Well, then, gentlemen, it's to be Mr. Dryden?"

One of the directors coughed. "But Secretary Dryden must understand," he said, "that the company cannot advance any large sum for this journey. It should take him about six weeks, including time on the high seas. I suggest the sum be limited to $250."

It was certainly no lavish allowance. The directors looked questioningly at Dryden. "That will be quite all right," he said quietly. "I shall leave as soon as I am able to arrange for passage."

Five days later, aboard the S.S. *Idaho*, Secretary Dryden set sail for Liverpool, England.

CHAPTER 4

Meeting of the Board

JOHN DRYDEN was in England for exactly two weeks. On Saturday, December 23, two days before Christmas, he sailed on the S.S. *Parthia* from Liverpool and on Sunday, January 7, 1877, landed in New York. The following morning he arrived early at the basement office at 812 Broad Street. Dr. Ward and Captain Bassett came in shortly thereafter, and the three men spent most of the morning discussing the results of the secretary's trip. That afternoon the clerks were set to copying a letter calling a special meeting of the board of directors for eight o'clock Friday evening, January 12. It was little enough notice and Secretary Dryden gave specific instructions that all of the letters be copied and mailed that evening.

The directors could hardly have received the notice with enthusiasm. Another meeting. Another discussion of the failing fortunes of this bargain insurance scheme Dr. Ward had talked them into. This time Dryden was going to report on his trip to England. Probably just more wasted time. The directors were substantial men whose time was well and profitably occupied in the day-to-day business of manu-

facturing and selling. They were interested in concrete
figures, not theories or abstractions. Each of them had an
investment in the new company, it was true, but none was
heavily involved financially. They felt that they had already
devoted more than enough time and attention to this little
marginal enterprise. If it was to fail, then at least it could
perish quietly and inconspicuously. A few more months and
the capital would probably be exhausted. When that happened, the directors thought, the company would be finished.

Well, let it go. Certainly there were few among the directors
that day who would have even considered risking additional
capital in this tottering little firm. There were better investments than that available.

And now this frantic meeting, this hope of getting English
secrets that would transform a failure into a success. The
directors pushed the letters back on their desks that morning
and got on with more profitable work.

In the office itself, however, there was an indefinable air
of expectancy, an undercurrent of tension that increased
as the week wore on. Captain Bassett and Mr. Dryden were
in almost constant conference. Several times a day young

George Gaston was sent scurrying to Dr. Ward's office with notes, or to Mr. Dryden's house to fetch piles of books and papers. On Friday afternoon the secretary called him over to his desk to give him special instructions about the preparations for the evening meeting. He told the boy how he wanted the desks moved to make more room in the crowded office, where to place the table with the material he would need for his report, how to shade the gaslights so they wouldn't shine in the directors' eyes. He produced a large rolled map from behind his desk and made a light pencil mark on the wall above Captain Bassett's chair to mark the exact spot he wanted it hung. Then he sent the office boy home—nearly an hour early—with strict instructions to be back at the office not later than seven o'clock to prepare for the arrival of the directors.

George Gaston remembered all of the earlier directors' meetings. None of them, he thought, had ever caused so much concern in the office—not even the meetings held in the big board room of the bank upstairs where his father was cashier. Later, when the elder Gaston came home from the bank, the boy told him of the meticulous directions he had received from the secretary. "I think Dryden sees that he's to have his last chance tonight," Mr. Gaston told him. "He wanted to go to England to find out why we're losing money, and now he has to give us the answer. From what I hear, the directors don't expect much." Young George knew what his father meant. Only a few nights before one of the directors who had been to dinner at the Gastons' had insisted that it didn't matter what Mr. Dryden learned in England, that nothing in the world would ever set this company on the road to big profits because in this country you just couldn't make money on three-cent and nickel policies . . . George felt a little sorry for Mr. Dryden.

Back in the darkened basement office the boy moved cautiously through the looming shadows of chairs and desks. At the back of the room he groped for the box of matches on the shelf. Swiftly, like some altar boy at his rites, he moved from one wall bracket to the next, holding the match to the gas jet and turning the valve until the flame grew bright. He realized that he was a little late and would have to hurry. The chairs he had carried down from the bank upstairs that afternoon were still piled in the corner, and he set about the business of arranging them in neat rows, as Mr. Dryden had directed.

Young Gaston pushed the bookkeeper's desk back against the wall to make a little more room. Then he stood on a chair and carefully tacked the edge of the rolled map Mr. Dryden had given him at exactly the height the secretary had indicated. Mr. Dryden always expected things to be done exactly right, not almost right.

George lowered the map slowly, unrolling it in his hands. Then he stood back and stared at it in surprise. It wasn't a map of England at all! It was a map of the United States, with all the states and territories right out to the Pacific. George stood there a moment shaking his head. The letters they had sent out to the directors had said that Mr. Dryden would report on his trip to England. How could he explain what he had seen in England if he used a map of the United States?

The boy was still staring at the map when he heard a heavy tread on the steps leading down to the door. He turned, picked up his dustcloth, and began to move quickly through the rows of chairs, straightening them and setting in order the basement headquarters of The Prudential Friendly Society.

It was no later than a quarter past seven when Noah

Blanchard, the first vice-president, stomped into the office grumbling about the snow which had just begun to fall. For a moment the burly tanner stood inside the door pounding the snow from his heavy boots and beating it from his shoulders with his enormous hands. He leaned forward and flicked the glistening flakes from his beard and then tossed his greatcoat across the bookkeeper's desk. He moved heavily across the floor and, with his hands locked behind him, solemnly regarded the map.

As he dusted the chairs behind the vice-president George caught the pungent odor of curing leather that always clung to the tanner. The boys said that even if they couldn't see him they could always tell when he was in the office and—when the wind was in the right quarter—when he was approaching.

George had finished his preparations before the other directors began to arrive. He watched them as they came— singly when they had walked from their offices and factories, in two's and three's when they had driven downtown after dinner. There were the two Wards, quiet Edgar, the attorney, and the hearty doctor who at once launched into a discussion with Mr. Blanchard. Mr. Moore and Mr. Wilkinson, looking cold and glum, came in together. Behind them arrived Mr. Murphy, Mr. Richards, and Mr. Whitty. Captain Bassett, meticulously dressed in a new gray frockcoat, circulated warmly about the room. They were coming faster now. Mr. Robotham, Mr. Burnett, Mr. Alling, and Mr. Romer. Mayor Yates and Mr. Campbell hurried in just before seven-thirty. Behind them came Mr. Dryden. George noticed that he looked a little thinner than usual and a little more tired. But perhaps it was only the trip from England. Mr. Dryden had told him about the trip. Fifteen days it was, and storming part of the way.

The men, gathered in close little groups, were chatting in low tones. To George they looked solemn and grim. It was almost as if they had already made up their minds that nothing Mr. Dryden said would change the prospects of the company. They were there merely as a duty.

Dr. Ward was the only one who looked confident. The tall, redheaded medical director of the company moved from group to group, smiling, talking to this one and that. "Worried? Why should any of us be worried?" he demanded of one director. "Wait till you hear Dryden. I've got an idea you're in for a surprise." Some of the men close by smiled at that. Always the enthusiast, Dr. Ward was. Always the optimist.

George was not permitted to remain during meetings of the board and when he saw Captain Bassett arranging his notes on the table at the front of the room he began to put on his coat. There was surely nothing unusual about the way this meeting was beginning. Suavely the president made a few pleasant-sounding comments about the high purpose of the society, and the intention to spread industrial insurance "as wide as this land." He reminded the directors that they had sent their secretary to England six weeks before to learn what he could about the British Prudential's operations, and assured them pleasantly that Mr. Dryden had returned truly "freighted" with information. As George closed the door quietly behind him he heard the president intoning rotundly, "Gentlemen, I invite your attention to the report of Mr. Dryden."

The minutes of the meeting that night were not perfectly recorded. Here and there a name or a figure was improperly heard or incorrectly entered. Occasionally a fragment of a sentence—a thought that was perhaps finished by a gesture—

stands unexplained. But whatever small failings there may be, those minutes preserve in their original form the words and concepts of John F. Dryden—concepts which were to alter the whole course of The Prudential Friendly Society.

Dryden began easily enough. For the benefit of the few who were unfamiliar with the background, he sketched in the reasons for the trip, the problems to be solved. He spoke of the crossing to Liverpool and on to London. Casually the secretary told the directors that within twenty-four hours of his arrival in London he had managed to obtain letters of introduction to the most prominent insurance men in Britain. Among them Mr. Henry Harben, head of the gigantic Prudential of England. There was a ripple of surprise among the directors at the statement that he had been able to obtain a letter to Harben. None of them had been able to furnish Dryden with such a letter. When he arrived at the British Prudential, Dryden continued, he was told that Mr. Harben was out of town. "But I was informed that the secretary, Mr. Lancaster, was in and that I could have an interview with him."

The directors glanced at one another. This was what they had expected. A world-famous figure like Harben, heading a company which did a business in hundreds of thousands of pounds, would hardly give much time to a minor official of an unheard-of little insurance company in Newark, New Jersey. Dryden saw the smiles of some of these men. He added quietly, "But I declined to see the secretary, preferring to wait another day to see Mr. Harben."

Smoothly, confidently, the secretary went on. On the following day he had seen Mr. Harben personally in the president's sumptuous offices. Mr. Harben had greeted him cordially. To Dryden's surprise, Harben had heard of the Newark company. To his further surprise, after Dryden frankly had stated his reasons for coming, the British insurance leader "cheerfully and cordially" agreed to answer any of his questions. Further, he had called in his manager, Mr. Dewey, and ordered him to furnish any blanks, forms, or information the American might wish.

The directors began to show interest. This Dryden had done better than they had expected. It was possible, barely possible, that the secretary might have some new knowledge. Just getting in to see Harben—that alone was something of a triumph.

Dryden knew that he had the directors' interest now and that he could hold it. He knew that in the facts he had assembled lay his future and the future of the company he had founded. With an instinctive sense of drama, Dryden chose to hold the suspense of that moment.

Dryden knew that these men were waiting for the facts he had brought back—the facts that might save their floundering company. But he proposed to give them more—the background to understand these facts. He turned abruptly from the meeting with Harben to a description of the friendly societies of England, tracing their origins, their growth, and their weakness. He sketched the steps in the development of industrial insurance from these societies. He quoted from the charters of old English companies, and even went to biblical times for examples of insurance practices among the Israelites. The directors stirred in their chairs. They hadn't come to the meeting to hear a history lecture. They wanted facts, practical facts.

Secretary Dryden was precise in his timing. He had given the directors the background they needed. As deliberately as he had turned from the story of the meeting with Harben he now returned to it.

He first pictured the intricate workings inside the offices of

ALLEN L. BASSETT

the English firm, the jobs performed by the various departments, the correspondence department, the registry department, the statistical, ledger, cashier, claim, and mailing departments. He turned then to the organization outside the
office, the six divisions into which Prudential had divided
Great Britain, and the subdivisions, each with its superintendent who, in turn, was in charge of the agents, "to see
that the field is well occupied, to see that these agents keep
their accounts correctly, to see that they make correct returns
to the company, to see that they take the proper kind of
applications, to see, in general, that they bring no disrepute
upon the company."

Detail by detail he took up in turn, as he unfolded this
story of how the highly successful English company
operated. Point by point he discussed the particulars in which
their own company differed, the mistakes they had made in
organization, the weaknesses in their understanding of industrial insurance and its practical operation.

Dryden pointed out that there were many differences between the American and the British company. For example,
in Newark they had divided the city into districts and rigidly
allowed the agent to work only within his assigned district.
"We had been informed that this was the practice of The
Prudential, but I find that we were greatly in error. They
appoint a city—Newark, for instance—and it is an open field
for every agent. They may work where they choose. . . ."

There was the vital matter of keeping books. In spite of its
large size, The Prudential of London was employing a system
far simpler than that used in Newark. It was based on only
three main registry books. Fluently Dryden outlined the
English method of recording policies issued and its advantages.

Marked like exhibits in a court, the material lay before the secretary on the table. One after the other Dryden held up the books and papers, explaining the purpose of each. Here was item Number 1, an application for a position as agent— age, occupation, character references. This space below for the endorsement of the supervisor. This form, item Number 2, gave the rules by which the agent was guided. There were fifteen such rules. Here were Numbers 4 and 5, application blanks for adults and children. Here was the premium receipt book, Number 7; the agent's ledger, Number 14; an office analysis form showing the policies in every district in England. Here was a form in regard to the medical examination required for reinstatement after a policy had lapsed thirteen weeks. A director broke in. Did the company have to pay for that examination? The secretary nodded and went on.

The secretary had now reached the heart of his report, and the directors had begun to realize that John Dryden had performed a minor miracle. In two weeks spent in England he had managed to collect and bring back every detail, every salient feature, all the facts and figures and forms used, covering this whole colossal operation called The Prudential of London. More, he had understood and marshaled all of these facts into a graphic, crystal-clear, exciting picture.

There was a new atmosphere in this crowded room now. The directors leaned forward, intent on the speaker. What they were hearing was not only the story of how some company operated in a distant country. It was also a picture of how this American company could grow and expand in success—just as Bassett had mentioned at the start—across the width of this land.

The secretary delved into the vital matter of sickness benefits. In England they had abandoned this form of insurance, having had "disastrous experience" with this branch of the business.

"I deem it due to you, gentlemen," he declared, "to state this matter frankly . . . and my opinion is that so far as females are concerned we ought to drop this branch of business at once. So far as the sickness business with males is concerned, it should be conducted with very great caution and we . . . should be extremely cautious as to the amount of the benefit we grant. . . ."

The secretary paused and looked around. "The Prudential of London sprang from a very small beginning. It was organized in a room not so large as the one we are in now," he said slowly. "The business has progressed from year to year, until they have been forced to break through one wall to another and go upstairs and downstairs, so that I got lost there one day and had to inquire my way out."

Dryden had come to the climax of his report. Now he must convince these men, he must show them what he had dreamed of achieving, what Prudential of London had actually done. "They had issued in 1851 less than 7,000 policies, in 1860 they issued 33,000 policies, in 1865 they issued 148,-000 policies, in 1870 they issued 297,000 policies, but they are now issuing them at the rate of over 1,500,000 a year. . . . From Liverpool alone they receive about $2,000 per week . . . in one year from now they expect over $5,000 a week. The premiums of The Prudential amount to over $5,000,000 a year, and they collect this vast sum of money from these infinitesimal amounts which are taken up by a string of 6,000 agents scattered throughout the country."

The pessimism had gone from this meeting. In its place was anticipation and excitement. "Now, then, this brings us to the practical question, whether we can apply this business —to America. Well, we are 40,000,000, in Great Britain they are 30,000,000. I think we have in this country all the elements of a successful business."

On the wall behind him hung the map young Gaston had tacked up earlier—the United States in that year 1877. Like a schoolteacher before a class of boys, the secretary picked a heavy black crayon from the table and turned to this map.

Dryden knew that uppermost in the minds of these men now was the question of expansion beyond the bounds of Newark. This was the problem they had put aside until his trip to England, until they knew where they were headed, or if they were headed anywhere at all. These men were worrying about tomorrow. Dryden would show them the future. "If you take the map, gentlemen, you will see that if you draw a line down the Missouri River and along the 35th Degree"—Dryden slashed heavy broad lines across the map—"all that part lying east and north of the lines embraces one third of the geographical portion of America . . . and 80 per cent of our entire population!"

Many of the directors were standing now, following Dryden as he outlined the routes of growth their company could follow across the nation. "This part of our country is accessible by railroads," he was saying. "We can arrive at the great points of population without serious inconvenience. The towns follow the railroad. . . ."

Dryden walked back to the table and began to assemble the scattered forms. The directors settled again in their chairs. The secretary waited for silence. "Gentlemen," he said softly, "we can reach those towns and cities.

"Mr. Harben said one thing further: 'Tell your men not to be afraid to spend money in the infancy of the company. There is a great field before you. It will surely yield re-munerative results, but you must spend money in the com-mencement. . . . Your men must not expect to realize great profits immediately. They must spend the money, and the profits will come.' " Dryden paused for the full effect. "Now, gentlemen," he said, "any questions you may desire to ask . . ."

As he finished, they all knew there was no longer any question of closing down. It was more a matter of how soon to advance—and where. But it is a curious fact—recorded in the minutes—that these gentlemen, finding themselves standing suddenly at the threshold of success, were still concerned primarily with problems of petty cash. Their first and most insistent questions centered on the matter of how much it would cost.

How many of these blanks he had shown them would they have to use? Only a few. How much would it cost to have them printed up? The cost wouldn't be high.

They kept at him about the expense of these forms. The secretary finally went through the forms one by one, picking out the few they would require. Would this mean changing the nature of the books now in use? No, the books could be adapted by adding special headings. Another director jumped up heatedly. Did the secretary imply they would have to discard present books and purchase new ones? Wearily the secretary repeated that there would be no need to purchase any new books. He smiled at the expression of relief on the director's face.

The questions came at him from all angles and on every aspect of the company. How about the rates? Were the rates they were using safe? How did they compare with the British rates? The British rates were higher. Should ours be raised? The answer was yes, and as quickly as possible.

What about Clark? Weren't they going to have to throw away Clark's tables? Mr. Dryden explained that Clark's tables had been based on the experience of ordinary companies. So the great mistake, boomed another director, lay in not realizing the vast difference between life insurance business and this business. That was correct. Then why not take the tables and rates of the London Prudential? Why not go right along? Why not follow right in their wake?

But Mr. Dryden said no. They weren't merely imitating the English firm; they were adapting certain of its principles to the American scene. You could sell insurance cheaper in America. People lived longer here, and better. You got higher interest on investments.

As the strenuous session drew to its close he reiterated his proposals: Abandon sickness benefits for women. Go slow with such insurance for men. Reorganize the system for keeping records, adapting the English system of divisions and subdivisions and the handling of correspondence with agents in the field. And revise their rate table with a view to wider expansion—all the way west to the Missouri and perhaps beyond.

It was more than merely a report he had made. This was virtually a blueprint for reorganization, based not on theories or fears, but on the practical experience of one of the most successful companies in the world. But it was more, too, than mere imitation. Whatever they borrowed from England they would reshape to fit the American needs.

The minutes of that meeting are only the cold words set down by the stenographer. They record merely that a director made a motion:

"Mr. President, I move that the report of our secretary be received and placed on file, and that the thanks of this board be tendered to the gentleman for his instructive and intelligent report."

And beneath that, in parenthesis, "The above was unanimously adopted."

Although the results of that meeting are not to be read in the minutes, they were evident in almost every activity of the company from that night forward. Within a few months the actuarial tables had been completely revised, the company had opened offices in Paterson and Elizabeth, and the president had been instructed to raise additional capital to permit the extension of the company's activities into New York and Pennsylvania. On March 15, 1877, the name of The Prudential Friendly Society was officially changed to The Prudential Insurance Company of America.

There was one other result not so readily seen. On the night of January 12 Secretary Dryden had made himself the master of Prudential. In his report he had shown the directors the promise of the future. These men of business were wise enough to know that their still somewhat shabby secretary was the only one who could lead them down the road to realization of that promise.

John Dryden was still listed as secretary in The Prudential Insurance Company of America. But the title had become a misnomer.

CHAPTER 5

The Battle for Debits

THERE are many ways in which the strength of a man—or of a company—is tested. The Prudential Friendly Society had been tested through the hard year of 1876, had been buffeted heavily during that time of deepening depression. It had lost money, and many of the directors had lost faith and all but given up hope.

On the surface the prospects for 1877 were worse. This was the bleakest year of the depression. Thousands of solid, reliable old concerns, after weathering three years of economic storm, were being driven onto the rocks. There was a rising clamor for help from the people, from the poor. There were riots and disorders. In Pittsburgh an angry, shouting mob of railroad strikers, brandishing clubs and bricks and shotguns, took over the city for three days and nights of terror. Even in Newark there were bread riots of the unemployed who marched and shouted their demands for work along Market Street and Broad. This was the very pit of the depression this year. And yet where others were failing this new company, The Prudential Insurance Company of America, not only survived but grew stronger.

Why? Why should it grow now, when a year before—when times had not been quite so stark—it had languished and all but died?

The answer was not hard to find. It was thriving now on the strength of an idea which had taken root—on the purposes, vision, persistence, and faith of the man who shaped that idea. John Dryden knew that industrial insurance was a workable plan. In spite of the red-ink record of 1876 he had been able to persuade the directors that it would succeed. Dryden knew that the roots of his plan were strong and sound, that it would spread in good times, that it would grow even in the worst of times. He and the men he was able to inspire set to work to prove his concept—in the mean, dirty, hungry year of 1877.

Every move, every step, was another challenge. Here were the tables—Clark's tables—which now they knew had to be revised completely. These tables of rates and benefits and commissions—these were the foundation stones of the business. If they were wrong or inaccurate, the whole structure would collapse.

Using Clark's figures, in addition to those he had obtained in England, and from their own experience in 1876, Dryden set to work. Day and night he labored on them, around the clock, working against the pressure of time and the eagerness of the directors to start their expansion. Several times Dr. Ward came into the office late to find Dryden bent wearily over these charts. "Slow up, John—slow up!" the doctor had warned. "Those figures will be dancing in front of your eyes if you don't relax a little." But Dryden kept on. He had finished much of the revision, actually, within a few weeks. Looking over this new rate table, he was rather pleased with the results. This was a sound table now, sound and well built. It would stand up a long time, the carpentering job he had done with rates and figures and years.

Premiums on policies for children under thirteen were limited to three cents and no benefit was payable until the child had been insured for three months. Later that was to be revised. But in that dark year Dryden felt the company could safely go no further.

There were other actuarial matters and details that demanded the secretary's attention in that chill winter. The matter of sickness, for example. After careful review of the figures, Dryden decided there was only one sound course: Abandon all sickness insurance for both males and females. The sale of all forms of sickness benefits was allowed to taper off. Within a few months it was stopped entirely.

In late February the secretary was able to present to the board his new tables, the new rates on which they would operate—and expand. Armed with these new tables, Prudential was now ready to move forward, to meet the next challenge—the problem of expansion.

Already people had begun to hear about the company in nearby towns. In Newark and neighboring communities many who had originally distrusted this "scheme" were watching with surprise letters and reports in the papers that this Prudential company was paying off its claims, paying them off in twenty-four hours, with no red tape either. Some of the people were beginning to drop into the basement office and ask questions. Residents of more distant towns were wondering when Prudential might be moving out their way.

The company made the first move carefully. After considering several possible communities in which to open its first branch office, the officers chose nearby Paterson. It looked like a good town to start with. It was like Newark in many ways, a city made up of a large industrial class, and, like

Newark, an area of smoke and factories and crowded sections of workers and their families. Most important of all, Paterson was near enough for a close watch to be kept on how it was running.

Bassett was sent to look things over in the new town, to find a proper location. Bassett was an old hand at real estate and would know a good value. He found an office at 114 Ellison Street. Before he started back to Newark, he dropped in to chat with some of his friends in the First National Bank. Casually he let fall a hint that Prudential might be moving into town shortly.

President Bassett's news had immediate effect. Word spread swiftly through the city that Prudential was coming to town—a new company selling industrial insurance. Many people had heard about this kind of insurance, but most of them were vague on the details. A group of the top men of the city—including the mayor, the city comptroller, the president of the Paterson First National Bank, and several other business leaders of the city, wrote to Prudential on April 6, 1877. "We the undersigned beg leave to request that you will address a public meeting of citizens interested in this new system of Insurance . . . and explain its peculiar features."

The meeting was held in the Paterson Odd Fellows Hall on Main Street over Michael Moss's drugstore on the night of April 12. President Bassett and Secretary Dryden were both there to address the hundreds who gathered to hear about this new kind of insurance. Secretary Dryden told them of the growth of the company and the fact that "even in these unprecedented hard times we have been able thus far to sell more than 10,000 industrial policies to the working people of our city." To the working people of Paterson this figure was astounding.

The Paterson office opened late in April 1877. In charge

was Christopher Blake, a young man groomed for the job by Dryden in Newark. But even then the officers were watchful. President Bassett himself used to come over every day to help Blake in the hiring and organizing. Carl Giese, who was still employed as a clerk in the home office back in Newark, recalled that "Captain Bassett went there every morning and did not return until evening, when I was expected to be in the office and report to him his callers and the incidents of the day."

Business began briskly in Paterson. And soon the company was looking for other new locations. The Jersey City office, covering Hudson County, was opened in August with George Babbitt in charge. Then it was Elizabeth, later in the same month, with T. W. Buttle as superintendent. Trenton was next, in 1878, with G. H. Brown as superintendent, and Camden in 1879 with J. V. N. Lyle in charge. The "peculiar little company" was spreading its wings across the state of New Jersey.

The figures for these years of expansion within the state tell their own story of Prudential's growth:

Years Ending December 31	Number of Policies in Force	Amount in Force
1876	4,816	$ 443,072
1877	11,226	1,030,655
1878	22,808	2,027,888
1879	43,715	3,866,913

Of course it was not all clear sailing. The growth was accomplished in the midst of chronic troubles and incessant crises. A portion of the press—notably the trade press—had begun to give serious and generally favorable attention to this growing company. But the woods were still filled with doubters and detractors who missed no opportunity to cast suspicion or ridicule on the company and its agents. Some of the agents themselves proved unreliable; many found the work too grueling, and a few yielded to the temptation to abscond with the collections. Some ministers still felt that insurance was defiance of Heaven's will. And as the company grew bigger, local governments began inquiring with zeal into its operations and talking of new regulations and taxes.

The job of hiring and training the staff of agents needed to keep pace with this growth was the second great challenge to be met in these years of beginning. From the start Dryden had been aware of the importance of the agent to the success of the venture. Since there were no experienced men in this new type of insurance, he had spent many long hours in the job of building a staff from the raw material coming into the office in answer to Prudential's want ads in the papers.

In the building of this agency staff Dryden found himself with a dilemma. To attract the kind of people needed, Prudential had to offer the possibility of reasonably good earnings. But here the difficulty arose. The cost of collecting premiums fifty-two times a year at the policyholder's home was heavy under the best of circumstances. If it were allowed to rise too high, the whole operation of industrial insurance would be jeopardized and possibly destroyed.

At the very beginning Dryden had adopted the rather complex system of commissions used in England. The agent would receive commissions on new business and on the weekly collections in his district or "debit," as it came to be called. In 1877 the American Prudential's commissions were a little lower than the English company's. On new business the agent received approximately three times the amount of the weekly premium. But to discourage him from writing worthless names—and to encourage him to work to keep premium payments up to date—lapses were deducted from the agent's earnings at the same rate. The agent was also paid 15 per cent of the total weekly premiums he collected in his district.

To take an example: For writing new applications with a total weekly premium of $3.00, the agent would be credited with $9.00. If policies totaling weekly premiums of $1.00 lapsed, $3.00 would be deducted from the $9.00, leaving him with $6.00. If, in addition, the agent that week collected $30 in weekly premiums, he would receive for this an additional $4.50. In this case his earnings would amount to $10.50.

Secretary Dryden knew that the scale of commissions would have to be revised upward. A few of the agents had done rather well, but the average had been far too low. As a result, it had been extremely difficult to build a permanent force. Shortly after his return from England he had increased the commissions, and within the next few years additional revisions were put through. Largely because of the increased opportunities he was affording his agents, Prudential was able to meet the trials of these coming years with a reliable, trained, and loyal staff in the field.

But entirely aside from the question of earnings the job of finding good agents was a continuing harassment. The agent had to be a special type of individual. He had to mix well and easily with the people on his "debit," the working men and their wives and kids. He had to understand them, and talk their language. He had to be their friend, and a little more than their friend. He was also their guide, their mentor, their adviser.

The agents also had to be ladies and gentlemen of sturdy constitutions, ready wits, and even tempers. They had to tramp the tenement stairs and the back streets of Newark and Paterson and Trenton. They learned to have quick answers in the give-and-take discussions with prospects and to brush off philosophically the slammed door or the sign: "No beggars, dogs, or insurance men allowed."

They were young mostly, these men recruited by Prudential. They came from all walks of life. One was a blacksmith and another a stevedore; there was a wheelwright and a glass blower, a tinsmith and a minister, a corset maker and an oysterman.

They belonged to the people, and that was why they could understand the people and their problems. They weren't interested, most of them, in the higher theories of insurance. Leave such matters to the home office. The business of the agent was the one indispensable job—selling policies and collecting the premiums. And to the great majority of the public the agent stood for the company. He was Prudential itself.

But it wasn't all work. The agent shared not only the grim moments of those on his "debit" route, but often the gayer moments, too, a christening or a wedding or a Saturday-night jamboree. And the agents themselves found time for social get-togethers, where the talk was mostly the swapping of stories and experiences.

Some of those stories came to be rather famous wherever Prudential men gathered. There was one about the new agent who insured a widow and her large brood of children, "including Tommy—don't leave out little Tommy," she had insisted. Later she told the agent to cancel the policy for Tommy. "He ran away. Poor little Tommy ran away. And with so many cats in this neighborhood, I just know we'll never find him again."

Another they told was of the lady who stopped the agent on the street. "When you asked me to take out a policy on my husband, I didn't do it—and, sure enough, he died. Well,

I've married again now, and I want a policy on my new husband right away. I wouldn't want to go through a thing like that all over again."

Or the story of the man who was dying and who begged his physician to keep him alive for two weeks. "If you do this for me," he breathed, "my Prudential policy will be in full force and my family will collect the whole $500."

According to the yarn the agents liked to tell, this story had a dividend. The physician worked so hard to keep the dying man alive for two weeks that the man recovered completely and lived for many years.

The job of keeping this widely scattered agency staff informed on the over-all picture—the developing programs and policies of the home office—sometimes was complicated. The agent in the field was a man of direct action. He didn't have much time for letter reading or writing. Even in those days the flow of circular letters from the home office was a sore subject with the agents. Still, these letters were important. The agent, as the company's representative, was the only one who could sit down in the living-room rocker and tell the company's side of the story to the worried or distrustful policyholders.

The agent had to be able to answer a whole series of recurring questions. What about these stories on the perils of infantile insurance, for example, "baby insurance," as the papers called it. Hadn't the Trenton *True American* stated that insurance on youngsters was actually an inducement to murder? Weren't there stories that mothers and fathers were neglecting their children in sickness or actually "putting them out of the way?"

There were such stories, of course, many of them. And it was the agent who had to answer these attacks. Patiently he would explain that the stories were sheer fabrication. Neither

NOAH F. BLANCHARD

in England nor America had a single case of child murder for insurance money ever been established. Would American mothers or fathers murder their children to collect a $10 or $15 burial fund?

Another line of attack which agents had to meet frequently was the matter of lapsed policies. There were many who believed the wild tales that Prudential was coining money from profits on lapsed policies. There was always the amateur mathematician who knew all about lapses. The agent would explain. There were no profits in lapses. The company lost because of the high costs of putting a policy in operation. The agent lost because three times the premium was deducted for every lapse in his district. And the policyholder lost his protection.

Sometimes the home office eased the agent's road by answering the attacks directly, as in the case of one letter to a Newark paper charging that the company was permitting large numbers of policies to lapse in the Eighth Ward in Newark. Was it the aim of Prudential to make money by allowing policies to lapse through non-collections? The editor permitted Secretary Dryden to reply. The secretary explained that Prudential made every effort to collect all dues and gave the policyholder every chance to save his policy. If the writer of the letter had any money he thought ought to be in Prudential's coffers, "our agent will cheerfully relieve at once his conscience and his pocketbook."

The most effective answer to these attacks was the success of Prudential. In New Jersey the company was beginning to attract wide attention. It was meeting its claims and paying promptly the full amount owed. Public confidence in the strength of Prudential—in spite of attacks or misunderstanding—was mounting.

"Six policies became due by the death of six persons insured by Prudential in one day of last week," ran a story in the Paterson *Guardian*. "The fact that six persons died in one day—that their friends took their policies to Prudential's office and got the money for them, all in twenty-four hours—is something that has never been seen in this or any other city of this country before. The brilliant success of this company is shown even in the magnitude of its losses. . . ."

But while they had met the test here in New Jersey, another challenge loomed immediately ahead—the problem of branching out still farther, into other states, across the river into New York and over the Pennsylvania border into Philadelphia. This required not only an enlargement of the staff, but also an increase in capital to $100,000.

The problem of raising these funds led to the company's first major internal crisis. President Bassett had assured the directors that he could raise the money easily. But as the months went by Bassett failed to bring in the required funds, as he had promised. Dryden and the directors fretted at this failure. The moment had come to advance and they were being held back, needlessly, many of them insisted. At length the directors took the matter into their own hands and solved the problem abruptly.

On the night of May 15, 1879, a special meeting of the board of directors was called by the president. Aaron Carter was there and Dr. Ward and his brother Edgar, Bassett, Noah Blanchard, Yates, John T. Leverich, Romer, Robotham, Whitty, Murphy, Wilkinson, William D. Carter, and John Dryden.

What happened that evening is quickly told in the terse minutes of the meeting:

> The President stated that he had called the Board for the purpose of considering the advisability of extending the business of the Company into Philadelphia.

Mr. Whitty stated that in order to get the matter before the Board he would move that steps be taken to commence business in Philadelphia but that he himself was opposed to the motion.

The motion was seconded and after remarks by several Directors the question was put and unanimously lost.

Mr. Murphy stated that some of the Directors felt aggrieved at certain acts of the President and thought the Directors would like to talk the matter over.

On motion Mr. Blanchard the Vice-President took the chair.

Mr. Robotham then presented a preamble of grievances against the President and a Resolution calling upon him to resign his office as President.

Mr. Whitty moved that the Preamble and Resolution be received. The motion was seconded and carried.

Mr. Robotham moved the adoption of the Preamble and Resolution. The motion was seconded by Mr. Yates.

Remarks were then made by the President and several Directors.

Dr. Ward then stated that the President wished him to say that if the Preamble and Resolution were withdrawn he would resign his office. On motion action on the Preamble and Resolution was postponed in order to give the President an opportunity to resign.

Mr. Bassett then handed the following communication to the vice-president:

NEWARK, N.J., MAY 15, 1879

To the Directors of The Prudential Insurance Company
  Gentlemen

I hereby tender my resignation as President of this Company.

I am yours Respfly.
(signed) ALLEN L. BASSETT

On motion of Mr. Robotham the resignation was unanimously accepted and his salary ordered paid until July 1st, 1879.

Adjourned
John F. Dryden   Sec.

There was more behind this sudden action against Bassett than appeared on the surface. Many of the directors felt that during the preceding months he had failed to put forth his best efforts. In the conflict arising from this failure, personal frictions had developed between Bassett and certain of the board members. It was a flare-up of this bitter feeling which resulted in Bassett's resignation.

The change in administration produced immediate developments. That evening Noah Blanchard was made acting president and twelve days later was named president. By October of that year they had not only raised the money needed, but President Blanchard was able to report to his board that they were already in operation across state lines. In New York they had opened offices at the famous old Astor House, at the corner of Ninth Street and Broadway with George Thornton, ex-president of John Hancock Mutual Life, as the first superintendent. They had opened offices in Philadelphia with John F. Collins—former secretary of the Republic Life of Chicago and one of the rising young insurance men of the country—as the superintendent in charge.

The reaction to this step across the borders was mixed. Most of the newspapers and the insurance press greeted the advance favorably, but there were others who regarded with disapproval the arrival of these "foreigners" from another state. They expressed their opinions bluntly, almost brutally. Declared the New York *Sunday Mercury*, for example:

> It may be known to some of our readers that a small one-horse insurance company, with its headquarters at Newark, New Jersey, is actually endeavoring to scoop in a harvest of victims in this city and state. With the grandiloquence which naturally arises from ignorance and presumption, it baptized itself The Prudential, after the great industrial assurance society of that name in England. Then it hung out its shingle,

published a wonderful prospectus, and on the 31st day of July 1879 its agents crossed the Hudson River and invaded this city like a microscopic pestilence of an army of worms or hornets. . . .

But if some of the press opposed, the people themselves approved. Criticism and praise alike served only to increase public interest in these "invaders from Newark." Back in the home office they watched the results carefully. This had been a major step for the young company, and an expensive one. It couldn't afford a failure. The officers were relieved when the new branch in the old Astor House began to show substanial returns. The applications from across the river were rolling in.

In 1879 the Metropolitan Life Insurance Company was under the domination of Joseph F. Knapp, a burly, muscular, hard-driving man who had guided the company through the depression of the seventies. Knapp was the antithesis of John Dryden of Prudential. He was a doer and a fighter, a stocky, stubborn man who drove tirelessly toward his objective.

The years of the depression had been hard for the Metropolitan, just as they had been for all the old-line insurance companies. Knapp watched the strength of his company ebb away and with it the solid personal investment he had in the firm. He saw the Metropolitan's assets shrink, had watched the applications dwindle. In the depths of the depression Knapp had strengthened the company with his own funds and set his mind to the task of recouping the losses.

One of the great figures in insurance history, Knapp would have been a tower of a man anywhere. At sixteen he had been apprenticed to a lithographer and at twenty-two he was a full-fledged partner in the business. He had moved from success to success. He was a man who made money easily and confidently. In the early seventies he had found himself heavily involved in the affairs of Metropolitan, and, characteristically, had taken over the direction of the company to extricate himself.

Knapp had been fully aware of the progress of industrial insurance in the United States. As early as 1876 he had suggested to the Metropolitan's board of directors that The Prudential Assurance Company of London was doing the kind of business which they, in America, might adopt. Nothing had come of that suggestion, but Knapp had watched John F. Dryden cautiously developing the idea across the river in Newark. He had seen The Prudential Friendly Society take its first unsteady steps and had watched Dryden correct the early errors and set the company on the road to progress and expansion. Observing Prudential's mounting success, Knapp saw in industrial insurance a way to salvage his own fortunes and Metropolitan's as well.

Joseph Knapp was not a man to circle about an idea. He moved in boldly. In the fall of 1878 he was off to England to see the workings of the English Prudential, and a few months later, like Dryden, he, too, stood before his board of directors with all the forms and ledgers and details of the business. Swept away by his enthusiasm, the directors voted $100,000, nearly a third of their surplus and capital, to launch the new venture.

Switching their efforts from ordinary to industrial was an enormous undertaking, a challenge worthy of Knapp's fighting talents. He had no time for experiment, no time to develop the idea in a limited space. Speed was essential. Overnight he hurled all of his own inexhaustible energies and all of the company's resources into the task. Knapp was determined to make Metropolitan the dominant company in industrial insurance, and that in the shortest possible time.

Knapp's entry into this new field precipitated one of the

historic battles of the insurance world—a struggle involving two powerful personalities, Joseph Knapp and John Dryden. No sharper contrast could have been found. Knapp the plunger, driving ahead to his goal, heedless of all obstacles in his path, and John Dryden, the cautious Yankee planner, thinking out carefully each move, every possible contingency.

Knapp was the first to move into action. He needed men trained in industrial insurance, needed them quickly. Some of them he found over in Newark. Brice Collard, British born, a top superintendent for Prudential, was one of the first to be brought over into the Metropolitan fold. Another was twenty-year-old George Gaston, already a veteran of the business, thoroughly versed in the organization of agency forces.

Knapp had special use for the British Collard. Metropolitan needed more trained industrial agents than Knapp could find in this country, and the only place to get them was in England. He sent Collard over with carte blanche to bring back as many men as he could persuade, with offers of free transportation, high commissions, and opportunities for immediate advancement to top-paying positions. Collard went over in January and by June had sent back more than 500 men and their families.

Building his agency force around this nucleus of men arriving from England, Knapp drove ahead. Within a few months Metropolitan's industrial agents were selling in an area three times the size of that patiently built up by John Dryden over the years since 1875.

Mr. Dryden watched Knapp carefully. Like Knapp, he, too, imported from England, but he was against bringing over English representatives wholesale. It was costly and uncertain as to results. He was not going to be rushed into tremendous, expensive, and often unproductive expansion.

Prudential was operating now in New Jersey, New York, and Pennsylvania. For the moment that was enough.

Raids on each other's agency forces continued, with honors about even. If Metropolitan sent men to Newark, seeking likely material among Prudential personnel, Prudential returned the compliment by sending men into New York for similar activity against its competitor. Staff losses and gains were about the same for both companies.

Knapp poured the assets of Metropolitan into building the agency force. When the company could no longer bear the strain, Knapp drew on his own personal fortune. During Metropolitan's first year in industrial, it wrote almost 214,000 policies for a total of $20,728,000. Premium income amounted to $157,000, expenses to $269,000, and claims to nearly $34,000. By the year's end only 110,193 policies for $9,103,000 remained in force.

In volume of business and territory covered Metropolitan had raced past Prudential. The Newark company had watched it go by and gone on about its business. Shrewd John Dryden was not alarmed. He said then, as he was to say many times later, "Prudential seeks only to surpass its own record." Nevertheless, Prudential countered when it was necessary. It raised agents' commissions to ten to twenty times the weekly net business increase, depending on the size of the debit.

By the end of the year 1880 Prudential's assets were up nearly $30,000, it had issued nearly three times the policies it had the previous year, and its income had climbed from $123,646 in 1879 to $258,322 in 1880.

At the top executive level there was an attempt on both sides to maintain a certain outward decorum. When things began to get too rough in the field, Vice-president John Hegeman, Knapp's next in command, wrote a politely worded but firm protest to John Dryden. Prudential agents, he said, were spreading stories that Metropolitan was on its last legs and was moving into industrial insurance only to try to save a sinking ship.

Dryden replied with a protest of his own—a denunciation of a campaign he claimed was being waged against The Prudential in Newark by Metropolitan's new superintendent in that city. The name of this Metropolitan superintendent, whose headquarters were just a few doors away from Prudential's home office, was Captain Allen Bassett, formerly president of Prudential.

It was on the level of the superintendents and particularly of the agents in the field that the struggle turned into a door-to-door Donnybrook. The agents of the rival firms were contending, not so much for principles or for the reputation of their firms, as for their own livelihood. To the agent every policy the opposition sold was one less commission in his pocket.

Throughout this struggle Prudential was aware that its one hope of holding its own with Knapp's Metropolitan was to continue at its own rate of growth, to refuse to be elbowed into extravagance and overexpansion. Even while Knapp was pouring in his tens of thousands of dollars, the Prudential's lumbering Noah Blanchard was priding himself on his numerous "small savings" for the policyholders.

George Williams, in those days the only stenographer in the office, remembered years later how the bulky tanner leaned over his shoulder one day as Williams was copying out a letter. "You write a beautiful hand, young man," Blanchard had said; "but the writing is too large. Cut it in half and you will save both ink and paper for the company." Blanchard was a thrifty man, but a good robust man to have at your side in a fight.

The office now was on Market Street—215 Market Street—
in a building that furnished three times the space of the first
basement office at two thirds the cost. The move was made
in 1878. The officers were as anxious for the money saving as
for the new space.

Prudential was at least holding its own in the fight and
continuing, in addition, the steady expansion of operations.
But even as it seemed to be gaining ground, the company was
struck a heavy blow. President Blanchard, the bulky, hard-
bitten fighter, was stricken suddenly, and, after a brief illness,
died on May 11, 1881.

Secretary John Dryden was the logical successor to Blanchard's post. But to many of the directors, in spite of their

respect for his brilliant understanding of insurance, Dryden was still somewhat an outsider. He was still the man from Maine who had come to town seeking funds to develop a new idea. Perhaps some one of their own circle would serve better.

A movement was launched by Elias Wilkinson to elect William Murphy president. Murphy was the father of Franklin Murphy, who would one day be governor of the state. Another favorite son, actually a second choice if Murphy should fail, was George Moore, who had originally been the treasurer of The Widows and Orphans Friendly Society.

Once again it was Dr. Ward who pushed the fight for his friend John Dryden. Dr. Ward was a powerful voice on the board. He held enough stock and controlled enough votes seriously to disrupt the Wilkinson forces.

Many years later the good doctor recalled vividly the meeting of May 13, 1881, called to elect a new president:

"Wilkinson was extremely bitter. He urged and persisted in his request that I, with my relatives, should vote their stock for Mr. Moore's election to the presidency when Mr. Murphy was eliminated. We became quite heated in our discussions on the subject.

"I insisted that Mr. Moore had no interest in the business and a comparatively small amount invested and that he had no qualifications whatever for the office and that my friendship for Mr. Dryden would not permit me to do such a thing. Finally, the meeting was held, and Mr. Dryden was elected on the narrow margin of one vote."

The young dreamer from Maine had finally won honor in his own back yard. He was now president of The Prudential Insurance Company of America—the company he had founded and built.

Yet even after his election the new president hardly fitted

the picture of a powerful financial leader. Dr. Ward was one day to write down his memories for the record. "His mode of life was of the simplest. He lived around in cheap boardinghouses; his health was poor. I was their family physician, and I can remember well rosy-cheeked Susie Dryden and little Forrest when they were small children, living in a small house on Walnut Street. Mr. Dryden's health was such that he had to live out of Newark in the summertime, and it was accordingly arranged to have him, with his family, go to Schooley's Mountain.

"At that time Mr. Dryden was getting $1,200 a year. He drew that amount for some time after he became president of the company. When matters got a little more prosperous, however, it was decided that he should have some kind of

a conveyance, so as to keep him out in the open air as much as possible. I remember that I undertook the assignment of purchasing a horse and vehicle for them. I went up here to the Old Bull stable and purchased a little pacing bay mare at a cost, I believe, of $100 or $125, and then went down on Market Street and bought a secondhand low phaeton, the combined rig making one of the most fantastic outfits you ever saw. . . ."

The struggle with Metropolitan came to a climax with the

publication in Camden of a letter which bitterly denounced
Prudential. The letter purported to come from a policyholder
who claimed Prudential had failed to pay on a policy he
held on his son who had been drowned. The letter declared:

"My object in writing this letter is to warn the public of
the tricks to which they expose themselves by dealing with
this company or its agents who . . . have proved themselves
utterly unworthy of public confidence. . . ."

The trouble here was that the man whose name was signed
to the letter hadn't written it. In fact he issued a public
denial to that effect. The policy he had held on his son had
been in arrears for months and nothing was due on it. He
had never seen the letter until it was printed and would
never have signed such a false document.

Armed with this, Prudential launched an investigation.
The letter was eventually traced back to a Metropolitan
superintendent. The man was arrested and convicted by a
Camden jury of libeling The Prudential.

In New York at this time Prudential's new superintendent
was John F. Collins, who had originally opened Prudential's
Philadelphia office. An able, sound thinker, with a long and
successful background in insurance, Collins realized the increasingly harmful effect that this insurance war was having
on public opinion. The whole thing had an ugly sound and
was beginning to have a highly detrimental effect on insurance in general and industrial insurance in particular.

A man of action, Mr. Collins determined to use his good
offices to stop this fratricidal conflict. The first step was to
see John F. Dryden. Ushered into the president's private office, he informed Dryden bluntly of his opinions. "I know
Mr. Hegeman—I know Knapp," he told Dryden. "Why not
let me act as emissary? Suppose I could arrange a meeting
between you and them?" The president leaned back thought-

fully. Perhaps he had been too close to the struggle to be aware of all its repercussions. Perhaps Collins was right. "If you can arrange the meeting, John," he said, "I shall be glad to attend."

There is no record of where this meeting was held beyond the fact that it was somewhere in New York. But these three big men of insurance—Knapp, Hegeman, and Dryden—did sit down together and talk out their problems. They agreed without question that this war was harmful to both companies, to all insurance. They agreed that the agents—the front-line soldiers of this war—had carried the battle far beyond what any of the generals in their offices had anticipated. The time had come to call off this useless, destructive struggle. America was a big, wide land. There was plenty of room for their companies and many more.

So that conflict was over, and insurance moved on to a new era. In the months immediately ahead Prudential, under the guidance of President Dryden, was to find its stride.

Almost before they realized, January 1886 was at hand. The annual report for the year just past was being prepared, and the figures were good. Total policies issued during 1885 had reached nearly 300,000. And the assets had risen to just a little more than $1,000,000.

Policy No. 1,000,000 was written on May 13, 1885. The amount was $500 and the premium was fifty-seven cents. It was written on the life of a man forty-five years old, six feet in height and weighing a hundred and fifty pounds. The application was written by Superintendent L. W. Frisbee and the medical examination was performed by Dr. L. D. Ward. The name of the policyholder was John Fairfield Dryden.

CHAPTER 6

New Figures and High Walls

THE years of the eighties were a time of growth in the nation, of consolidation, of a deepening sense of national pride. The wounds of the Civil War had healed a little, and the turbulent speculation of the seventies had begun to subside. These were good years, by and large. Wall Street suffered from occasional lapses and minor panics. But getting a job was not too hard, and there were new fields opening up all the time for younger men.

These were the years of marvels and the years of contrasts. In 1883 Brooklyn Bridge, the then longest suspension span in the world, was opened to the public. The following year newspapers were reporting a startling new development: long-distance phone service between New York and Boston. In 1886 the Statue of Liberty was unveiled. Out West the frontier had almost ceased to exist. The thresher and the self-binding reaper clattered across the plains, changing thousands of square miles of grass land into endless fields of wheat. And the Democrats finally elected a president—a reformer named Grover Cleveland.

The new age of mass production began to supplant the era of craftsmanship. Immigrant workers and their families continued to pour into the eastern industrial areas, and the movement from the farms to the cities began to accelerate. The number of America's industrial workers rose from hundreds of thousands to millions. Trade unionism—a militant new trade unionism that was part Old World class struggle and part American individualism—began to take root in the soil of discontent. There were strikes and in some places there were riots. Here and there were alarmed industrialists who were saying that unions would wreck the nation in another ten years. Here and there the dissidents complained of the increasing materialization of life in America. There were ups and downs, abuses and evils, but still the economy of the nation expanded. In spite of fears and felonies, weaknesses and evils, American industry prospered. Smoke poured from plants spreading across the land.

The roots of insurance now ran deep in the social and economic structure of the nation. It was no longer a new device designed primarily for the wealthy. Insurance—industrial insurance—had become one of the powerful forces in the war on poverty and pauper funerals. The workingman now turned to industrial insurance—"prudential insurance," as he often called it, regardless of what company he bought it from—as the best available protection for himself and his family.

As the smoke of the battle with Metropolitan began to clear in 1883, Prudential found itself in the strongest position of its history. Its growth had been steady and careful; it had thrown no vast sums of money into too rapid expansion. But its assets now totaled more than half a million; it had nearly 200,000 policyholders, and they were increasing at a rate of more than 1,000 a week.

The "peculiar little company" in Newark, in fact, was bulging at the seams and once more had to move. This time it took over the old Jube Building, at 880 Broad Street, an old-fashioned roomy four-story structure located only a short distance from the bank and the basement where it had begun.

As always, there were a few conservative members of Prudential's board of directors who viewed the move with misgivings. A nine-year lease on a building as big as that, with all that space it would never need. It was, actually, more than it needed, in spite of its rapid growth, and at first the company occupied only the two lower floors.

Down in the basement, and even under the sidewalk out front, vaults were built for the storage of the thousands upon thousands of records which were piling up. The carpenter who built the shelves in those vaults was the same man who had built the shelves in Prudential's first basement office. "I said then and I say now," the carpenter is reported to have told one of the company officials, "building them shelves is just a pure waste of policyholders' money. Why don't they just throw them papers away?"

But the press in Newark and the insurance journals of the country took the occasion to remark on Prudential's growth. The new building, the vaults for records, and the ever-mounting figures were all outward visible signs of the almost unbelievable achievements of the "peculiar little company." But most of the stories concentrated on the man behind this success—President John Dryden. They were unanimous in their praise of this man, and there was a new note now, a new tone of high respect in these stories. "The full measure and extent of the beneficence of such a plan of insurance can scarcely be told in language," ran a typical story. "And if the plan merits praise, the man who first introduced it . . . likewise merits the warmest recognition. . . . That

man is President Dryden. . . . The success achieved by him
is almost miraculous. . . ." The man and his company had
reached a new stage of development and maturity. It was no
longer a question of survival. The company was here to stay.
It was only a question of where it was going.

Dryden was barely forty-four the year they moved to 880 Broad Street, yet he seemed much older. His hair and beard were almost entirely gray and the lines of his face had deepened. But the tall, erect figure with the long, striding walk was well known in Newark now. Even the old-line families of the city, who had once regarded this whole concept of industrial insurance with mild contempt, accepted him. Sometimes they would call on President Dryden at his office, seeking his advice and guidance on some important financial problem.

Dryden had changed a good deal. His understanding of the business had grown and he had become aware of his responsibilities to the public. He had launched the business primarily because it had seemed like a sound and profitable venture—offering value received for those who bought as well as those who sold. Now he had begun to achieve the mature concept of the business statesman, the custodian of vast aggregations of funds. He realized that beyond a reasonable margin of profit and reserve against future claims this money belonged not to President Dryden, not to Prudential, not to the stockholders, but to the policyholders themselves.

Prudential was no longer a basement experiment. It was no longer a novice company. It had behind it years of experience and the records, the figures of premiums received and claims paid out. Now it was able to determine where it was going. It could gauge the costs and measure the benefits. At last, after years of uncertainty, Prudential was on firm ground.

President Dryden would have been the last to claim that the extraordinary growth of the company was the achievement of one man alone. It was true that the responsibility was his, but the attainment was the result of many hands and many minds. He had brought together able lieutenants who were directing the detailed activities of the various departments.

Dr. Leslie Ward was perhaps the closest of these associates. Early in the 1880s the doctor had given up his private medical practice and devoted himself exclusively to the work of the company. He was still Prudential's medical director. But more important than that, he had been made first vice-president and active head of the agency staff.

Dr. Ward's manner was a little more serious now. He had the worries of the field staff on his mind, and often in the evenings he and President Dryden would sit together in the new offices at 880 Broad Street, thrashing out the problems of the business as they had done so often in the past. Outwardly, in spite of the marks of time, they were still the same two men: Dryden the dignified, precise, brilliantly clear thinker, and Dr. Ward still the optimist, the enthusiast, ready to plunge ahead.

It was a big job Dr. Ward had to handle. He didn't take his responsibilities lightly. For weeks at a time he would be away from his desk in Newark, traveling from one district office to another, familiarizing himself with the problems of the field and untangling the intricate details of administration. Dryden knew better than anyone else how tremendous was the contribution of Dr. Ward, original investor and closest associate.

Dr. Ward was also still overseeing the activities of the medical department, where a staff of doctors carried on the work of examining and deciding risks on individuals seeking policies.

There were other departments too. Dryden tried to keep a close watch on all activities, but as the size and complexity of the business increased he was forced to delegate more responsibility to the lieutenants. Edgar Ward, who had been the counsel for some years, was running the details of the young "law department." He had also become Dryden's chief adviser on investments. This matter of investments had assumed tremendous importance as the assets mounted. Dryden's philosophy here was extremely simple. He wanted as high a rate of return as possible while avoiding unsound risks which could jeopardize these funds.

The holdings were sound and solid—railroad bonds, federal bonds, state and local securities, reliable holdings yielding a steady return, gilt-edged bonds in which a policyholder could have absolute trust.

The mailing department had also become a major operation. It was handling some 5,000 to 6,000 pieces of mail a day, pouring in from agents and policyholders. It had come a long way from the time when a boy named George Gaston, who had since become vice-president for Metropolitan, had sorted and opened the mail himself and personally licked and stamped the envelopes of the outgoing mail in the late afternoon.

And there was the cashier's department. At the end of 1885 Prudential was receiving premiums of $28,000 per week. It was paying an average of $35,000 per month in claims.

The business was becoming more complex and there were many new departments in operation or in formation—the editorial and printing and supply department, the auditing and bookkeeping department, and the still amorphous but highly active claim department.

No division had contributed more to the purpose and stability of the company than the actuarial department, whose dry-as-dust figures were the navigational charts without which the company would have floundered, as many other firms had before it. Curiously, the most important figure

in this field, traditionally reserved to seasoned veterans of the
business, was one of the youngest executives in Prudential—
one of the youngest, indeed, in the profession. Back in 1880
there walked into the Prudential offices on Market Street a
husky, broad-shouldered youth by the name of John B. Lunger. He was nineteen years old at the time, and he had little
to offer beyond his enthusiasm and remarkable comprehension of the intricate theories of the business. Dryden was impressed by the youth's abilities. He was reminded of his own
younger days, of the years at Yale when insurance had been
to him as it was to Lunger now, a complex of theories and
abstractions and hopes. Dryden had hired Lunger and given
him the chance to test himself and his theories against the
realities of the insurance business. Lunger had met that challenge brilliantly. In 1889, when he was not yet thirty, Lunger
was appointed actuary.

Lunger's brilliance was not confined to actuarial compu-
tations. Being younger, he was not a captive to the thinking
of the past, as were some of the older men. He was closer to
the needs of the moment and to the social and economic
trends pointing the way to the future. Lunger was more: he
was a planner and thinker. He was a man who could project
his ideas into the future.

One early autumn afternoon in 1885 young Lunger
walked into the president's office and calmly laid before him
a thoroughly iconoclastic proposal: Prudential, he told him,
should begin selling ordinary insurance.

As Lunger expected, the president objected to the suggestion. He and the men around him had grown up with industrial insurance. "The people know us as an industrial company," Dryden declared. "There are other firms entrenched
in the ordinary field. Why should we venture into a business
where we start at a disadvantage?"

The president had listened, however, and had agreed to present Lunger's proposal to the directors. Edgar Ward and Henry Yates objected vociferously. Their views were echoed by the directors, always cautious, not anxious to take needless risks. But young Lunger had carefully studied his field and he continued pounding away at his idea.

A week or so later there was another meeting, and young Lunger expounded his ideas and the reasons which made them seem to him compelling. Times, he told the directors and executives, had changed radically since 1876.

People accepted insurance now, on all sides, as a part of the pattern of living. Industrial insurance had helped to raise the whole level of the working classes. People who could afford only pennies ten years ago were making more money now, could afford more, and had learned to want protection, not only for a burial fund, but also to provide for family needs in the critical months after the loss of the breadwinner.

Lunger pointed out, further, that many people preferred to pay quarterly or semi-annually by mail. This was not mere guesswork. The proof lay in the fact that millions of dollars' worth of ordinary insurance was being sold in the very districts in which Prudential was strongest.

"Times have changed. Mr. President, I've heard you talk of total coverage for a family as a goal—providing full coverage of all insurance needs. Wouldn't this be a step, sir, in that direction?"

Lunger was a brash young man and he presented his proposal forcefully. When he had finished, it was the one to whom industrial insurance had always meant most who stood up. President Dryden looked around him and stated slowly, "Gentlemen, we may have been overhasty in our reaction to this suggestion. We may not have been considering the needs John speaks of. But we must consider them. An institution which does not change to meet new needs of new times cannot survive. I think we must examine into this suggestion with much care."

The ordinary insurance branch of The Prudential Insurance Company of America was founded only a few months later, on January 18, 1886. Mr. John B. Lunger was appointed to head the new branch.

The first year only 551 ordinary policies were sold, for a total amount of insurance of $727,500. By the end of 1890, however, Prudential had a tidy $4,079,156 of ordinary insurance in force. Premium income rose from $14,733 in 1886 to nearly $125,000 in 1890. Mr. Lunger's little idea was growing fast.

The tide of increase swept on through the years of the 1880s. The story of that growth was told year by year in neat rows of figures, mushrooming ever larger. Even in that age, when rapid development of industries was the norm rather than the unusual, the advance of Prudential was extraordinary.

By 1886 it had 422,671 industrial policies in force for a total of $40,266,445. But by the end of 1890 it had 1,228,322 industrial policies for a total of $135,084,498, more than trebling the amount in five years. At the start of 1886 the total assets had been a mere $1,040,816. By the close of 1890 those assets read $5,084,895. In 1886 its industrial premium income had been $2,099,522. In 1890 it was $5,513,898. In 1886 payments to the industrial agency staff totaled nearly $600,000, but by 1890 the cost had climbed to $1,500,000. Claim payments climbed from $593,272 in 1886 to $1,794,714 in 1890.

Perhaps the clearest picture of the growth of those years can be seen in Prudential's record for the five years following the introduction of ordinary insurance:

Years Ending Dec. 31	INDUSTRIAL INSURANCE		ORDINARY INSURANCE		ASSETS
	Number	Amount	Number	Amount	
1886	548,433	$ 59,328,627	427	$ 585,500	$1,425,720
1887	736,909	81,694,088	735	945,000	1,967,369
1888	850,064	92,418,854	915	1,242,929	2,874,163
1889	1,099,312	117,357,415	1,839	2,328,862	3,924,295
1890	1,228,332	135,084,498	3,272	4,079,156	5,084,895

Prudential had grown financially and the physical plant had grown, too, as the company had reached out, extending into new states and territories. By 1887 it was operating in eight states, as far west now as Missouri, where it had opened an office in St. Louis. In 1880 the total field staff had been only 483. By 1885 it had climbed to 1,262 and by 1890 it was more than 3,000. In 1883, when it had first moved into the old Jube Building at 880 Broad Street, the home office staff had numbered only 89 and occupied only two floors. By the end of the eighties the staff numbered nearly 250.

The statistics tell part of the story, but only part of it. They do not tell of the tremendous job of organizing required to keep this American institution operating smoothly, so that claims could be paid promptly, usually within twenty-four hours. Nor do they tell of the troubles which still harassed the president and the directors—the constant carping of certain elements of the press, the varying regulations with which they had to comply in different states, and the bewildering increase in restrictions and rulings to which insurance companies were subject.

But these, in the main, were minor troubles. Mostly, it was a time of adjustment to changes—changes in program and theories, changes in methods and techniques. The telephone had come in. Back in 1880, when the first phone was installed in the Market Street office, it had been treated like some special object of art which only the high officials could touch. A decade later phones were a commonplace in the office.

The typewriter was in use too. The old office force had fought against it at the start, back in the days when George Williams was the only stenographer in the office and took all his notes by hand, and all letters and forms were handwritten on "multiple-writing" forms, providing a number of duplicate copies. Typewriters now had taken over.

Women, too, had come into the business world by now. At the start President Dryden had frowned on the idea of women employees in the home office. He had been forced finally to give ground before the sweeping feminist movement, and young lady clerks and stenographers began to be employed in the offices.

Watching these changes and developments, Dryden sometimes thought of the older harder days and traced in his mind the steps by which the company had grown to its present eminence. He liked to remember the personal associations which had grown over the years. It wasn't just a business relationship. It was a camaraderie based on the recollection of old battles and old scars.

Perhaps it was not unnatural that a man who had risen from poverty, as Dryden had, should seek to build some continuing symbols of the loyalty he had inspired in those about him and to set up some durable landmark of the success he had achieved. Others might provide cold monuments to themselves. John Dryden wanted more. He wanted some visible signs of the place he had won in life and in the hearts of his fellow men.

In 1888, at the company's thirteenth anniversary dinner, Dryden made a suggestion for a new kind of organization within the company. "The records show that we have 168 persons who have been five years or upward with continuous and honorable service with the company. It has occurred to us that it would be a pleasant thing, an honorable thing, if we could have within the Prudential organization an association based simply on long and continuous service."

After a man had been continuously employed with the company for five years, the president explained, he should be entitled to a badge, a neat bronze badge perhaps, specially designed, admitting him to membership in the association. "After he has been in service ten years he should be entitled to a badge of the same description, except of a different metal—say silver. At fifteen years it should be gold. At twenty years he should have a badge ornamented with diamonds."

He was talking of men with twenty years' service. A few in his audience smiled at this projection into the future. There were no men who had been that long with the firm, of course: This was only the thirteenth anniversary.

He was thinking of a fraternal organization, the president said. "It should be a bond of good fellowship, of good will, a union which should bind us all together, whether it be agents, assistants, superintendents, directors, or officers. . . ."

They called it the Prudential Old Guard. President Dryden himself chose the name. It was strangely reminiscent of Napoleon, of the trusty little band of officers who clung to him through the hard years and on to the heights—and even after.

Prudential Old Guard was one symbol. There was another, more tangible, more practical. Ever since its founding Prudential had lived in rented rooms—from the basement of the bank, to Market Street, to the old Jube Building on Broad. They had been adequate, these quarters, but for a number of years now Dryden had nourished the idea of a place of their own, a Prudential building that would exemplify the lofty achievements of insurance and of the company. In the late eighties Dryden proposed to the directors that the time had come when they could undertake such a project, and plans for the new building were set in motion. Leading architects were invited to submit designs for a new building—one that would be the finest and most outstanding in the whole state of New Jersey.

The design chosen was one submitted by George Post, the well-known New York architect—a design based on an ancient French château which had stood for centuries on the Loire River. It would be a high-turreted, gray-stone structure, of Romanesque pillars and arches. And yet it would be modern, of steel and stone and mortar.

In 1890, as construction actually began, Prudential's new building was the chief topic of conversation in Newark. It was the biggest thing in New Jersey, people said. It would take 5,000,000 bricks and twelve miles of beams and girders and iron posts, and it would have more than 600 doors and 500 windows and elevators that sped up at 500 feet a minute but stopped without even a jar, and phones in every office, and gas and electric lights both.

They watched it grow. Watched it rise out of the ground in that year 1890 and soar above the three- and four-story office buildings which occupied much of that area of the city in that day. It was a vast monument of gray stone and steel —a monument to a man and his dream.

The day the new building was formally opened, December 2, 1892, there was a parade in Newark and all Newark turned out to line the streets and cheer. The field staff for one hundred miles around was there, superintendents and assistants and agents, and the home office staff, nearly 4,000 all together, marched up Broad Street and past the new building decorated with bunting and flags.

Peter Egenolf, superintendent of the Fourth New York District, headed the parade, riding a white horse and wearing a sash given him in the Civil War by General Winfield Scott. There were five military bands blaring as they marched past

the reviewing stand, where President Dryden watched with his son Forrest. The Wards were there, and other directors and officers of Prudential, and city dignitaries including Newark's mayor, Joseph Haynes, sitting beside President Dryden.

But perhaps the greatest event of this occasion was not the parade or the bunting or the dinner for 2,256 people served out in Caledonia Park, or the stories and editorials of commendation in the papers. The great moment to Dryden was not a public event at all, but a formal dinner given the night before the dedication ceremonies. It was held at Delmonico's in New York, the most fashionable restaurant in America. Nearly 200 were present at that banquet, the top men of the insurance world.

It was a dinner de luxe, of course, squabs and soups and wines of rare vintage—"of an excellence for which that house is celebrated," stated one report of the affair. They drank toasts in champagne, and the guests stood at attention as the famous Hatton Quartet sang in close harmony, "My Country, 'Tis of Thee."

There were speeches after the meal by Aaron Carter, Jr., John B. Lunger, Edgar Ward, Dr. Ward, John F. Collins, and a number of others. President John Dryden sat at the head of the table and listened and smiled. They had rarely seen the president in so mellow a mood as he talked with them, chatting and joking, praising this one or that. He seemed pleased and anxious to bestow praise on others. It was right that the world should appreciate the role of his associates.

Dr. Ward was standing now. The others in the room grew quiet and there was a hush, an air of expectancy. "Gentlemen," the good doctor declared, "there is but one man in this country who needs no introduction to an audience of industrial insurance men." He paused, then added, "He will now address you."

At once they were on their feet with cries of "Dryden! Dryden! Dryden!" At the table the tall, white-haired guest of honor arose slowly. He tried to speak, but they would not let him at first. The bank presidents and insurance presidents, the dignitaries of New York and New Jersey, of all the insurance and the financial world, were standing and cheering.

They grew quiet as he began to speak. This celebration, he

told them, was not for a building but for what it symbolized. He traced the history of the company and the tremendous role it had come to play. They were doing business now in seventeen states and their policyholders numbered 1,000,000 —"a number greater than the entire population of New Jersey, greater than the population of this great metropolitan city. . . . To fidelity, to principle, to fair and honest dealing

with all . . . I attribute largely the success which has been achieved."

At intervals throughout the speech the guests broke into applause. But as he neared the climax of the talk there was a change in Dryden's tone. Delmonico's dining room with its glittering glasses and silverware seemed to grow quieter, the guests more intent upon the tall man speaking.

"Our names," he said, "may be forgotten; those whose brains have planned, whose hands have builded the great structure, may pass into oblivion and be forgotten. . . ."

There had to be a way of summing up for these people all of the ideas which had burned within him from the earliest days—at Yale, and out in Ohio, and coming back East to New York a failure, and struggling through those years in Newark in the basement office.

"The iron pillars which support the structure may topple

to the ground," he said slowly. "But after we are forgotten and after the building itself is leveled to the dust the principle upon which The Prudential is founded, the immutable principle of the brotherhood of man and that love of family which binds society together—that principle will live, for it is divine and eternal."

CHAPTER 7

Growth and Crisis

"NEW occasions teach new duties and man's thoughts widen with the progress of the sun," John F. Dryden said once in a talk to insurance men. The statement was almost autobiographical. In the life of Dryden himself it reflected a profound personal struggle which arose early in Prudential's history and persisted throughout the gaudy era of the nineties—an era of fast fortunes and reckless speculations. The struggle was not to be fully resolved until the early years of the new century.

For Dryden the sun was rising toward its zenith. He and the company he had founded were approaching the summit. It had been a long, wearying, winding road to the top. Through all of his adult life Dryden's thoughts and attention had been focused on insurance and its problems. But years of varied activity enriched by ripe experience remained before him. His own personal business interests began to require some attention. In later years he served as a director of several companies—United States Steel, Fidelity Trust Company of Newark, Union National Bank of Newark,

Public Service Corporation of New Jersey, and others. As a prominent citizen he was called upon to participate in civic activities. He was active in Republican political circles and from time to time was asked to serve on various committees. But whatever extraneous demands might be made upon his time and energy, his one consuming interest remained unchanged.

Insurance was his life. He was at his desk daily, actively directing the business, constantly searching for new ideas, new methods, and new people. New departments were added to the organization, and the system became ever more complex, more intricate and far-reaching. No one man could, of course, have been personally aware of the myriad details in the day's operations. Yet no one in the company could ever have doubted that the directing mind and hand behind this vast operation remained, as it had always been, John Dryden.

Even on his few brief vacations insurance was never completely out of the president's mind. At the urging of Dr. Ward he and Mrs. Dryden took a trip abroad in the summer of 1895, supposedly a vacation, to see Europe's castles and cathedrals and drink in the Old World culture. But for Dryden it was a busman's holiday. He stopped off in England and, while he was there, went to see President Harben of the British Prudential. The two men talked back across the years to that time when the English company had opened its books and forms and methods to the American and told him to take back what he needed. "Perhaps the day will come," President Dryden had said, "when we in America can repay you for the help of those early days."

The busman's holiday had continued. On the liner coming home that fall he had met Charles Austin Bates, the advertising man. Bates had been enthusiastic about the new role advertising was beginning to play in American life, and he had availed himself of the chance to discuss his ideas with this important business leader. Throughout the voyage Bates and Dryden had promenaded the decks talking insurance and slogans and trade marks. The president had always believed in the efficacy of advertising, and these leisurely talks awakened in him a realization of the impact that the new techniques were to have on American business methods. There was something in Bates's arguments. The company that fell behind in the promotion of its product would certainly lose out to more aggressive competitors. It was time, Dryden thought, to turn his attention to the development of more modern methods of reaching the public.

Back in Newark again he asked Bates to find a symbol, some sign of lasting, enduring strength which would stand for Prudential. Bates spent some months in the effort to discover an appropriate emblem, but eventually admitted that he had failed. But not President Dryden. Having decided that a symbol was needed, he proceeded with the search, confident that it could and would be found.

It was about this time that a new firm in New York, the J. Walter Thompson Advertising Agency, approached Mr. Dryden with several suggestions for the more effective handling of the company's advertising program. A young account executive of that firm, Mortimer Remington, was set to work to find an acceptable symbol, and it was he who finally produced the trade mark which Prudential was to make world-famous. There is no positive record of just how Remington happened to hit on the right idea. Some say the advertising man stumbled upon it while searching through books in the library. A more colorful story has it that Remington got the idea while riding back to New York on the train from Newark. On the way he passed a landmark familiar to all commuters, an abrupt shelf of rock, known locally as Snake Hill, which juts upward from the Jersey meadows. It suddenly occurred to Remington that here, almost within sight of the Prudential Building, was the symbol all of them had been looking for. A rock! In all the world nothing was more enduring than rock. This hill was only a crumbling, inconsequential pile, but somewhere there must be a famous and

enduring shaft. The Rocky Mountains? The Matterhorn? Or—Gibraltar! That was it. The Rock of Gibraltar!

Whatever the true story of the discovery of the emblem, Gibraltar exactly suited President Dryden. No one could fail to understand quickly this sign of enduring strength and invulnerability. Gibraltar was the strongest fortress in the world. It was a fitting symbol for Mr. Dryden's "peculiar little company."

From his office in the Prudential Building President Dryden personally directed the advertising campaign the company began that year, employing the "Rock" and the slogan "The Prudential Has the Strength of Gibraltar." The campaign which introduced the symbol was one of the first great advertising campaigns in the nation. Through magazine advertisements, newspapers, posters, and direct mail, it made Prudential and the Rock of Gibraltar synonymous words in virtually every home in the land. It has continued to this day to be known as one of the great business symbols of the world.

Prudential was big now and growing bigger each year. By the end of 1896 Prudential's assets totaled nearly $20,000,000. Both ordinary and industrial branches were growing steadily. There were nearly 2,500,000 policies in force and total insurance had climbed to more than $300,000,000.

President Dryden could well take a personal pride in the success of the enterprise. Here at last was the incontrovertible proof of the soundness of his plan. Above all else John Dryden was a businessman, and he had a businessman's pleasure in watching his plans mature. This was the solidity and security he had dreamed of when he and a few investors had started their little company on this venture into untried fields. They had moved cautiously and built always for stability. At times it had been possible to strike out with daring, but for the most part they had necessarily pursued a conservative route. The primary objective was clearly the establishment of a financial position so secure that no conceivable series of unfavorable events could ever swamp the company. Certainly that objective had now been attained.

But the achievement of stability itself had in the course of time produced problems, complex and vexatious problems, which were to disturb the management of the company for many years to come. There was the handling of surplus, for example. This surplus had been built up carefully and deliberately. At the inception the rates had been set high enough to cover the unknown contingencies in a field that had never been explored. From time to time necessary adjustments had been made, but the company's experience was limited as yet, and there was always the necessity to provide absolute protection to the policyholders. The substantial surplus had come from better mortality than had been anticipated, higher interest returns than they had expected, and an enormous increase in volume of business. Only when the surplus began mounting at an accelerating rate had the management of the company come to realize that much of this money was in effect the result of the necessarily conservative premium rates charged policyholders and ought to be returned to them as experience demonstrated that lower charges were sufficient. Almost as soon as the company was on its feet and growing steadily Dryden had launched a series of "concessions" to the policyholders. These concessions were essentially gifts, freely given.

The concessions were not wholly unselfish in motive. The need to meet the prices and promises of the competition, the effect on public opinion, and the building of good will had all played their part in influencing the decision of Dryden to follow this course. Above all, Prudential had launched industrial insurance in America, and he was determined that it should maintain its leadership in the business of protection for the public.

From the first there had been a few within the company who objected. Dryden's ideas were well in advance of the freebooting era of the eighties and nineties, and some of Prudential's stockholders didn't understand this concept of concessions. The policyholder had signed a contract promising specified benefits and nothing more. Certainly the policyholder had no legal rights beyond the contractual terms. Any surplus, they insisted, belonged to the stockholders. But

Dryden, with his strong personal leadership, had been able to carry his program.

As far back as 1880 he had launched this project of voluntarily given benefits and added protection for policy-holders. Adult policies in that year had been placed in immediate benefit for one half the amount of stated insurance and in full benefit after six months. Previously no benefits were paid if the policy had been in force less than three months. Immediate benefits were also provided for infantile policies in the same year. In 1884 the directors under Dryden's urging had approved new concessions, removing restrictions on travel and occupation "except military or naval service in time of actual war." The policies had been made incontestable after two years—the company agreeing it could not contest the validity of the policy after it had been in force for that length of time. That same year—noting that there had been complaints about the legalistic phrasing of the policies—Dryden had ordered them revised. The policies had to be plain and straightforward and easily understood. And so Prudential's policies were rewritten—with all "unnecessary verbiage" omitted.

In 1886 a special adult policy was introduced, for amounts of from $500 to $1,000, with a non-forfeiture value consisting of a paid-up term policy to take effect in event of lapse after the policy had been in force for three years. In 1892 a new industrial policy was written granting a non-forfeiture paid-up value upon lapse after premiums had been paid for five years. The company further announced that all policies outstanding would be entitled to the paid-up concession, whether or not it was actually written into the contract.

Insurance journals cheered this "enlightened leadership" of Prudential. "The great importance of this voluntary concession," declared the *Insurance Monitor* on one occasion, "lies in the fact that it anticipates and effectually meets what might, in the near future, prove a serious menace to the business. . . . Sooner or later a legislative agitation would have been started in the ostensible interest of the poor man to compel surrender values. . . . The action of Prudential will almost inevitably be followed by the rest, and there will be no occasion for legislative interference. . . ."

More advances by Prudential were to follow. In 1892 endowment policies were inaugurated, payable after periods of time ranging from fifteen to thirty years, or at death if it should occur prior to the stated period. Later would come the child's endowment policy, in 1893. In November of 1893 a depression struck the country, and during the ensuing hard times the concessions granted by the company assumed increasing importance to those who found it difficult to keep up full payments on their policies. The *Insurance Journal* declared that Prudential's liberality was "unexampled in the history of life insurance."

On January 1, 1897, Prudential announced more liberal policies of such a startling nature that President Dryden in his circular letter to the agents called it the beginning of "a new era in industrial insurance." Under the new policies an additional benefit would be paid, over and above the actual policy value, if death occurred after the policy had been in force for five years; still more if death occurred after ten. After fifteen years a cash dividend would be paid the policyholder, another after twenty years and at the end of each five years thereafter.

The immediate cost to the company of these voluntary concessions totaled hundreds of thousands of dollars. But this was only a beginning. By these new grants the company had obligated itself to pay millions more in deferred payments over the years. Praise poured in from all sides at the tremendous scope of these concessions. The Prudential was showing the world that this business was being run not just as a private venture for gain but also as a public trust.

The significance of the concessions lay primarily in the recognition of the moral right of policyholders, whose funds had earned large profits for the company, to a share of these profits. But the minority who had originally opposed Mr. Dryden on his program of concessions had year by year grown stronger within the company. His conception of the relative rights of stockholders and policyholders, far in advance of contemporary thinking, was challenged by these men.

From 1875 on the capital of the company had been increased, by successive stock dividends, from an original authorized amount of $100,000—of which only $91,000 was ever contributed by stockholders in cash—to the sum of $2,000,000 in 1893. For some time prior to 1893, and continuing thereafter until the company's ultimate mutualization, an annual dividend of 10 per cent was paid on the par value of the stock. It might have been supposed that this enormous increase in capitalization, coupled with the high rate of annual dividends, would have satisfied stockholders who had contributed so small a proportion in cash, or whose holdings had been inherited from some early director who had died.

But the strong minority group who opposed Dryden's liberal attitude toward the policyholders had far different ideas. The prosperity of the company and the immense returns on so trifling an original investment seem only to have excited their cupidity. Their incessant demands for high annual dividends and further stock dividends grew louder. Such extra payments could have been made only if policyholders were denied further concessions.

Dryden continued to oppose these demands which grew increasingly "clamorous and threatening," as he was later to describe them. By 1898 this minority group had grown so strong it was able to push through an affirmative vote of the directors to increase Prudential's capitalization from $2,000,000 to $5,000,000—the extra $3,000,000 to come from surplus and to be distributed as a bonus on a pro-rata basis in new stock to the stockholders. Dryden's doubts about the wisdom of this move were bolstered by a deluge of protests which followed announcement of the plan. By taking what was called "an extremely firm stand in this matter" Dryden was able to halt the proposal at a stockholders' meeting called shortly thereafter to pass on the directors' action.

The white-haired president was becoming increasingly concerned over the future of the company he had founded and built. The greatest danger was that outsiders, speculators or stockjobbers, might get control of the company and exploit it for their own selfish interests. Already he had observed what seemed to him the cupidity of some of the directors now on the board. He wanted to find a method by which he could give some degree of permanence to the conservative policies by which he had built the company to its high position.

This apprehension for the future of the company he had founded was a matter of ceaseless concern to him in the closing years of the century. The outside world knew little about that. They saw only a distinguished gentleman going about the daily business of running the great company he had built. Honors continued to come to Prudential's president. In 1896 he had been a presidential elector and again in 1900. In 1902, on the death of Senator William J. Sewell, President Dryden was elected to the United States Senate by the New Jersey Legislature.

But his concern for Prudential and its future remained

uppermost in his mind. Some method had to be found of making sure that the control of the company would stay in the hands of those who would protect the institution from the rapacity of self-seeking stockholders. In 1902 Dryden evolved a peculiar scheme by which he believed he could continue the control of the company in the hands of its friends. That involved scheme, which shocked the insurance world on its announcement, was probably the great blunder of John Dryden's career.

The plan—for which he won approval from Prudential stockholders, with the support of Dr. Ward and other large shareholders in the company—provided for the sale by Prudential stockholders to the Fidelity Trust Company of Newark of a bare majority of Prudential stock and the subscription by The Prudential to a new increase in the stock of Fidelity Trust in amount sufficient to give Prudential voting control of Fidelity. By this novel scheme, in which each company held a controlling hand over the other, Dryden was convinced that he could place the destinies of Prudential forever beyond the control of the dissident Prudential stockholders still clamoring for higher profits.

Almost as soon as the plan was announced a suit was brought by two dissatisfied Prudential stockholders seeking to enjoin Prudential from carrying out this extraordinary "fifty-one per cent" merger plan. In answer to their charges that the plan was illegal, Dryden contended that his sole aim was to protect the interests of more than 4,500,000 policyholders by placing the assets of the company beyond the reach of reckless speculators.

Representing the complainant stockholders was a brilliant corporation lawyer whose legal successes had already won him a national reputation. His name was Richard V. Lindabury of the firm of Lindabury, Depue & Faulks. This was the kind of case Mr. Lindabury enjoyed; it provided a number of angles of attack which made it possible for him to demolish the plan.

Lindabury contended that the plan as proposed actually provided for a merger of two companies not empowered to merge. Even if they could merge, the method here was illegal. They would be setting up a situation in which a small group of men—each conceivably holding no more than a share of stock—could actually control the destinies of a company and its millions.

The injunction Mr. Lindabury asked for his clients was granted. Prudential was forbidden to purchase Fidelity stock. But the court did not enjoin the first step in this merger plan, the agreement of the majority of Prudential stockholders to sell part of their holdings to Fidelity. Since this part of the plan was not affected, it had to be carried out. But the court proceedings and the injunction had disturbed many of Prudential's stockholders, and nearly 40 per cent of them refused to sell at the price agreed upon. Dryden, Dr. Ward, and others in the "Dryden group" had to dip heavily into their own holdings in order to meet the terms of the contract with Fidelity.

Dryden's original plan for interlocking control involving Fidelity and Prudential had envisioned perpetuation of the management of both companies until death or internal dissension should bring about a change in personnel. And even though Prudential was not allowed to acquire additional Fidelity stock, it already held 4,800 out of a total of 20,000 Fidelity shares, and these holdings, together with the personal holdings of Dryden and his close friends, constituted a large block. The personal influence and prestige of Senator Dryden effectively held the reins of both Prudential and Fidelity, and there was no question at that time but that the

Prudential stock held by Fidelity would be voted in favor of the Dryden management.

But the granting of the injunction had undoubtedly been a serious personal defeat for Dryden. He found himself and his motives bitterly assailed in many sections of the press. Even the insurance press, which had praised him for the long series of concessions, had difficulty in understanding this new maneuver. Some of them were almost apologetic in tone. "In an interview with Mr. Dryden on last Monday morning," one weekly insurance journal stated, "he declared that the sole motive . . . was the future welfare of 4,500,000 policy-holders of The Prudential. Mr. Dryden said these words with much intensity of feeling. We believe he meant what he said."

But there were many who made no effort to justify Dryden's position, and instead lashed out at him with violent abuse. After reading one particularly bitter denunciation of himself and his plan one afternoon, he walked out of his office to the desk where George Williams, his personal secretary, was finishing up the day's letters. "Williams," Dryden declared, "I'd like to ask you a question. You've been reading about the merger plans and the various things they've been writing up in the papers. I want to know—what's your own personal opinion of that plan, Williams?"

The secretary looked up. "You want an honest answer, Mr. President?" And when Dryden nodded, the secretary went on, "I think it was wrong. I think it was a wrong thing to do, to start a plan like that, Mr. President."

Dryden turned from him without speaking, walked back into his office, and closed the door.

On July 20, 1905, the New York State Assembly and the State Senate passed a concurrent resolution authorizing the establishment of a committee to look into certain aspects of life insurance companies operating within the state. The precise purposes of the investigating committee were declared to be: "To investigate and examine into the business affairs of life insurance companies doing business in the State of New York, with reference to the investments of said companies, the relation of the officers thereof to such investments, the relation of such companies to subsidiary corporations, the government and control of said companies, the contractual relations of said companies to their policyholders, the cost of life insurance, the expenses of said companies, and any other phase of the life insurance business deemed by the committee to be proper for the purpose of drafting . . . such a revision of the laws . . . as said committee may deem proper."

The need for this investigation, which was to be directed by State Senator William Armstrong, had become increasingly apparent as the boom in life insurance had gathered momentum. Many companies had grown to undreamed-of size and wealth, enormous sums were in the care of these companies, and the question of how this money was being handled and invested, used or misused, had become one of vital public concern.

There had been, moreover, rumors and public accusations of mismanagement, of risky investments and juggled figures, of extravagance and other malpractices. The press had been demanding a thorough probe and, if necessary, a revision of insurance regulations.

The actual spark which set off this investigation had been a violent dispute between contending factions on the board of Equitable Life of New York. The contention had developed from a struggle of two powerful groups for control of the company. So bitter became the conflict and so abusive the charges and countercharges that they very shortly developed into front-page news, and the headlines grew larger as the allegations grew more vitriolic and lurid. The Armstrong investigation had become inevitable as public concern over this quarrel—and over the entire question of how the companies were operating—had risen. The committee had been asked by the Legislature to look into certain specific alleged abuses. But so far as the papers were concerned—and, for that matter, so far as the public attitude was concerned—life insurance itself had been placed on trial.

The public hearings, which began on September 6, 1905, and continued until the end of the year, had all the ingredients that the sensational press demanded—scandalous rumors involving vast sums, respected and powerful financiers to be interrogated by a hostile and suspicious committee. As an added fillip, the examination of witnesses was to be conducted by the brilliant and resourceful Charles Evans Hughes, who had just completed a similar clean-up job for a committee investigating activities of the Consolidated Gas Company.

The Great Armstrong Investigation was staged in the council chamber of New York City Hall, and the newspapers treated it with all the special attention—feature writers, cartoonists, sketch artists, and photographers—usually reserved for the more sensational murders. It made good reading as these top men of the insurance world came under the penetrating scrutiny of Mr. Hughes.

For insurance it was an embarrassing public ordeal. Executive after executive of the biggest companies in the city, in their halting testimony, appeared as men who either did not know what manipulations were going on, or preferred not to remember. Some of them did not even know the basic operating figures of their own companies.

In addition to this picture of business ineptitude pieced together from a maze of evasive testimony, the public was also titillated by lurid stories of expenses, of wild and costly parties, of waste and extravagance of an unprecedented nature. One party described by witnesses was said to have cost more than $100,000.

The hearing had been on for some weeks, with one headline disclosure after another, before the committee got around to calling the Honorable Senator John F. Dryden, president of The Prudential. As Prudential's president was both a senator and a resident of another state, there was the delicate question of jurisdiction involved. The Armstrong committee avoided the issue by not sending Dryden a subpoena, as they had others. Instead, they wrote him a letter inviting him to attend the hearings if he cared to present his views. It was an invitation Senator Dryden had no desire to decline. He replied that he would be pleased to attend. He would also like to bring along his attorney, a certain Richard V. Lindabury whose talents Mr. Dryden had first witnessed —from the opposite side—when Lindabury had defeated the Prudential-Fidelity merger.

The announcement that Senator Dryden was about to face Mr. Hughes's diligent and urbane inquisition produced something of a sensation. The meeting of these two polished antagonists promised to be the climax of this sensational exposé. The erect, dignified, white-haired senator, head of the multi-million-dollar Prudential, would face the perceptive and relentless young attorney. The attempted Fidelity-Prudential merger had cast a lingering shadow. There were some who wondered. There were some who said wait until Mr. Hughes starts in on that.

The hearing room at City Hall was jammed on Tuesday, December 12. Senator Dryden, accompanied by Lindabury,

Actuary John Gore, and a few other Prudential executives, pushed his way toward the row of chairs reserved for witnesses. People craned for a look at this world-famous figure of insurance. The reporters that day said in their stories that John Dryden—Senator Dryden—was slightly nervous as he sat down in the witness chair. They reported that his hands fidgeted on the arms of the chair as Hughes, polite and formal, began his interrogation with the usual routine questions of identification. But their stories reported also that the nervousness quickly disappeared, that Senator Dryden's whole manner, his whole bearing, seemed to change as he began to talk about the insurance business. The reporters, of course, could not know that John Dryden had been talking insurance since the days when he and a girl named Cynthia rode the horsecars to the end of the line in New Haven. But they did recognize the curious animation which seemed to come over the white-haired man. They did notice that he had only a few notes in his pocket and yet seemed to have all the answers at his fingertips, even the most minute figures, that only on the rarest of occasions was it necessary for him to ask Actuary Gore to check some detail for him.

There were a number of avenues of attack, and Mr. Hughes was expert in finding the most vulnerable routes of approach. But if he was expecting evasions and forgetfulness and I-don't-remember responses from this witness, as he had had from others in this turbulent hearing, he was mistaken.

The subject of surpluses had proved highly embarrassing to earlier witnesses. Mr. Hughes pressed this quickly after a brief reference to the original investment of a mere $91,000:

Q. Is it a fact that all the increases . . . to the present time have been through stock dividends? A. That is a fact.
Q. Yes. A. If you will allow me to explain, The Prudential

was organized as a stock company purely and simply; there never was at that time a thought of its doing a mutual business. Its business was confined exclusively to industrial insurance; following the precedent of The Prudential of London, from which the company took its name and system of business, whatever surplus might be created out of the business was then considered as the property of the stockholders of the company. Out of this surplus thus created and belonging to the stockholders from time to time dividends were declared until, as I said, the capital amounted to $2,000,000.

Q. So that capital of $2,000,000 represented $91,000 originally paid in, and the profits upon that investment? . . . A. About $91,000. . . . The story has been told to the public many times, and I have no objection, I am sure, to repeating it here.

The straightforward, simple statement of fact by Dryden was surprising. The man was confident in his answers. He felt no necessity to apologize. The spectators and reporters settled back to enjoy the performance. They watched as Hughes tried another tack, still on the same subject of surplus, but bringing it up to date, up to this day of huge funds.

Q. Now, to come back, your company has in a comparatively short period of years made out of its profits over and above all that it has distributed to its stockholders and its policyholders an amount which at the end of 1904 was $13,000,000, and during the past ten years or so I understand it has been paying 10 per cent on its capital. A. Yes, sir. Let me—are you through?

Q. Certainly, go on. A. I want to say a word with respect to that so-called surplus. For twenty years we have been issuing participating policies in the ordinary branch, about twenty years. Since 1897 we have been giving a participation to the industrial policyholders. The surplus of $11,000,000, less the capital, is not in the strict—is not in that sense a surplus to stockholders, but it is a large part of it a surplus to policyholders. And the actuary estimates that if we continue

to pay to our industrial policyholders and our ordinary policyholders the same rate of dividends that we have been paying
for the last few years, 90 per cent of that surplus will ultimately be returned to the policyholders. . . .

I wish in this connection to call your attention, Mr. Hughes,
to this important fact, that we have upon our books some
millions of policies on the industrial classes, the original contract of which never called for one cent of return in the way
of dividends. We have already paid out to such policyholders
voluntarily over six millions of dollars, and we expect in the
future to pay a vastly greater sum than that, and from year
to year we are now doing that by the action of the board of
directors.

This sort of answer did not fit the pattern Attorney Hughes
or the headline readers had grown used to. There was no
hedging and no equivocation. Nor did this change throughout the grueling two days of questioning.

The matter of lapses was important. This was a highly
technical, complicated business, requiring lengthy interrogation. The claim was that lapses had been a source of high
profits to the companies. But Dryden was able clearly to
show that lapses were a burden to Prudential. Again and
again he stressed this important fact. At length Hughes
turned to other matters.

Costs were supposedly the most vulnerable weakness of
industrial insurance. It was said that industrial insurance was
unconscionably high, that it bled the poor. Here was the
man who had started the system in America. If Mr. Hughes
was to expose the evils of industrial insurance, this was the
moment. The attorney began by pointing up the wide dis-
crepancies between costs of ordinary and industrial insurance. Dryden admitted this condition existed. He added
that there was "very sufficient reason" for it. Mr. Hughes
was interested.

Q. You might state that now, if you desire to. *A.* In the case of the ordinary policy, there is, in the first place, a careful selection of the risk. We have a most thorough medical examination by at least one doctor, and if the amount is large enough, by two doctors. Then the premiums are paid not less frequently than once a quarter . . . and the cost of making these collections is, of course, inconsiderable.

In the case of the industrial policy, we send an agent at least fifty-two times a year to a man's house or shop, to collect his premium. Frequently the agent, on account of not finding the party at home, or in his shop, will have to go two or three times a week to get that premium. That makes it expensive. Then the machinery for taking care of that business at the home office is very elaborate, and somewhat complicated, and necessarily must be so, because we require a report from each agent among all the thousands of agents in the employ of the company, scattered all over the country. . . .

Now, in addition to that, it is a fact, Mr. Hughes, it is not a theory, but it is a fact, which a vast amount of experience has demonstrated beyond all question, that the mortality among that class of people is higher. Unfortunately they are not as well clad, nor as well fed, nor can they surround themselves with the comforts and the necessities of life, that people in better circumstances can. That increases the mortality, and in a business of this kind it all has to be taken into consideration.

Later, Hughes and members of the committee pressed the point more sharply:

Mr. Cox: The question is raised as to whether the business is worth doing if such a large percentage of it has to be consumed in getting it and doing it.

Mr. Hughes: And so many, if I may add, through their lapses, get nothing from it.

The Witness: Well, looking at it from a theoretical standpoint, I am well aware that it has been criticized, and that there are very excellent persons who have raised that question, and I suppose will continue to raise it, but look at it from the standpoint of the workingman himself. That is the point of view, Mr. Hughes, that we should consider it from.

Isn't it worth something to him that the facilities for getting this insurance, even at the cost involved to him, are laid before him at his very door? Isn't it of some consequence to the public that we can offer this insurance to these people, and inculcate in them, as I said this morning, a feeling of self-respect, and enable them to protect themselves from a pauper's grave? That is the public's point of view, from which I think we should look at this question.

Prudential was no simon-pure company of angels and Dryden did not attempt to present it as such. This was the most surprising fact of all. He was making no attempt to withhold information that might be embarrassing. It had, he frankly admitted, contributed modest sums to three presidential campaigns. But that, he pointed out, was entirely legal; it was a general practice. Prudential had once employed a man who might be described as a lobbyist. But year after year legislative expenses had continued to be remarkably low. Mr. Hughes appeared to be surprised and a little later again questioned Dryden closely on the scope of his legislative interests. Dryden was pleased to come back to this point:

A. Never to my knowledge has there been one dollar of the company's money spent in legislative matters except in a legitimate way and upon matters that affect our own company. Never has been one dollar improperly expended. Never has been one dollar spent in any way than in legal, legitimate, open ways, in appearing before legislatures and legislative committees in reference to the matters.

You asked how it happened that we had kept our legislative expenses so low. I have time and time again personally been before the legislatures and committees of the legislatures to argue upon bills and explain the nature of our business, and to do my best to satisfy the committees, not to pass inimical and hostile legislation. That of course cost the company nothing.

Q. And you generally found it effective?

A. I am happy to say that in most cases we were successful, sir.

Discussion of legislative and legal expenses brought them by a roundabout route to the big question—the abortive Prudential-Fidelity merger plan. There was one point where reporters noted a curious intensity in the senator's answers:

Q. In the statement of legal expenses you have in . . . 1904, $49,000 in connection with litigation; an amount considerably in excess of the expenditures of earlier years. What was the occasion for that? A. The expenses for the litigation in 1904 grew out of the attack on the Prudential-Fidelity arrangement. As I say, that matter was taken into court and bitterly fought. The very action that was taken in that matter only confirmed the fears that I had had before, which led me to seek some plan which would safeguard the policyholders of the company.

I did not believe and I do not now believe the litigants in that case were the real litigants. I am satisfied that there were influences and powers and resources behind that attack which did not come to the front. I had that suspicion, and I believe it to be true. We made a stubborn fight to carry that matter to success.

Dryden's first full statement on this merger provided the high moment of the hearing. This had been the big question from the moment it had been known he would testify: What explanation could he give for the scheme? Hughes led into it with a few extraneous questions about personalities:

Q. Mr. Edgar Ward and Mr. Leslie D. Ward are brothers? A. They are brothers, and they have been associated with me from 1875 when the company was organized upon its present basis.

Q. Is Mr. Jacob E. Ward also a relative? *A.* He is a brother of the other two gentlemen named Ward.

Q. And Uzal H. McCarter and Thomas N. McCarter are brothers? *A.* They are.

Q. What arrangement was made in or about 1903 for the transfer of the control of the stock of The Prudential to the Fidelity Trust Company? *A.* I suppose you will allow me to make a little statement, will you, explaining the transaction?

Q. Certainly. *A.* For some time I had been apprehensive as to the distribution of the stock of the company. The founders of the company, those who were associated with me, and my other co-workers were getting older and dying off, and the stock was passing into the hands of their estates or it was being sold and distributed. I saw that the time might come when that would be a very dangerous situation for the policy-holders of the company.

The company had been my own lifework, and I had my pride in it, and in addition to that I was extremely anxious to protect the great mass of policyholders who had shown their confidence by insuring with us. I consulted counsel as to various schemes. My first proposition was to extend to the policy-holders the right of franchise, the right to vote at the annual meetings. I was advised that without the unanimous consent of all the stockholders, and in the face of the objection of any stockholders, that that scheme could not be carried into effect.

I think it was several years that I had that scheme in my mind and talked at different times with counsel as to the matter. Finally I was compelled to abandon it because I knew it was impossible to get the unanimous consent of all the stockholders. I then began to inquire as to some other plan by which that stock could be concentrated and held together for the protection of the company, and as a defense against the attempts of any selfish interests to get control of that company for selfish purposes. A number of different schemes were proposed and rejected. This plan of selling to the Fidelity a majority of the stock of The Prudential and then in turn of purchasing of a new issue of stock of the Fidelity a sufficient amount for The Prudential to own a majority of that stock, and thus control the situation, was proposed, and after careful consideration was adopted.

This matter was talked over very fully with the managers and members of the board and enough of the stock of The Prudential entered into an agreement with the Fidelity, under which they bound themselves to sell to the Fidelity a sufficient amount of Prudential stock to lodge in that company the control.

I was about to take steps to carry out the other part of the scheme, viz., the purchase by The Prudential of enough of a new issue of the Fidelity stock to give it control of the Fidelity, when action was taken before the court and the court intervened, and an objection was raised, and sustained by the court. In the meantime this other part of the contract, as to purchasing The Prudential stock by the Fidelity, had become a contract. Every party including the Fidelity was bound to carry out that contract.

This scheme I advertised widely; it was not done in a corner. I published it in the newspapers. I sent notices of it to every stockholder; I notified every insurance superintendent in the country; I sent out circulars to our entire field staff, so that they might circulate it among our policyholders, and I gave to it in every way the widest publicity that I could.

It had been an amazing performance. He had been a smiling, self-assured witness, answering the questions freely and completely. He had attempted to present no whitewashed picture. What had emerged was the picture of a company that, in spite of faults, was strong and secure and well run.

The results of the Armstrong hearing were widespread. Insurance, it is true, had suffered damaging blows in the eyes of the public, but in the long run the investigation served to strengthen confidence. New York laws were rigidly tightened. Limitations were placed on the types of investments, on expenses. A closer scrutiny of insurance operations was ordered and even the amount of business a company could write in a year was strictly limited. Many of the evils which had plagued insurance in New York and elsewhere were eradicated, although it was admitted that some of the new regulations—which set the pattern for legislation in other states —were too severe, and in later years many of them were modified.

Less important, perhaps, but certainly more dramatic was the personal vindication of John F. Dryden. The newspapers were unanimous in their verdict that the senator had done well. They said he had made one of the best witnesses of any of the heads of the large insurance companies and had given renewed confidence to the whole country on the fundamental soundness of Prudential and of the institution of insurance.

That afternoon, as the senator left the hearing room, there were those who noted a certain jauntiness in his long stride. They should not have been surprised. After all, Prudential was the company he had founded and in which, as he had explained, he had his pride.

CHAPTER 8

Death and Storm

Richard V. Lindabury was one of the great lawyers of America. He was the man who had drawn up the papers that put together the composite parts of the United States Steel Corporation. He was the special counsel for many of the giant industries which had grown up in America—in the galloping decades at the turn of the century. He was a man of substance and fiber and quality. The men who had assembled the great corporations he served admitted that Mr. Lindabury was really more than a lawyer. They would make no important move in their business, they declared, without first consulting him and assuring themselves that he approved. For the great corporations who were his clients Mr. Lindabury was a moral force—a kind of walking conscience.

For Prudential he was to be even more.

His full name was Richard Vliet Lindabury. He was born of Dutch and English stock on a farm in a place called Peapack in Somerset County, New Jersey. The date was October 13, 1850—exactly twenty-five years to the day before the birth of an organization known as The Prudential Friendly

Society. His parents were hard-working farm people, and almost the first lesson he learned from them was that work— work on the land, most of all—was an obligation, a kind of duty to God, a religion in itself.

He wanted to be a minister. He had gone to the public schools in the district, but they ran only through the grammar-school grades. After that he had won the interest and friendship of a local minister, the Reverend Henry P. Thompson, pastor of the Dutch Reformed Church where the boy and his parents worshiped. Reverend Thompson had an eye for the fundamental qualities of character. He said young Lindabury had a good head on his shoulders and a heart that knew right from wrong. He said he would make a fine preacher. Reverend Thompson had offered to tutor him for college. The elder Lindabury was pleased, and the farm boy was permitted to leave his chores in the fields and go over and sit in the pastor's study, where he worked with him over history books, algebra, Latin, and Greek.

Young Richard's parents were proud of him, but they fretted about him sometimes. They said he studied too much and worried that he would get what was called in those days "brain fever" if he kept on. The youth didn't heed the warnings, and after three years of intense study his health did suffer a breakdown, just about the time he was ready to enter Rutgers. He had to give up all plans of college and all ideas of the ministry.

It was after he recovered that young Lindabury turned to law. Being a lawyer wasn't the same thing as being a preacher, but it was still the business of right and wrong. He spent four years clerking in the office of a former congressman named Alvah Clark. Four years of reading law and studying under Mr. Clark, an experienced lawyer, had given this young man the basic equipment. In 1874—

about the time a man named John Dryden was calling on a druggist named Dr. Ward—Lindabury passed the New Jersey bar examinations and opened law offices in a little town called Bound Brook.

The rise of Richard Lindabury was no meteoric record of achievement, but even in the first small cases he began to get in Bound Brook, and a few years later in his new office in Elizabeth, New Jersey, people began to notice something special about young Lindabury. It was more than the way he looked, more than the flashing black eyes. Young Lindabury seemed to exert a kind of moral dominance and authority. When he cross-examined, he did so with a quiet firmness that disconcerted the witness. He knew what he wanted and he kept on driving past distortions and evasions—with a polite, merciless persistence—until he got his answer. Young Lindabury knew how to prepare his case too. He worked day and night learning everything he could about the subject at hand, absorbing facts until he knew more about the matter in litigation than his clients or opponents.

In 1892 Lindabury was chosen to be an associate counsel with the distinguished Joseph H. Choate in a litigation between the Singer Sewing Machine Company and the state of New Jersey on a matter of taxation. The case dragged on for three years, but when it was finally settled the verdict was in favor of the Singer Company and Mr. Lindabury's reputation as a corporation lawyer had begun. He was later retained, along with Choate, by the American Tobacco Company for a suit brought by the New Jersey attorney general, accusing the company of operating in restraint of trade. Choate eventually had to withdraw from the suit and Lindabury carried on alone. The case at length reached the Court of Errors and Appeals, where Mr. Lindabury made a plea which is still regarded as a classic of skillful argumentation in the best tra-

ditions of the law. The American Tobacco Company was
awarded the decision and Mr. Lindabury attained national
stature.

In Newark, where Mr. Lindabury had moved his offices—
by coincidence, to the Prudential Building—many of those
who saw him in action felt that the lawyer had never really
given up the ministry. The law to him was something sacred,

they said, and he preached it not from a pulpit, but from behind a big desk to a congregation of clients that was beginning to include some of the most powerful enterprises in
America. Mr. Lindabury was a busy man. Those who had
business with him went to see him at his offices. In the ante-
chambers of the firm of Lindabury, Depue & Faulks, the
directors and officials of America's top corporations waited
for a chance to talk with the law firm's senior partner.

The president of Prudential had been watching the career

of his distinguished tenant. He had tasted some of what they called the "Lindabury fire" in the Prudential-Fidelity merger business, and had been impressed. There was a place for a man like that in Prudential, Dryden thought. Later he had engaged Lindabury's services, as had other insurance executives, during the Armstrong hearings. A year after those hearings, in 1906, he was to call in Mr. Lindabury again, on a matter of even more urgency.

They were a curious pair, these two men in the president's office. Behind the desk—the senator, dignified and proper, a self-made patrician who had achieved success of an unparalleled nature for himself and an idea the world now recognized as noble. On the other side of the desk sat his caller, the younger man, still in his early fifties, an erect, craggy man who seemed on the surface severe and cold, who lived by the pure light of reason and justice, and who would make no compromise. Senator Dryden needed Mr. Lindabury. He needed this sort of man, this sort of intelligence and integrity, for the future of the great Prudential enterprise. The senator was a man who understood insurance. For Prudential, Mr. Lindabury was a kind of "insurance."

At the moment of that meeting the need was rather pressing. Edgar Ward, who had been with the company for more than thirty years as its general counsel, had decided to retire. As the senator explained to the taciturn lawyer, Mr. Ward had always been its attorney, but the company never had had an organized law department. The senator was at his most persuasive as he outlined his ideas. Would the lawyer consider the possibility of taking over Edgar Ward's post in the company and, in addition, the responsibility of organizing the company's law department?

It was an attractive offer the senator made. But Mr. Lindabury was a busy man. He had a number of commitments, particularly with United States Steel, which required his attention. He could not conceivably devote his time to one company.

"I would be willing," he told the senator after some consideration, "to assume the duties of general counsel for your company. I could also undertake to find some young lawyer of outstanding capabilities who would be able to carry out the assignment of organizing your law department." Three weeks later Prudential was able to announce that it had a new director and general counsel: Mr. Richard V. Lindabury.

It was quite a feather in John Dryden's cap, bringing in Lindabury. Men of this caliber were needed. Forrest Dryden would probably take over after the senator was gone, but he would need all the help he could get. Senator Dryden had been bringing in new men, new blood, for the company. John Gore was as fine an actuary as could be found. And there were others. Robert Burrage, the medical director; Frederick Hoffman, the historian and statistician; Wilbur Johnson, the comptroller. And a number of young men in the agencies who were rising up through the ranks.

There was another name added to this list shortly after the arrival of Lindabury: Edward D. Duffield, the man Lindabury picked to do the actual job of organizing Prudential's law department. Duffield was a towering broad-shouldered son of a Princeton professor. A Princeton graduate himself, he had been winning favorable comment and attention as assistant attorney general of the state. Lindabury was impressed with Duffield's ability. He told Dryden that there wasn't another man in the state, or over in New York for that matter, who would be better for the job of organizing the law department.

For the senator, the later years were not unkind. He

divided his time between Washington, Newark, and Stronghold, his summer estate. The Drydens enjoyed the social life
of Washington, the colorful diplomatic gatherings and
parties, the occasions when Senator and Mrs. Dryden would
call at the White House for dinner with President Roosevelt
and the first lady.

In the Senate Dryden had done rather well. One bill he
had introduced on insurance had been tabled, to be sure. But
he had won the esteem of fellow senators by his brilliant
work on committees, and a speech of his on the projected
Panama Canal had upset the majority report favoring a sea-
level canal and won the senators over to the lock canal which
was finally put through. On that occasion the senator put on a
forensic display, marshaling facts and figures as brilliantly as
he had done on a night years past, at the gathering of
directors in the Broad Street basement office after his return
from Europe.

He enjoyed the give-and-take of politics in Washington
and back in New Jersey. But the political situation at home
was confused, and during his term internal conflicts developed within the Republican party. Senator Dryden, as a
wealthy man and the head of an insurance company, presented an excellent target for the darts of the reformers.
When it became plain he could not be re-elected without an
extended and wearing campaign, and possibly not even then,
the senator chose to retire from the political stage gracefully.
In 1907 he came home to Newark and insurance.

At Prudential the "old gentleman," as they called him, still
held the reins. The company he had founded continued its
growth. It was operating now in virtually every state, including the District of Columbia and the Territory of Hawaii, and
plans were under way to open offices in Canada by 1909. It
had won a gold medal at the Paris Exposition in 1900 and a

silver medal at the Pan-American Exposition in Buffalo in 1901. It had continued its policy of more and more concessions to policyholders. In 1903 Prudential had paid the highest claim thus far in its history: $93,475 on the life of Judge Henry B. Tompkins of Atlanta, Georgia. The sum paid out was more than the paid-in cash of the original investors in the company.

Yet strong as the company now was, there remained a weakness: Prudential was a stock company doing business for profit, and some of the stockholders were still insisting that these profits should be far greater than they were, that the dividends paid to stockholders should be the first consideration of the management.

In 1909 Leon Blanchard headed a group of the Blanchard family—all descendants of Noah Blanchard—in an action against The Prudential for the purpose of obtaining a far greater share of the profits of the company than Dryden was willing to grant. What these stockholders asked for now was a complete reversal of Prudential's past policy. They wished the court to order Prudential to distribute at once $2,500,000 from the company's surplus to the stockholders. In addition, they entreated the court to order Prudential to cease granting any benefits to policyholders of any nature beyond those specifically stipulated in the policies.

The legal position which the stockholders assumed was clear. The directors of Prudential were arbitrarily and illegally "in a way fraudulent in law and subversive of the rights of stockholders not assenting thereto" withholding funds which should have been turned over to the stockholders. Or so they claimed.

Lindabury handled the case, of course, with Duffield to aid him. Lindabury had no reservations about the issue. He insisted that they would fight this thing all the way up to the

Supreme Court if they had to. It was a bitter legal fight before Vice-Chancellor Howell in the Court of Chancery. Two
able lawyers were opposing them: John R. Hardin and Robert
H. McCarter, who had once been Duffield's superior when he
was assistant attorney general.

The long and costly court battle wound up after weeks of
testimony in what the newspapers called an "even split."
Actually the decision was a serious setback for Prudential's
policy of retaining surplus earnings for the protection of
policyholders. The court agreed that "concessions" were a
legal and necessary part of operating the business of insurance and as such might be continued. But it declared that
Prudential was in an extremely sound and stable condition
and therefore could easily pay the $2,500,000 dividend to the
stockholders as Mr. Leon Blanchard *et al.* were demanding.
Both sides immediately filed cross-appeals to the New Jersey
Court of Errors and Appeals.

Out at Stronghold, in Bernardsville, where the Drydens
spent much of their time now, "the old gentleman" took a
few weeks' rest after the first round of this case. He liked being out there in that great massive building, with its solid
walls and tower, the quiet, secure place behind stone fences
and iron gates. Mrs. Dryden wasn't in the best of health and

they went out but rarely. A network of roads was laid down on the estate to provide secluded drives. The portico with the high white columns they had glassed in so that Mrs. Dryden could sit out there in the afternoons in the sun.

Dryden, aging and tired, felt secure in that country castle of his with the great doors which seemed to shut out the world. Not many miles away, at Florham Park, was another house, a rambling, informal house overlooking a serene landscape of lakes and rolling hills—the estate of Dr. Ward. The doctor was still a force in the company, though he was less active in its day-to-day affairs. He spent an increasing amount of his time abroad in the summers and in recent years had become a familiar figure at the Ritz in London.

Down the hill, just a few miles from the Dryden estate, was another house, the home of Attorney Lindabury. It was a big, middle-aged house of an indefinite style, a plain, simple house built to be lived in. Lindabury wasn't a man who could enjoy an elaborate estate. He chose a farm instead, a low-lying place with rich summer pasture watered by a strong stream. The lawyer was proud of his prize Guernsey cattle and the timber along the ridges above the fields. He worked late on his cases here, and at six was up and out riding on his big bay hunter.

Often in the evenings Mr. Lindabury would ride in his carriage up the hill to Stronghold to see the senator, and the two would sit and talk by the great fireplace. Sometimes of a fine summer evening they would go up in the great square tower room with its windows on all sides providing a sweeping, commanding view of the landscape with its scattered country lights.

More and more Dryden had come to rely on this man. In him he found no soft answers, no devious motives. Mr. Lindabury was his own master, a man of deep convictions and in-

corruptible ethics. His opinions were based on clear reasoning backed by moral judgment. They were not always the
answers Dryden wanted to hear. But he listened because he
knew Lindabury was a man whose decisions were based on
fundamentals. He had a way of being profoundly right that
provided a sense of security the senator needed in these late
years.

There were no records kept of these meetings. They didn't
need transcripts. They were moving now in a field of morality
and ultimate purposes, and both of them would know when
they had reached a conclusion. From what is known of the
actual history of the relationship one can almost reconstruct
the long talks, the slow unfolding of a new concept from an
old problem. The talks began on the matter of the Blanchard
case in the fall of 1909. This was the thorn that Dryden had
not been able to tear away—this desire for profits on the
part of these stockholders. From the beginning they had
stood astride his path—the path of Prudential. They weren't
evil men, Dryden thought, so much as shortsighted men
—they did not realize that business morality had deepened
and changed, and that if Prudential was to survive and
grow, it, too, must change. "Social institutions, like political
institutions," he had said in the introduction he wrote for
his collected addresses and papers being issued that year,
"can endure only . . . if they prove their social utility by
successful adaptation and re-adaptation to the ever-changing
conditions and circumstances of political and social life."
Dryden believed that, and knew that it was important to
the future of Prudential. He knew, too, that those who opposed him would never understand its meaning.

The case now before the court was not Dryden's principal
concern. Prudential would win on appeal. Lindabury had
told him that. Lindabury knew his case and his grounds.

There was no doubt in his mind. But this would not be the last case, the last attempt. They would keep on with their demands, he knew.

Often in these evenings the attorney would discuss this point with him. Actually it had been Lindabury, the man of reason, who had persuaded him that only a basic change could remove the danger. "Senator," he would say, "you have been plagued with these cases for years and they will go on. There is no way out because you are a stock company and stockholders want their profits. The only way to end this clamor and destroy this threat is finally and irrevocably to take the company out of the hands of those who endanger it."

But hadn't the senator attempted that? Hadn't he tried to give the policyholders a voice in the running of the company, a vote at annual meetings, and found it impossible? One can hear Mr. Lindabury's answer, "Senator, you have got to give them more than the vote. You have got to eliminate the stockholders." And after a pause, "There is only one final, lasting solution—mutualization."

The senator hadn't wanted to accept Lindabury's views. He was willing to distribute the proceeds, to continue and to expand his program of concessions and dividends. But to give up the company entirely was another matter. After all, it was his company. He had built it, and he could and should control it. There were perhaps other, less drastic solutions to this problem. Sitting there by the fire, he had suggested several possibilities. Lindabury had listened and asked questions. It hadn't been necessary for him to do much more. Dryden saw the flaws in the plans even as he presented them and, in the end, he realized there was no escaping the soundness of Lindabury's reasoning. One by one he abandoned the alternatives he had put forward. Slowly, reluctantly, and with reservations, Dryden was forced to admit that mutualization of Prudential was the answer.

Months before his discussions with Lindabury the senator had stated his position on this Blanchard matter very clearly to the directors of his company. It had been perhaps a kind of valedictory for the senator. "The faith and confidence of three generations," he told them, "are today placed in this institution, and no words of mine can do justice to my sincere desire to impress upon the board of directors the solemn responsibility which rests upon us all, to administer the affairs of The Prudential for the best interests of the vast aggregate of our insured. No one can question the right of the stockholders to derive from their investment a proper and legitimate reward, but it requires no argument to prove that in this respect the stockholders of The Prudential have no just cause for complaint. It should not be a difficult task to do justice both to stockholders and policyholders, and the great success of the company itself is evidence that good care has been taken of both interests. Our position of justice and equity in all our dealings with our policyholders is neither new nor novel, but traditional with The Prudential, and this will ever be our policy so long as my voice prevails and so long as I am sustained by the judgment, good will, and good faith of those who throughout these many years, in unison and without a dissenting voice, have administered with rare skill the affairs of The Prudential, in due appreciation of the great trust committed to their care."

This was the statement he had made, and the words summed up his views at the time. But now, watching the Blanchard case move to its conclusion, he began to see that there was no compromise, that the company could never survive divided against itself. As Lindabury had said, they would never be satisfied, there would always be some group demanding more. Mutualization was the road—the only road to security.

It would be a lengthy process, the old gentleman realized. There would be so many details to consider in such an involved business. It would require months, even years, after the methods of mutualization were worked out. It would take time.

But there was very little time left.

Many of his friends, as he had explained some years before in his statement at the Armstrong hearing, were growing old and dying. On July 13, 1910, he had lost the man who had been his closest friend, Dr. Ward. The doctor had died in London, and Dryden had written the statement announcing the death to the field force and the home office.

"Personally," he had written, "I have lost in Dr. Ward a friend and companion through a long association not often paralleled in the relations existing between men in business affairs. I can bear testimony to his valuable services in the building up of this great company, to his integrity, to his fidelity to principle, to his lovable and charitable disposition, to his optimistic and enthusiastic temperament. . . ."

Dryden felt the loss of Dr. Ward heavily, more heavily than he had the passing of the others. They had been close for all these years, and it was like losing a part of himself, a part of his past. The shock of Ward's death troubled him for months.

On Saturday, November 18, 1911, Senator Dryden underwent a serious operation. He rallied in an encouraging way until Tuesday, when what was then known as ether pneumonia set in. The reports state that the senator made a valiant struggle, but in spite of every medical aid he continued to sink, until he sank into a coma. He died late Friday afternoon, November 24, at his residence on Broad Street, only a few blocks from the site of the old bank building where he had launched The Prudential.

Messages of shock and grief came in from the mighty and humble. President Taft sent his condolences, and former President Roosevelt and Mrs. Roosevelt, senators and governors and businessmen, heads of great companies, presidents of insurance concerns. There were resolutions passed by the boards of many of the great banks and business houses of the day.

Letters came also from agents who had worked with him back in the early days, superintendents and others who had grown up with the company. Some of them had gone on and won high honors for themselves. George Gaston was one. He was a vice-president now, at Metropolitan. And John Lunger, who was a vice-president at Equitable.

The funeral took place on November 27, at the Third Presbyterian Church, and was described as "plain, simple, and unostentatious." But many of the most distinguished men of the time were there. Heading the honorary pallbearers were J. Pierpont Morgan and Richard Lindabury, and following them were notables of that era—Chief Justice William S. Gummere of the New Jersey Supreme Court, New Jersey's former Governor Franklin Murphy, Judge Elbert Gary of United States Steel, George Perkins, the financier, Haley Fiske, vice-president of Metropolitan, Uzal McCarter, president of the Fidelity Trust, Thomas McCarter, president of the Public Service Corporation, Frederick Frelinghuysen, president of Newark's Mutual Benefit Life Insurance Company, Moses Pyne, head of the Princeton Board of Trustees, and a number of others.

The high and the low crowded into the church to pay their last respects to John Dryden. Some of them knew him as the senator. Others as the president of the great and powerful

Prudential. Still others remembered him as Mr. Dryden of years past, an insurance man who came to town, a frayed young dreamer with a new insurance idea he claimed would be of considerable value to the working people of America. . . .

He had left his company in sound shape. The total number of policies in force was more than 10,000,000 and the amount of insurance on the books had climbed to two billion dollars. The company was well organized now. Departments were running smoothly, and little difficulty was anticipated in adjusting to the new administration. John Dryden had set the pattern for the future. Forrest Dryden would take over the presidency and there were experienced men to guide him in his new duties.

But there was one flaw that Senator Dryden appeared to have overlooked. Back in the trying time of the Prudential-Fidelity merger plan the officers of Prudential had been compelled by agreement to sell the majority of its stock to Fidelity. The management of Fidelity, therefore, was clearly in a position to assert working control of the insurance company. So long as Dryden lived his personal prestige and power were sufficient to force agreement among all factions. With Dryden dead, the entire situation changed abruptly.

The storm broke only a few days after the senator's funeral. At the December meeting of the Fidelity directors they bluntly announced that they proposed to appoint a proxy committee which would vote the Prudential stock at the forthcoming annual meeting of The Prudential in January in favor of ousting the management and placing its own nominees in control of the Prudential board.

It was a stunning assault. But it had one great weakness. The plan was not acceptable to Richard Vliet Lindabury.

CHAPTER 9

Of Men and Mutualization

A<small>T THE</small> December meeting the Fidelity group did not, as a matter of fact, appoint the proxy committee, according to their boldly announced intention at the start of the meeting. But they did set in motion a series of events which were to result in a dramatic change in the ownership of Prudential.

The meeting exploded in bitter acrimony following the announcement of Fidelity's plans. The Dryden group violently assailed the proposal, and before the meeting ended they had effectively countered the program put forward by the trust company's officials. Fidelity had the shares to control Prudential. But Prudential would have overwhelming public opinion on its side and very likely the insurance commissioners in addition. Faced with this impasse, the two factions finally agreed to the appointment of a committee of three members from each side to study the problem and find a solution fair to all parties involved.

The actions of this committee did not make the strident headlines which years before had greeted the announcement of the projected Fidelity-Prudential merger. But in the final accounting the plan they set in motion was ultimately to result in the complete elimination of the stockholders and the mutualization of the company for the benefit of the policyholders scattered across the nation, in its towns and cities and on its farms.

The seeds of mutualization had existed in the original charter of the company, which declared that "each stockholder shall be entitled to one vote for each share of stock by him held, and every member of the corporation, though not a stockholder, shall be entitled to one vote." A further section provided that "all persons making contracts with said corporation for any of its objects or purposes shall become and be members of said corporation, subject, however, to all . . . regulations which may be made or prescribed by said directors. . . ." Policyholders were apathetic about their voting rights, however, at that time; none actually had even exercised his right to vote at an annual election. In 1880 New Jersey had passed a bill, with the backing and approval of Prudential's stockholders, providing that all elections of directors of any stock insurance company should be by stockholders only.

Opposition by some of the stockholders to Dryden's long series of concessions led him later to regret having supported this bill. As he had declared at the Armstrong hearing, and later before the Hillery Committee of the New Jersey Senate investigating life insurance in 1906, he had sought to give policyholders back their vote and found it was now illegal. The report of the Hillery committee, published some months later, declared:

> Upon full consideration of this subject, we are satisfied that it is not feasible for so great a number of policyholders to vote at the election of directors of their company. The expense and difficulties make it almost impossible to secure a general ex-

pression of opinion, and the desire to take part in the selection of directors does not seem to exist to any considerable extent among the policyholders. . . . But we think that where the interests of policyholders are so great . . . some directors should be selected more particularly charged with looking after the interests of policyholders. . . . We have, therefore, prepared a bill providing for the appointment by the governor of three directors of each stock life insurance company. These directors will be persons having no interest in the stock of the corporation.

This recommendation—with the exception of the substitution of the chancellor for the governor as the appointing power—was enacted into law by the Legislature in 1907. This was the extent to which policyholders legally could participate in the company's operations. As Lindabury had shown Dryden after the opening round of the Blanchard case, mutualization was the only way to bring in the policyholders on a sound basis of full participation.

Senator Dryden had died in 1911 before any actual plans for a mutualization program had been set in motion. His sudden death had brought to an end any plans which may have been in the back of his mind, and precipitated the acute crisis in the affairs of Prudential and the Fidelity Trust. The dragons' seeds sown by Dryden with his merger plan of ten years past cropped up now in a harvest of dissension and brittle insults exchanged across the table.

It was to be the job of the committee appointed at that stormy meeting to find a way out, a method of separating the interests of the two companies in a way that would be fair to both sides. The acrimony of the Fidelity meeting gave way to more sober reflections on the probable consequences which would follow the drastic and reckless action the Fidelity group had originally proposed.

Neither side—even on this new committee—was prepared

to retire from the arena, and it was apparent that the Fidelity group was still ambitious to control the great Prudential if it could.

It was here that the clear reasoning of Richard Lindabury held the ground for Prudential. Patiently Lindabury explained to the Fidelity members of the committee the untenable situation in which they would find themselves if they attempted to ram through their original proposal. They would have to face not only hostile public reaction but almost certainly the opposition of various state regulatory authorities. Neither the public nor these authorities would tolerate the conversion of The Prudential, with its vast assets held for millions of policyholders, into a mere subsidiary of a banking institution, to be exploited for profit by the latter.

Throughout the difficult and delicate deliberations faced by this committee there was always Lindabury in the background to advise Forrest Dryden and to help him chart the Prudential course and map its legal strategy. In the end, this program was successful. The committee, recognizing the practical realities of the situation, agreed finally to recommend to the Fidelity board that Fidelity should vote its Prudential stock at the Prudential annual meeting in January 1912 for those who constituted the present Prudential board. In return, the Prudential management, including Forrest Dryden, the new president, and those associated with him, agreed to vote the Fidelity stock held by them and by Prudential in favor of those who constituted the then existing Fidelity board.

The achievements of the committee were far wider in scope than might have been anticipated. Under Lindabury's guidance the committee had also arrived at a further agreement whose importance was tremendous. A concerted effort would be made by both interests to devise a method of mutualizing The Prudential.

The committee report was received by the Fidelity board of directors and won the immediate approval of both the Fidelity and Prudential factions. The bold design to take over Prudential had been halted.

Faced with these tremendous technical and legal problems the new president, Forrest Dryden, made no pretense of being touched with the same stamp of genius which had set his father apart from other men. But the younger Dryden was a sound and well-trained executive. He had risen through the ranks of this company and knew its problems and its working mechanism. As an executive he was also wise enough to gather about him men of vision and ability.

Certainly the most outstanding of the men around Forrest Dryden was Lindabury himself. Thrust into the foreground of action with the crisis which arose immediately after the senator's death, Lindabury within those first months became a decisive figure in the new administration, guiding and advising Forrest Dryden in every major question which came across the new president's desk. Even in later years, as President Dryden grew more sure of his ground, there was never any question but that Lindabury was the guiding mind, the "prime minister of Prudential."

Mr. Lindabury and his associate, Mr. Duffield, the general solicitor of Prudential, set about the problem of devising a plan of mutualization which would secure the endorsement of the commissioner of banking and insurance, the approval of the Legislature, and the co-operation of the Fidelity and of other Prudential stockholders. Assisting them in this was William H. Hotchkiss, former superintendent of insurance in New York, who had been retained by the company for this purpose.

During the rest of 1912 these men labored over the plan with Forrest Dryden, while the uneasy truce continued between the opposing camps. There were many obstacles to be surmounted. It would not do merely to acquire a majority of Prudential stock for cancellation; this would have placed absolute control of the company in the remaining minority groups which might then easily have carried out the very policies Senator Dryden had always opposed.

The problem was to find a method of mutualization which would eliminate the dangerous possibility that some minority group, or clever outside manipulator, might be able to seize control at some vulnerable moment in the mutualization process.

It has been said that Edgar Ward, the retired general counsel, first suggested to Forrest Dryden the plan which was adopted—the placing of all stock acquired by the company in trust for the policyholders until all the outstanding stock had been acquired. Whether the suggestion was Ward's or came from some other source, it is certain that Dryden and Lindabury at once seized upon it as the ideal solution.

Prudential's situation had been eased a little by the fact that in April of 1912 the New Jersey Court of Errors and Appeals had finally reached its verdict on the Blanchard case —with a complete victory for the company. The court held that Prudential had properly exercised its discretion in the matter of granting concessions as well as in withholding from distribution the fund of $2,500,000. This finding meant that Prudential was free to pursue the program of mutualization without further harassment in this particular matter at least.

Prudential's board of directors—on January 13, 1913—appointed a committee of several of its own members to prepare and present to the Legislature a bill providing for the acquisition by the company of its stock to be held in trust for policyholders until all of the stock had been acquired. The committee consisted of Lindabury, William J. Magie, former chancellor of New Jersey, and Bennet Van Syckel, former justice of the New Jersey Supreme Court. The bill was drawn by Lindabury and Duffield, was approved by the committee, presented to the Legislature, and duly enacted that same year.

This act provided for a proceeding by the company before the chancellor for an appraisal of the value of its stock. The act further provided for the purchase by the company of any stock which might be offered to it at the appraised price, but only after approval of the plan by stockholders and policyholders, at meetings to be called for this purpose. It was further stipulated that the plan would not be operative unless and until the chancellor had determined that such purchases could be made out of the company's surplus without impairment of the rights of stockholders who did not elect to sell.

The legislation made it compulsory for the company to purchase all stock offered at the appraised price. But for the stockholders it was "permissive" only. It did not in any way obligate them to sell. The practical success of the plan, therefore, depended, to a large extent, on the fairness of the appraisal and the resulting inducement to stockholders to sell. All stock thus purchased by the company would be transferred to a policyholders' trustee who would receive all dividends thereon and repay the same to the corporation, to be used for the benefit of policyholders. The trustee would also vote the stock at elections of directors for those persons the policyholders might select at a meeting called for that purpose, and at other meetings would vote the stock as in his judgment would best promote the interests of the policy-holders.

To some of the directors and company officials the plan seemed too complicated. Why couldn't they get a forced condemnation of the stock and have the whole thing over with and settled quickly? But Lindabury and Forrest Dryden held out against this. Such a plan would be a bold invasion of private property rights. It would certainly be opposed by many stockholders with resultant delay, not to mention a serious risk of failure. "We must follow the safe route even if it takes longer," Lindabury told them. "We cannot afford to risk the danger of a misstep—with hundreds of millions of dollars in our trust."

After approval of the act on March 24, 1913, the company filed its petition before the chancellor for the appointment of appraisers pursuant to the act's provisions. The objecting minority of stockholders was still to be heard, however. They protested to the chancellor that this entire thing was illegal and would deprive them of their property rights. Over their protests the chancellor appointed three men to appraise the value of the stock: former United States Senator James Smith, Jr., former Governor John Franklin Fort, and William M. Johnson, insurance expert. At the same time he appointed former Governor John W. Griggs and Merritt Lane, prominent attorney, as counsel to represent policyholders before the appraisers and in any further proceedings which might be taken under the act.

The objecting stockholders pressed the battle. Seeking to have the order appointing the appraisers declared a violation of their constitutional rights, they appealed to the Court of Errors and Appeals. This action was dismissed in October on technical grounds. The question was not of a judicial character but the act of a legislative agent and therefore reviewable only by a writ of certiorari. One of the objecting stockholders, Julius S. Rippel, prominent Newark financier, at once obtained a writ for review of the order in question by the New Jersey Supreme Court. The court affirmed the order without touching on the merits of the case on the ground that it would be "premature to adjudicate the validity of a mere order appointing appraisers before any further action had been taken pursuant to the terms of the act." Lindabury and Prudential had won another round.

In the spring of 1914 hearings began before the appraisers. A large body of testimony was presented and elaborate arguments were heard on behalf of stockholders, policyholders, and the corporation. In June the appraisers filed their report. The total value of Prudential stock they declared to be $18,174,108.89. This was approximately $455 a share, or 910 per cent of the original par value of $50. In July, again over the objections of minority stockholders, the chancellor confirmed the report of the appraisers.

In October, in accordance with the terms of the act, the stockholders—by a vote of 30,899 shares in favor and none opposed out of 40,000 shares outstanding—authorized the company to purchase such shares as might be offered at the appraised price. This action was confirmed by the policyholders in December by a vote of 940,797 in favor to 208 opposed.

The unanimous vote of the stockholders was the result of a curious series of behind-the-scene moves and countermoves. When the mutualization plan was first launched, informal discussions with the Fidelity interests had indicated that the Fidelity group would approve the plan and tender its Prudential holdings to the management if the appraisal were satisfactory. Certain Fidelity directors, however, were unwilling to go along unless Prudential would agree to sell to them 800 shares of Prudential's holdings in Fidelity. This would give these directors clear control of Fidelity.

This was not unreasonable. Under a law passed in 1907, limiting the amount of stock a life insurance company might hold in any one corporation, Prudential was under compulsion to sell 800 shares of Fidelity stock, and the bank's officers were anxious to keep this block of shares from outsiders. If Fidelity were to relinquish its control of Prudential under the mutualization program, certainly Prudential ought to be willing to turn over the 800 shares to one of the Fidelity directors, to offset the chance that outsiders might seize control of that company.

Prudential was willing to sell this stock to Fidelity, but a serious dispute developed over the price. This led to a series of delays, and the chancellor had to extend the time limit Prudential had been given to get rid of these holdings. In the end, because of the need to remove a serious obstacle to mutualization, the commissioner of banking and insurance approved an agreement of Prudential to sell the stock at a price substantially below the market value. The Fidelity officials, under the circumstances, were willing to accept the appraiser's evaluation of the stock of Prudential.

Another side light of the stockholders' meeting was the fact that none of the minority group which had been opposing every step toward mutualization raised a dissenting voice. At least one of the group was present at the meeting. The fact that neither he nor any of the others voiced a protest was regarded as possibly a sign that they had given up the fight. This was not borne out by later actions of the minority group, however, and to this day no explanation has been given for their silence on that occasion.

On December 22, 1914, following the approving votes of

the stockholders and policyholders, the chancellor confirmed their action and authorized Prudential to buy stock of the company at the appraised price. The chancellor also ruled that the purchase could be made out of surplus without impairing the rights of stockholders who did not desire to sell. On that same day he appointed Austen Colgate as trustee for the policyholders.

Prudential's annual meeting of January 11, 1915, was the last controlled by the individual stockholders. Substantial blocks of stock soon afterward began to come in, and were transferred to the trustee as required by the law. On January 22, 1915, Fidelity Trust tendered its holdings—19,993 shares. This block, together with other shares coming in, constituted a solid majority. The shares continued to come in throughout the year. At the next annual meeting of January 10, 1916, Trustee Austen Colgate appeared for the first time and voted the stock transferred to him as directed by the policyholders' meeting of December 1915. The shares voted by Colgate constituted 93 per cent of Prudential stock. In spite of the 7 per cent of stock still outstanding, Prudential had become in effect, in practice, and in purpose a mutual company.

But the situation was somewhat complicated. Although in effect mutual, it was still technically a stock company. In compliance with a law passed in 1907, requiring it to elect whether it would do a participating or non-participating business, it had, as a stock company, elected the latter. Now, virtually owned by its policyholders, it seemed anomalous to go on doing a type of business designed for a stock company, the writing of policies the holders of which did not participate in profits except by company "concessions."

To accomplish a change, it was necessary to have an amendment written into the law enabling Prudential to reverse its previous position about the type of business it would do. The amendment was passed in March 1915; in April the company began doing business on a strictly participating basis with its policyholders.

By the end of 1915 there remained only 2,707 shares outstanding. Of these shares, 2,400 were held by various members of the Blanchard family. According to the stories of that time, the animosity between the Blanchards and the Drydens dated all the way back to the time when John Dryden was elected president following the death of Noah Blanchard— and in the face of opposition by a number of stockholders including members of the Blanchard family. In any case, the earlier lawsuits of the Blanchards were well remembered. Their opposition to mutualization itself was to continue over many long years. It would be almost three decades before this matter was finally settled by the purchase of the last remaining Blanchard holdings.

Mutualization of Prudential had become an indisputable fact in practice. "From this time on," Forrest Dryden declared in a letter to the field staff early in 1915, "all Prudential policyholders, except the holders of policies issued in exchange for lapsed policies, will receive their proportion of the company's earnings, which will be distributed among them in the form of dividends."

As a result of this practical completion of mutualization, Prudential at the end of 1915 was able to apportion about $4,000,000 more in dividends to its policyholders. And that was only the start. Year by year the millions paid out as dividends to policyholders would climb higher and higher. A new era had begun.

CHAPTER 10

Gibraltar —
of Main Street, America

PRUDENTIAL put its offices where they would be close to the people—along the Main Streets of America.

During the opening decade of the twentieth century the roots of the company spread wide and far across the country. As early as 1890 the eastern states had been opened up and the westward expansion was well under way. At the turn of the century there were Prudential offices already operating in Alabama, Florida, Georgia, Tennessee, Texas, and Nebraska. The next five years brought in states all the way to the Coast—Montana and both Dakotas, Wyoming, Idaho, California, Washington, and Oregon.

The little company that had once been bounded by the city limits of Newark, New Jersey, now reached into almost every village and town in the country. The Prudential sign with its Rock of Gibraltar was a familiar sight on any Main Street, as well known to the farmers and ranchers of the Middle West and West as it was to the factory workers of New Jersey and New England.

The people of these cities and towns and farms knew Prudential. They could tell you where to find the local office; they probably knew the superintendent personally and, probably, some of the agents who worked the debits. There was a reason for that too. When the home office sent out a superintendent to open up a new office, it wanted him to make himself part of the community, to take a role in civic activities, to do his share in the building of that community. He was often a member of the school board, or a Sunday-school superintendent, or a member of the town council. He knew that it wasn't enough just to be in the community; it was his job to be part of the community.

The Prudential man's office was never ostentatious. It was likely to be somewhere near the center of town, but it was usually upstairs over some business place. It might just as well be in a farmhouse, or over a country store, or in the back of a real estate office. It didn't seem to make much difference where the offices were. The people knew Prudential, and they knew the agents, and that was what was important. Even in big places such as Chicago, Detroit, St. Louis, Fort Wayne, and Salt Lake City, the offices were inconspicuous. People seemed to like the fact that Prudential didn't put on any glitter. Its offices were plain and simple and reassuringly solid.

"The superintendent's office was very plainly furnished," one Prudential old-timer, who broke in at the start of the century, was to remember. "There was a huge oak roll-top desk with a high-back swivel chair, an iron safe, a table upon which proudly stood a typewriter (built in 1898), back of which was a straight-back chair of the 'kitchen' type. There was a telephone fastened to the wall farthest away from the superintendent's desk. The room was large and barny, but four pictures on the walls, in wide gold frames, helped to reduce the emptiness a little bit. The pictures were of John

Dryden, Dr. Leslie Ward, the home office, and the Rock of Gibraltar. In one corner of the room stood a wooden costumer upon which hung the superintendent's hat, overcoat, and umbrella.

"Through the open doorway one could look into another large adjoining room. This was the agents' room. It had brown battleship linoleum on the floor and was furnished with three small-sized roll-top desks, three swivel chairs, three oak tables, and about a dozen wooden chairs. There weren't any pictures in this room, but several bulletins and calendars were pinned on the wall. There was a large blackboard on the longest of the walls and a box of chalk on the window sill near by."

These were the offices that were opening all across the United States in the early 1900s and on into the teens. While they were being dotted across the map, the bustle and the parasol disappeared. The brown derby and the celluloid collar came in and barbershop quartets flourished. The telephone was accepted as a business necessity, and in some towns a few of the wealthy and daring citizens began to appear in sputtering motorcars. But these new mechanical marvels were not for the fieldman. Mr. Ford's "Tin Lizzie" was still a few years away, and the agent traveled for the most part on bicycle or on foot, and by horse and buggy over the unpaved roads outside the cities.

But by whatever means they traveled, Prudential agents were reaching every corner of the country. There was an office in Gallitzin, Pennsylvania, and in Red Wing, Minnesota. There was one in Chillicothe, Ohio, and in Ardmore, Oklahoma; in Middletown, Connecticut, and in Pueblo, Colorado; in Webb City, Missouri; Berlin, New Hampshire; Ogden, Utah; in Terre Haute and Vincennes, Indiana; in Buffalo, Elmira, Glens Falls, and Binghamton, New York;

in Madison, Wisconsin, and San Jose, California. In 1909 Prudential crossed into Canada and a whole new list of names began to appear—Levis and Montreal and Trois-Rivières in Quebec; Winnipeg, Manitoba; Regina, Saskatchewan; Saint John, New Brunswick.

The names run on. From one end of America to the other, along the main roads and the back roads as well, Prudential was reaching the people.

There were good districts and bad, rich and poor, but for the agents there were no easy districts. In the hundreds of county-seat towns where Prudential set up the sign of the Rock the agent made his rounds, meeting his friends and neighbors and chatting with the members of the families he served. It was pleasant, sometimes, as serene as an English landscape, but that was only part of it, the better part. There were the sprawling metropolitan areas, too, with their blocks of tenements and stores and stands and markets. There were the dank hallways and the endless flights of broken stairs, the littered slum streets. In blackened coal towns the agents walked among people who lived in fear of disaster and poverty. Strikes were sudden, violent, and bloody. And everywhere there were days and weeks of rain, of cold and ice, of snow that clogged the frozen streets. Summer was no better. There was the blistering sun on the sidewalks, the airless halls, the sweltering kitchens. Prudential was reaching the people of America, but it was a hard job and often a thankless one.

Prudential put offices out in the byways of America, but it was the fieldmen who made Gibraltar a familiar symbol in every home. They made their rounds regularly, sold insurance, were there in moments of need and crisis. They did a little more than their duty, and there were many stories of their deeds. People told how one young Prudential man had crossed the frozen Ohio River on foot to pay a death claim in Milton, Kentucky. He had nearly been carried to his own death, they said, as he leaped from one floating cake of ice to the other on the way back, as the ice pack began to move out. There was another man in Colorado who made an appointment with the pit superintendent to go down in a mine and talk to the men on duty. He was late for his appointment because his car mired down in ruts. When he got to the shaft it was nearly noon, and he found others waiting there—many others. There had been an explosion. No survivors, they thought. There was the story, too, of the claim man who was escorted to a Kentucky mountaineer's cabin by a squad of rifle-toting marksmen. There were stories of all kinds about the work and the danger and the difficulties. They all added up to one thing—the determination of the men to reach all of the people everywhere.

The more successful the men were in the field, the more the story of Prudential spread into every town and village, the greater became the volume of work back in the home office in Newark. From 1892 on it had been necessary to expand the staff again and again, as hundreds of policies grew into thousands and then into millions. The outward symbols of this progress were the additions to the home office buildings. Four more were put up in 1901: the twelve-story Main Building addition, the twelve-story North Building, the eleven-story West Building, and the ten-story Northwest Building. But even this was not enough to meet the needs of the growing staff and the increasing number of departments. In 1910 the North Building addition was erected.

The new buildings were the most visible signs of Prudential's growth, but more important was the change and expansion that took place in the home office staff. By 1910 there

was in Newark a trained group of more than 3,000 office
workers. Year by year the numbers had increased as new
departments were added and new services were developed.
There was the whole enormous business of keeping in regular contact with every agent. The mailing department had
now become a vast enterprise in itself. Tens of thousands of
pieces of mail were received and sent out daily. To help keep
the men informed, the company regularly published *The
Prudential Record* and *The Bulletin.* Millions of records
had to be filed, indexed, and obtainable at a moment's
notice. Thousands of forms had to be printed—in the Prudential's own printing plant, incidentally—and stored, ready
to be sent to the men as needed. The home office was now a
complicated mechanism and growing more complicated
every year.

New services were added constantly throughout these
first decades of the century. In 1914 the Prudential longevity
service was established to provide special examinations of
policyholders by which diseases might be discovered in their
early stages.

In almost every branch of the business new departments
were added to facilitate the handling of the increasing volume, and older departments were expanded. The investment
departments were extended to find profitable employment
for the funds being built up, and the law department, now
a sizable section with a battery of attorneys under General
Solicitor Duffield, was engaged in handling the problems
arising from investments. More and more space was being
given to the farm mortgage branch. A few years later, in
1916, a whole new field of coverage was opened up in the
"group insurance" branch. This was a different kind of insurance that had developed in recent years, and John K. Gore
and James F. Little worked out the details for Prudential.

Group insurance was a new thing that very few in those days thought would grow very much. The business was still divided between industrial insurance and ordinary, and that seemed the way it would continue. By the end of 1914 ordinary had passed the one-billion-in-force mark and total insurance was more than two and a half billion.

The home office was a thousand forms and blanks and papers, a myriad of details and notices, of bills and payments and checks. Yet if it had a surface appearance of confusion, it was, as one old-time agent declared, "the most brilliantly organized confusion ever seen—because it was doing the job it was supposed to do, and even more."

In the field and in the home office Prudential was now a part of the bloodstream of America. It went wherever men and women were seeking a way to provide protection for themselves and their loved ones—human security in its highest and truest sense.

The service Prudential gave to the people of the United States was constant and inconspicuous. The agent quietly went his rounds and just as quietly appeared in times of difficulty and despair. Insurance agents had become an accepted part of America, part of its growth and history. The need they filled was seen dramatically only when some national disaster struck, some moment of terror which flashed in headlines across the country.

Back in 1898 it had been the blowing up of the battleship *Maine* in Havana Harbor, the explosion which set off the Spanish-American War. Two hundred and sixty lives were lost. Prudential paid death claims to the families of seventeen of those men.

When the excursion steamer, the *General Slocum*, took fire going through Hell Gate in New York's East River in 1904, more than 1,000 lives were lost. Of those who died, 212 persons carried 336 policies with Prudential. Benefits went to the families of some of the persons who died in the San Francisco fire and earthquake in 1906. Prudential paid claims on the lives of some of those aboard the *Titanic* when it struck an iceberg in the North Atlantic in 1912. When the steamer *Eastland* overturned in the Chicago River in 1915, with 812 lives lost, the families of 243 victims of this tragedy received benefit checks from Prudential.

Prudential's aim, as always, was to meet the need of its policyholders at the moment that need was greatest. An emergency—a disaster, a train wreck, an explosion—meant a tragic loss of life. For the families of victims it also meant urgent expenses. As a matter of course, when one of these disasters struck, Prudential men on the scene paid what benefits they could in the quickest possible time. Actually, however, these men were more than bearers of money. They aided in whatever way they could, caring for the needs of victims wherever they found them, working side by side with nurses and doctors and volunteers giving first aid.

In April 1917 the United States entered World War I. In December of that year Halifax, Nova Scotia, was rocked by a tremendous explosion resulting from the collision of the *Mont Blanc,* a munitions ship, and another vessel. Fifteen hundred were killed and thousands of others maimed and injured. Three thousand homes were wiped out.

Immediately Prudential men set about their specific jobs— to seek out victims and their families entitled to benefits. But they did much more. They were not only insurance men —they were also a part of the army of rescuers helping to carry out the wounded, leading the injured and blind to temporary aid stations, distributing food and clothes and blankets.

All the time they were giving their aid they were also

carrying on the job of finding and identifying victims and paying out claims to grief-stricken, destitute families. It was a heartbreaking task which became for these men a grim daily routine, until all claims in that havoc-ridden city had been paid.

Even before the United States declared war, Prudential had been involved in the conflict through its personnel in Canada, which had been a belligerent since 1914. Already everyone in the United States was talking about "doing his bit" for the Allies, everything from enlisting to sending packages. And when America found herself actually in the war, emotions soared even higher. It was a time of enlisting and parading and flag waving, of knitting sweaters and socks, of folding bandages at the Red Cross, or helping in the canteens set up for the "doughboys" soon to go "over there."

Before America's entry Prudential people had been enlisting for overseas service in the armies of the Allies, in the Red Cross, the YMCA, or the Salvation Army forces. Beginning in April 1917 hundreds of the younger men were called up to the colors. Before the war was to end the great service flag waving between the Main Building and the North Building was to boast 1,729 stars—the men of Prudential who were in the service of their country. Several hundred of them were overseas in active combat. Fifty died in service to their nation.

In war, as in any activity affecting the nation, Prudential's role was bound to be many-sided now. It was not only a question of men from the company's staff going overseas, or employees rolling bandages on the home front. Prudential was an organization devoted to insuring lives, to paying claims. Many of the policies written before the outbreak of war in 1914 had clauses excluding coverage in actual war. But Prudential, like other life insurance companies, waived this right on all such policies. On new policies, war clauses or war risk premiums were required.

On July 16, 1917, three months after our entry into World War I, Second Lieutenant John McCahey, U.S.M.C., died at the Marine Barracks, Quantico, Virginia, of a gunshot wound. This, Prudential's first United States war claim, was the forerunner of payments aggregating almost $7,000,000 on 20,264 industrial policies and 2,553 ordinary policies. The amount involved represented one per cent of the claims paid during the war years.

Prudential had another vital job in the winning of the war. As an investment institution handling vast sums, the company was able to contribute to the national war chest through the purchase of bonds. A large part of investment money now went into Liberty Loans, $5,000,000 in the first loan drive, $10,000,000 in the next, $15,000,000 in the third, and $60,000,-000 in the fourth. In addition, the employees of the company themselves subscribed or obtained subscriptions for nearly $50,000,000 more.

But even as the people of America were cheering the war's end, a new disaster was to take a toll even greater than that of war itself: influenza. This world-wide epidemic, perhaps the worst America has ever known, before it was over was to take a total of nearly 500,000 lives in the United States alone.

Actually, it had begun even before the end of the war. Death claims had trebled in October 1918 because of the spread of the illness which struck all classes and claimed its victims almost overnight. From September 26 to October 19 Prudential paid out $1,000,000 in death claims. In one day alone the company paid out $506,000, the largest total ever paid in a twenty-four-hour period up to that time.

Throughout America, in the months of November, December, and on into the following year, the horror spread. Doctors, working until they collapsed, were unable to answer their calls, so great were the numbers of sick and dying. Coffins became a rare commodity selling at scarcity prices. Many were burying their own dead, hammering together rude pine boxes for their loved ones. In cities and towns across the nation the death rate climbed to undreamed-of heights.

If the war had left Prudential and other insurance companies remarkably unaffected, this swift and disastrous epidemic was a far different story. To Prudential it was without question the great moment of testing, for Prudential was the company which boasted that it always paid quickly, within a few hours, a few days at most. But death claims were pouring in, agents in the field were harassed and sleepless, and the need for money by those who suffered losses was never greater.

For some reason the death rate in Philadelphia ran a little higher than in most cities along the east coast. But the scenes at the Prudential offices there were typical of those in any field office of the company during that dread winter of death. Claimants stood in lines at the windows, sometimes all the way out to the street. Agents, claim representatives, and superintendents worked on a round-the-clock schedule to keep up with the ever-increasing claims.

One of the agents in Philadelphia at that time was a man named Harry Leonard. Leonard was young and strong and unafraid. He was a kind of unsung hero making his rounds during the epidemic, going on his own debit, and in addition going where he was needed on claims. He was just another insurance man, but wherever he went he brought confidence. Where he had to, he filled out a form that meant a check for some family with a load of grief and expense.

"The influenza epidemic," he was to recall long after, "is

FORREST F. DRYDEN

something I'll never forget. The deaths were so sudden that it was almost unbelievable. You would be talking to someone one day and hear about his death the next day. The doctors were worn out and weary and many of them died. The undertakers could not handle all the people to be buried. The cemeteries had stacks of coffins piled up, as the gravediggers could not dig graves fast enough to dispose of them."

Agent Leonard worked through all that time of sickness and sorrow and sudden death. Etched in his mind was one incident: "I talked to a man on the street who had a box under his arm. The tears were running down his cheeks. I asked him about his trouble, and he told me his little baby was in the box. He was unable to obtain an undertaker or a permit for burial and he was going to bury the child himself. His wife, he told me, would probably be dead when he returned. 'I only pray that I can get back in time or that I go next,' the man sobbed."

A man couldn't think too much about himself during those weeks. It was his business to be where his people needed him, and it didn't matter much how he did it. People asked Leonard how he managed to keep going. His answer: "I'm taking a rare old stimulant, about a pint a day. And I'm 'way ahead on my prescription."

What was happening in Philadelphia was repeated in scores of cities and hundreds of towns across America. And to The Prudential Insurance Company this was its war, the company's war, in a very special way. It was in the business of paying benefits—John Dryden once had called it a "great factory for paying claims"—and here was the challenge. It was only money it had to give, not aid or succor. But money was needed, and quickly.

As soon as the extent of the epidemic began to be clear, orders went out from the home office: Pay all claims as quickly as possible. Cut all red tape. Clear the claims within twenty-four hours—*don't let them pile up.*

Across the nation Prudential offices stayed open late into the night, and superintendents and cashiers, often wearing gauze protectors over their faces, paid out claims as fast as it was humanly possible. Field claim payments were being made so rapidly that in more than one instance there was neither time to reconcile nor to replenish the company's bank balance. But the reputation of Prudential was such that even when accounts were overdrawn, banks continued to honor checks until new deposits had been received. Only the fact that the field superintendents were able to pay a substantial part of the weekly premium claims made it possible for the company to keep up with the avalanche of claims that poured in from every part of the country.

Back in the home office in Newark it was the same story. Hundreds of workers from all departments were enlisted in a special drive. Night after night they worked clearing the rush of claims which came in great stuffed mailbags from the field offices. The claim papers were fumigated on arrival, distributed among the workers, and matched with home office papers after tedious hours of searching through the files. Routine methods of handling the work were completely disregarded in the rush. Written memoranda and the regular reference of claims to qualified supervisory authorities were superseded by a new entity—"the Floor Walker Claim Adviser"—a claim specialist who circulated among the volunteer examiners and advised them on specific problems.

Claims, records, files, and clerks filled the department to overflowing. Room was made available in the adjoining recreation hall, and soon that space, too, was crowded. Typists couldn't keep up with the demands of the work; clerks spent entire days writing checks and records and documents in longhand. The work went on from eight in the morning until eleven or twelve at night, Saturdays, Sundays, and holidays. At the height of the epidemic there were those at Prudential who worked for two days and nights without rest. This was the service Prudential had promised, this was the moment it was needed most, this was its duty to the country and to the people of America.

With the help of the home office and field staff alike Prudential met the demands of that dark moment. It was a challenge not of cash reserves—it had the reserves needed and many millions more—but of time. Prudential was able to do the job—the heart-rending job—expected of it in those grim months. The challenge was faced daily and hourly. And through all those weeks, claims were processed, approved, and speeded on their way—on time.

It was finally over. The number of cases began to fall off as the winter of 1919 ebbed, and by the summer of that year the epidemic had passed. As a result of influenza deaths in 1918 and 1919 Prudential paid upward of 85,000 claims for a total of more than $20,000,000.

In Muncie, Indiana, and Pottsville, Pennsylvania, in Waterloo, Iowa, and Sioux City, in Vancouver and Sacramento and Walla Walla, across the Main Streets of the continent, the agents went about their appointed rounds. Some of them rode now in Mr. Ford's new flivvers.

Business was going rather well. The war was over, the dreadful epidemic was past, the world was returning to civilian life and normalcy, as Mr. Harding would call it. By 1920 assets had climbed to almost $600 million, policies numbered nearly 19,000,000, and insurance in force had climbed to more than $4,400,000,000.

By and large, the times were good, in spite of some major

strikes and disturbances and dislocation of prices, as the economy adjusted to peace. Agents returning from the war enjoyed going back to the old routes and routines. Life was settling down again.

Actually, an era was dying in these months after the end of war. And a new age was in process of birth, a hectic, lavish, cocksure age. The crisis and challenge of the twenties were at hand.

CHAPTER 11

Mr. Duffield's New Horizons

In AUGUST 1919 the House of Representatives passed the Volstead Act and the age of prohibition in America was under way. That same year the Boston police walked out on strike and Calvin Coolidge won national fame with his declaration that there was no right to strike against the public safety "by anybody, anywhere, any time." On September 16, 1920, someone set off a bomb in Wall Street. Thirty people died and hundreds were hurt. One fall morning in 1922 the Reverend Edward Wheeler Hall and Mrs. James Mills, choir singer, were found shot to death on a farm near New Brunswick, New Jersey, providing the country with one of its most sensational murder mysteries. Tennessee staged an epochal trial over evolution in the blistering summer of 1925, and in 1927 a gangling youth named Lindbergh flew from Roosevelt Field, New York, to Le Bourget in Paris, and thereby became the modern world's most famous hero. On Valentine's Day, 1929, in Chicago Al Capone's triggermen lined up seven rival gangsters against the wall of a garage and shot them dead.

The age of the twenties was a bitter, bewildered one. It was an era of astounding contradictions. Americans piously passed a prohibition act and turned to drinking bad liquor in dirty little basement hideouts. Women boasted of new intellectual equality, but gloried in playing the role of the brainless flapper. People talked one way and acted another. Morals and manners were changing.

Morally, spiritually—and financially—the country was on a week-end binge of reckless living and speculation. Radio and Westinghouse and American Tel and Tel and New York Central and scores of other market leaders climbed up and up. And the great financial minds, most of them, said the spiral of rising prices on Wall Street was sound.

It wasn't. It was to culminate in a new Black Friday on Wall Street, in sudden panic and a profound depression which was to change the whole course of history.

Companies, like nations and individuals, are molded by the times and the circumstances in which they exist. In them are reflected the purpose and the values of the age. But no company, no institution, is a rudderless thing, adrift and driven only by the current of the time. It responds to the hands of those who guide it, and in those hands rests the responsibility for its ultimate direction.

Prudential, during most of the reckless years of the twenties, was in the hands of a new president, a lumbering giant of a man called Ed "Duff" Duffield. It wasn't always easy to think of Ed Duffield as a powerful executive. Big and genial and warmhearted, he was always ready to find an excuse for the other fellow's fault or to discover a way of straightening him out. It was only after one looked at the record Duffield built for Prudential and for himself during those bewildering years that one realized the true extent of his achievements, the achievements of a man who found new ways through which the might and power of a great institution could serve America.

Many people who knew Ed Duffield said he should never have gone into the insurance business at all. Duffield was Princeton, they pointed out, his whole family was Princeton for generations back. On his mother's side he traced his ancestry all the way to Jonathan Dickinson, the first Princeton president. His father, Professor John Thomas Duffield, had taught mathematics at Princeton for more than fifty years, and his brother, Henry Green Duffield, was Princeton's treasurer. Ed Duffield had grown up in the shadow of university elms and had gone to Princeton himself. He did all right in his studies. He got a diploma at Princeton and then went over to New York Law School and obtained a law degree.

Though he was big, Duffield had never done too well in sports. The only one the tall young man went in for was tennis. An accident in a match had broken a ligament and resulted in his having an awkward gait. His classmates in college had called him "Paddlefoot" because of that walk, and the nickname clung to him over the years.

After he got out of law school there were those who still felt that young Duffield would follow along in the family tradition and find a place for himself in the academic world of Princeton. But Duffield had different ideas. He decided to find his own paths in the world of law and politics. He started by serving a clerkship first with J. O. H. Pitney, a distinguished member of the New Jersey bar, and later in another office before setting up business with a partner. All the time he was practicing law he was building friends, particularly political friends. The politicians liked this young man. They liked his manner and his honesty and his way of getting along with people. In 1903 he was elected to the New

Jersey Legislature and in 1905 he was appointed an assistant attorney general under Robert H. McCarter.

One of the cases the brilliant young Duffield was allowed to handle brought him up against Richard Lindabury. Duffield lost the case but he won the respect and friendship of his opponent. Lindabury remembered Duffield, and a year later turned to him as the keen young mind to organize Prudential's law department.

The odd part about it was that the job was supposed to be only a temporary one. Duffield had made that clear to Lindabury. He liked the excitement of politics and his regular law practice and didn't want to settle down in any kind of safe and conservative environment. He'd take the job, to be sure, but only on the understanding that it was temporary. That temporary job was to last for thirty-two years.

When Forrest Dryden had taken over from his father, it had been Lindabury and Duffield who stood at his side, and it was to their advice and sure hands to which Forrest Dryden had turned. He had done well in the job. He had kept the company strong and built it even stronger. Certainly the figures would have borne this out. When Forrest Dryden took over, the assets of the company had been hardly $300,000,000. By 1922 the assets were nearly $800,000,000. But the strain of the responsibility had broken the health of Forrest Dryden. On his doctor's advice he had gone on a long ocean voyage early in 1922.

Lindabury and Duffield handled the business of The Prudential during Forrest Dryden's absence. Duffield, who had been vice-president since 1918, was made acting president. Lindabury, his hair now steely-gray and the lines of his face deepened by time, still refused, as he always had, to become an official of the company. A general counsel, he insisted, should be able to sit on the outside, to give his advice objectively—judicially—without being personally concerned.

In August of that year 1922 Forrest Dryden came home, but his health was still too uncertain for him to resume the duties of president. So Forrest Dryden sat down and penned a note of resignation. The board of directors accepted it regretfully, but with appreciation for the job this son of the company's founder had done. At that same meeting they unanimously elected Edward Dickinson Duffield president of The Prudential.

The new president was a man of faith. This was the dominant theme and credo of his long years of service, this fact of faith—faith in himself, his fellow man, his country, and his God. These were simple things, often derided in the tinselly years of the twenties, but to Ed Duffield they were tangible and real. He wanted the confidence and friendship of the people who worked for him in the home office and in the field. When a man gets to be president of a great institution he sometimes inspires a certain awe, becomes a remote symbol of an impersonal thing called "the company." Duffield didn't want it that way. He wanted the doors open.

It was a new era for Prudential. John Dryden, the founder, had been a crusader, and his interest had been not so much in individuals as in the great huddling masses of the poor. Forrest Dryden had carried on as a kind of trustee of the great idea, but it was Duffield who brought new horizons and new humanity to this great business.

Duffield's humanity was seen in many ways. First of all with the Prudential staff itself. He wanted to know them and sent out word that if any man were thinking of quitting, let him write his whys and wherefores to President Duffield. Perhaps together they could straighten things out. They believed him, and many wrote to him of their doubts and problems. The president's answers to these letters often saved a man or a woman for Prudential. More important was the effect on the morale of the entire staff. The simple fact of Duffield's interest was a tonic in that world of figures and percentages and rate tables and all the mechanical calculations of insurance. The people working for Prudential, now numbering nearly 20,000, recognized this new relationship. Mr. Duffield was their personal friend.

One of his first major actions was to make a tour of all the states and of Canada, dropping in to sit with his superintendents and agents to get to know them. They found him a sincere man who seemed to take his insurance almost as a religion. And he would talk to them about the power they had to do good, to bring help and protection and solace to people. He would chat about business or politics or even religion. He often talked about religion in one way or another and about the need for observing the commandments of Christ. Insurance men said that Ed Duffield was a curious blend, an unusual personality to be running a billion-dollar business. But they had to admit the tremendous effectiveness of Duffield's new personalized approach.

Vice-president and Actuary John K. Gore had long been interested in the problem of providing wider coverage at lower rates, particularly for young families. With his associates, he was instrumental in having The Prudential bring out a modified form of whole life policy which, while providing lifetime protection, called for a premium during the first five years of only half the subsequent rate. This was the policy known as Modified 5, the full title of which read "Modified Whole Life with Change of Rate at the End of 5 Years." It was a policy which fitted admirably into Mr. Duffield's program of new horizons and service. It gave the young family man a chance to obtain more nearly adequate permanent protection at a price he could afford to pay with the higher premium coming due at the end of five years when, in most cases, he would be in a better position to afford the increased cost. Modified 5 was first presented in 1924, and it quickly became one of the most popular of the ordinary life policies.

One of Mr. Gore's associates at this time was James F. Little. Little was a brilliant actuary who had turned the business of rate computation into an adventurous profession. Australian born, he had begun his insurance career "down under" in Sydney and later had gone over to England and established himself as a consulting actuary, associating with some of the foremost British actuaries. Still seeking excitement in the rate tables, Little went to Mexico as the first actuary in the Mexican Insurance Department. He had been there only a few months when Mexico had another revolution. Bullets began to splatter around the charts on his desk and Mr. Little hastily packed up and came to the States. Things were a little quieter and safer in the office he found with The Prudential in Newark.

For some time Mr. Little had noted that the participating ordinary life policies, as they were then written, had a distinct disadvantage as compared with non-participating policies. They called for a higher initial premium, which had to be paid in full, before dividends became payable at the end of one, two, or three years. He therefore conceived the idea of an ordinary life policy with a premium for the first three years 15 per cent lower than the ultimate rate. At the time the increased premium became payable, dividends would also be payable and would be available toward offsetting the increase. Thus was the Modified 3 born. The policy was introduced in 1928 with the title "Modified Whole Life with Change of Rate at the End of 3 Years." Since the initial premium in many cases determines the amount of insurance an individual can secure, by lowering the premium at the outset this plan made it possible for the individual requiring permanent insurance protection to secure more insurance right at the start than he could on other participating life policies then available. The new plan was welcomed by Mr. Duffield, who saw in it a way to provide sound permanent life insurance at the lowest possible rate from the very beginning. This Modified 3 contract continued as one of the best whole life policies on the market.

Another new form of insurance which Mr. Duffield helped to build was group insurance. Duffield saw group as a way of bringing coverage to many more thousands of people who might not be able to receive protection in any other way. Group was new and still the infant prodigy of the insurance world, but Duffield was willing to give it the opportunity it needed.

But in Mr. Duffield's mind insurance divided itself into two broad social aspects. The matter of coverage and protection for the individual was of prime importance. This was the aspect on which the company had concentrated from the very beginning days. The great sums of money which had poured in had been carefully invested with about equal division between bonds on the one hand and mortgage loans on the other. But Mr. Duffield realized that the funds themselves had become a source which could be used, not merely to protect policyholders' interests, but also to promote the public welfare. More and more of Prudential funds from here on would go into factories, new farm operations, new homes. Prudential under Duffield would play an ever-expanding role in the building of this new era. But it would not depart from its policies of caution. Investments would be sound.

They were speculative years, those years of the mid-twenties. Fortunes were being made and lost in reckless plunging, and there were those who felt that even a cautious program of mortgages was a dangerous investment. Ed Duffield's answer was that he put his faith in the people, and the money Prudential lent on homes, on farms, and on factories was safely invested, regardless of what economic storms lay just ahead.

Here, as elsewhere, Duffield's concern was in seeing that the company fully realized the opportunities before it, that it fulfilled the national responsibilities he had set for it. Nobody understood better than he that no one man could direct the details of a vast enterprise such as Prudential had become. But no one believed more firmly than he in the duty of those in control to set the moral and social objectives which must be the common goal.

When Ed Duffield took over the presidency of Prudential, Richard V. Lindabury remained in many ways his guide, confidant, and adviser.

The aging attorney was still active as the nation's outstanding corporation lawyer. He was still the general counsel for Prudential, United States Steel, and other large companies. At well past seventy he continued to manage the details of his farm and was up and out at six o'clock in the morning for a ride on his hunter.

Early on the morning of July 15, 1925, his horse galloped back to the Lindabury stables riderless. A little later Mr. Lindabury was found, lifeless at the side of the road. Just how the accident occurred no one ever actually knew. Doctors stated that death was due to apoplexy superinduced by his being thrown from the horse. Abrasions on the animal indicated it had fallen.

The death of Richard V. Lindabury was a tremendous blow to Prudential and to his close friend, President Ed

Duffield. It happened that Duffield was traveling in Europe when word came of the death of his friend and associate. Duffield packed up his grips and came home. It was a sad homecoming, but with Lindabury gone, Duffield was needed all the more in Newark.

The Prudential law department which Duffield and Lindabury had started in 1906 was a strong and going department now. It had nearly 100 employees and more than thirty attorneys handling matters of law. Assuming the commanding role of general counsel was a man Lindabury and Duffield had brought in back in 1915—Alfred Hurrell. Before he came to Prudential, Hurrell had practiced law in Buffalo and had been district attorney of Erie County, New York. He had later been counsel for the New York Insurance Department and for the Association of Life Insurance Presidents, now the Life Insurance Association of America.

Hurrell was a tall, rangy man who looked, many said, like Lincoln must have looked. He had, too, the same undeviating devotion to what he believed to be just. Lindabury and Duffield had brought him into Prudential because they felt the company needed men of his caliber, and he had worked closely with them on many vital legal matters during the closing years of Forrest Dryden's regime. After Lindabury's death, Hurrell was to be one of Duffield's closest advisers. In addition to his position as general counsel, he was a vice-president and a member of the board of directors. Throughout his long term of office until his death in 1938 Hurrell played a tremendous part in the development of Prudential itself. One of his greatest contributions lay in handling the new legal questions that arose in connection with group insurance—novel questions of law imperfectly understood even by members of various state regulatory departments. He contributed greatly to the solution of the complicated legal problems connected with the company's expanded mortgage business.

The influence of this man and his character upon the company was profound. Charles B. Bradley, who served with him in the law department and who was himself later to be Prudential's general counsel, remembered him as a man of "cold judgment born of hard experience, tempered by an intense human sympathy and understanding." He freely gave of his knowledge to his colleagues, to younger officers and employees who looked to him for advice and help in every conceivable sphere from the most serious problems of company policy to the petty perplexities of personal and domestic life.

Hurreli was Duffield's kind of man because he was human and warm and because he liked people as Duffield liked people. This was the key to the whole Prudential family in those years, this warm, personal, human approach to the vast problem of protection and security for millions of people. This same warmth which dominated Duffield's program of new horizons in Prudential was reflected in the president's own personal life. It was said that Duffield's life had in it four P's—Princeton, politics, Presbyterianism, and Prudential—and in spite of the heavy burdens which the last of these placed upon him he managed to keep up with the other three also.

His interest in the church remained an outstanding part of his life, as did also his interest in Princeton. During the twenties Duffield served as a life trustee of the university. Later, in 1932, he was named acting president, on the retirement of Dr. John Grier Hibben. This was announced as only a temporary job, and Duffield found himself commuting to Princeton on Tuesdays and Saturdays from his South Orange home, while devoting the balance of his time to Prudential. People remembered that Duffield had come to Prudential on a temporary job in 1906, and they began to speculate about how long he might be at Princeton. Mrs. Duffield on one occasion was said to have remarked, while trying to determine whether Duffield was at the university or Prudential, "I do wish Princeton would find itself a full-time president." It finally did, a year or so later, and Ed Duffield could take it easy with the simple job of running a company whose assets now totaled more than $2,800,000,000.

Duffield also kept up his interest in politics over those years, serving as a presidential elector in 1920 and again in 1924. There were those who said that Duffield could have been senator any time he wanted, and there was no doubt of the popularity of this ambling, soft-spoken man among the people of New Jersey. But Duffield enjoyed taking part in politics rather as a civic duty than as a profession. His profession, as he once told the New Jersey political leaders, was Prudential.

Down through the years of the twenties and into the trying era of the thirties Duffield and his "new horizons" were to set Prudential on new paths of service, service to its policyholders and to the country. Almost from the beginning he himself appears to have understood plainly where he was steering, what roads this company under his command would follow.

On October 13, 1925, the buildings of the Prudential home office in Newark were decorated with flags and bunting. It was a rather special birthday party. The Prudential was fifty years old.

It was an elaborate affair, that birthday party. Leaders of government and business and the professions gathered to celebrate the golden anniversary. The Vice-president of the

EDWARD D. DUFFIELD

United States, Charles G. Dawes, was present at the lunch-
eon held in the Prudential North Building. Also among those
present were Senator Walter E. Edge, Haley Fiske, president
of Metropolitan Life, and President Ernest C. Heppenheimer
of the Colonial Life.

In the afternoon the directors of the company and the
officers and hundreds of the employees gathered in Newark's

Mosque Theatre, a building located on the site of John
Dryden's home on Broad Street. There was a nostalgic air
about that meeting. Some of the old-timers present had
fought The Prudential in years past. Some of the McCarters
were there, and the Blanchards, and Julius Rippel, and
others.

Dr. John Grier Hibben, at that time still the president of
Princeton, spoke of the great asset of dependability which
the company had won with its record for the past half century. And John Hardin, president of Newark's Mutual Benefit
Life Insurance Company, brought greetings "from an older
brother." The company's founders, he declared, were "men

of vision . . . enduring benefactors of human society." And
New Jersey's former governor, the Honorable Edward Caspar Stokes, traced the early history of the company and the
efforts of John Dryden in those beginning days to convince
the world that this idea was sound. Robert McCarter remembered the days of strife in the company and praised the
vision and determination which carried Prudential forward
to strength and unity.

It was a moment for recalling the long uphill road to the
high place the company had reached. Duffield also remembered some of the men who had contributed to that
success, men who should have been there at the meeting and
weren't. Wilbur Johnson, the vice-president, who had died
that year. And Vice-president Fred Tasney, also lost to them
that year. And General Counsel Richard Lindabury.

It was also a time for looking ahead. There was ample
reason to be proud of accomplishments to date. But President Duffield in his address at the birthday party pointed
to the new horizons, the new responsibilities and the duties
of this insurance company. The president cited the need for
recognizing "the character of the business in which we are
engaged and our relation to it." The company, he said, had
no funds of its own. "The Prudential has been entrusted
with vast sums of money by those who confide in it, and the
duty that rests upon us is to resolve every question as it is
presented—will this or will this not benefit those who have
trusted in The Prudential. . . . Their welfare and their welfare alone is to be our guide.

"Our first duty, as I see it, is to invest their funds so safely
and securely that they will yield to them the greatest possible
return commensurate with safety." Mr. Duffield paused. "A
second duty, however . . . after the discharge of our primary duty in the administration of that fund, is to invest it

in such a way as will best benefit the people of these United States and Canada; to see to it that more loans are made to those who need our aid; to see to it that money is placed so that productive enterprise is enabled to carry out its mission; to see to it that in making our investments we have an interest not only in our own but also an interest in the country of which we are a part.

"Every premium that was ever paid on a policy of life insurance represented a sacrifice made by someone for the benefit of someone else. It is a business based on self-sacrifice. It is a business in which selfishness can find no place. It is a business calling for the highest that man has to give, recognition of the claims of others overtowering any claims of self.

"In such a business can we not realize the ideals that permeated this company from its foundation? Can we not, if we are but true to those who have gone before, carry on its work in the years to come? May God in His infinite goodness grant that those who are entrusted with the administration of its affairs may have the vision to see, the wisdom to understand, and the courage to perform."

Such was Mr. Duffield's vision of the new horizons.

CHAPTER 12

A Roof Over Their Heads

THE first and most important function of a life insurance company, after insuring lives, is to pay claims. For the protection he receives the policyholder pays to the company certain stipulated premiums, and the benefits which he or his beneficiaries receive come in part—but only in part—from the premiums that the policyholders pay in. A substantial portion of the money paid out by an insurance company in claims comes from the returns realized on the investment of funds in thousands of enterprises throughout the country.

It follows, then, that the safe and profitable investment of the funds in its control and the proper use of these funds throughout the years are of the utmost importance not only to the company, but to the policyholder as well. Today, when these funds have reached enormous totals, where and when and how they are invested are of the greatest significance to the nation as a whole.

Without investments and investment opportunities no insurance company would be able to furnish adequate protection at a cost within the reach of the average American family. This simple fact is difficult for many to understand: premium rates are based not only on age, health, occupation, and amount of protection, but also on the interest earned on the invested part of the premiums paid in. This money is put to work to help pay for the protection the policyholder gets. This concept is fundamental to the operation of life insurance. If funds were not profitably invested, insurance rates would be enormously increased: for example, a $1,000 straight life policy for which a man of thirty today pays an annual premium of about $20 would cost him about $30.

The funds of a mutual life insurance company are invested for the benefit of the policyholders and their beneficiaries. The investment of those funds by the directors is in the nature of a trust. Restrictions are imposed by law to safeguard the interests of the policyholders. In the main, the investment of insurance funds is grounded on three basic considerations: security, yield, and diversification.

Security, of course, is the prime consideration. Investments which are in any way speculative or hazardous are not for a life insurance company, nor are enterprises which involve the possibility of large profits offset by the possibility of large losses. The rules and regulations governing investments which have developed through the years are strict and often specific.

Within the limits of safety, however, the aim of the insurance company is to obtain the highest possible return on its investment, as higher returns obviously mean lower rates on insurance. For several decades prior to 1930 the average rate of return was 5 per cent or more. Since then it has dropped to less than 3 per cent.

Obviously a company with billions to invest is bound to suffer a few losses. Not every investment will work out to a profit. The company may lose on one house or farm. On the

next the investment may yield a substantial and continuing
return. The average—the over-all picture—is the significant
factor. And for this reason diversification is the third vital
safety rule in insurance investment. In a broad sense, diversification means simply the spreading of funds over a wide
geographic area and in a variety of classes of investments as
insurance against the possibility of reduced productivity in
any one industry or section of the country.

Such, reduced to simplest terms, are the basic principles of
insurance investment, the fundamental "golden rules" on
which life insurance companies in the United States operate
today.

But for The Prudential Insurance Company of America
still another consideration developed over the years, a consideration which grew enormously in importance and significance during the decades of the twenties and thirties and
forties down to today. It was not a new consideration, really.
It had its roots in John Dryden's early realization of the ever-
widening responsibilities of the company which he controlled. This broadening consciousness of responsibility was
reflected in the first tentative steps of concessions and later in
the prolonged struggle for mutualization. The philosophy of
social responsibility was enlarged to embrace the growing
millions of Prudential policyholders. Later, under the guiding
hands of Lindabury and Duffield, the increasingly important
role of the company in the economy of the nation became a
decisive factor in the investment story.

By 1925 nearly 17,000,000 policyholders—almost a sixth of
the entire population—held one or more policies with The
Prudential. Insurance in force totaled $8,149,707,406—a sum
almost half as large as the national debt. The assets of Prudential totaled $1,196,348,261.

The policyholders of Prudential were no longer a limited

group. They were a vast cross-section of the people of America. The company was deeply affected with the public interest. The investment and management of its assets were matters of immense significance in the growth of the country —and in the protection of America and its ways of freedom.

Investments had not been so weighty a problem back in the early days. Funds were strictly limited when the company was starting out, and scarcely affected with any national interest, and the main effort had been to find safe investments yielding sufficient to keep up policy reserves. Under John Dryden's guidance the company had invested its funds in safe fields which guaranteed good if conservative yields. In 1878 it had invested in eight small mortgages on property close by the basement office on Broad Street. The total mortgage investment amounted to $8,700, which at the time represented more than 50 per cent of its investments. This was the beginning of a mortgage program which in the years to come was to provide financing for thousands of apartment buildings, commercial and industrial properties, and hundreds of thousands of homes and farms. By 1949 the company was to have granted the staggering total of more than $6,000,000,000 to almost 800,000 borrowers throughout the United States and Canada.

It was much less in volume in the 1880s. But they were boom years, and, like every other insurance company, Prudential had sought out properties in which to invest. Some it found as far away as the Midwest. There newcomers to America, Swedes and Poles, Irish and Germans, and Finns were helping to build up the new cities. Prudential began investing in mortgages on city properties in Chicago and Wichita, Leavenworth, Denver, and Pueblo.

It was a new adventure, this investing in the homes and the

business plants of the nation. By 1887 mortgage loans had reached $1,000,000, a total which represented more than 70 per cent of the company's total assets. In 1898 Prudential extended its investment program to include mortgage loans on farms.

It was soon apparent from the increasing volume of work in connection with various aspects of the mortgage loan business that the company had to have someone in the field to look over properties. A young man by the name of Archibald M. Woodruff, later to become vice-president in charge of mortgage loans, was selected to be the company's first mortgage loan "inspector." In 1894 he was sent out on the first inspection tour of properties in which the company was interested.

He was a zealous worker who carried out his duties with painstaking care for details. In addition, since he was an amateur photographer, he took along a camera and made actual photographs of every piece of property inspected. Back in Newark these photographs proved so helpful that what was done merely as a hobby became a part of company routine. In addition to his regular duties as an inspector, Mr. Woodruff was charged with supervising the management of a certain amount of property which the company had taken over because of delinquency.

A company report on the earnings of the properties while in Prudential's hands was as follows: "The most unprofitable property was a church, while the two most profitable, from a management standpoint, were livery stables—one in Pueblo, Colorado, and the other in Elizabeth, New Jersey. The theaters and opera houses account, which consisted mainly of the famous Pueblo Opera House, also made a relatively good showing; all of which may lead to a good deal of reflection—either humorous or melancholy."

The Pueblo Opera House, on which Prudential held a mortgage of $191,214, was an interesting case. About 1894 conditions in Pueblo deteriorated because of the closing of a large manufacturing plant. The loan on the opera house became delinquent and Prudential was forced to take over. The situation on this particular property looked bad. As one Prudential official put it, "There was hardly a very active market for slightly used opera houses." Nevertheless, Prudential found itself a buyer interested in theatrical arts who took over for the sum of $190,225, a loss of only $989.

These loans continued to grow, in spite of setbacks, years when property values dropped precipitously, and money was short. By 1912 Prudential's loans in force had reached almost $20,000,000 on city property alone and almost $38,000,000 on farm property.

Throughout the decade of the teens, the importance of mortgage loans increased, although the company continued its policy of investing a substantial part of its funds in railroad and government bonds—the latter particularly during the years of the war. Not until the war was over and the boys came marching home did the period of Mr. Duffield's expanding horizons in investments get under way.

By 1920 America was going through its usual postwar problems. There was a mild depression, a sharp fall in farm prices, and a tremendous housing shortage which was to grow worse in 1921 and 1922. An increasing amount of Prudential's funds was made available to enable small homeowners and prospective owners to meet this critical situation. Prudential's mortgage loans were at that time handled through "correspondents" located in cities and towns across the country. These correspondents, frequently banks or other local financial institutions, were charged with a variety of duties. It was the correspondent who arranged to supply the homeowner or farmer with needed funds through a Prudential mortgage. He was responsible to the company for the quality of the risk, and in addition it was his job to collect the interest and the principal as they fell due. It was also his duty in case of delinquency to contact the borrower and to work out a satisfactory liquidation of the current indebtedness.

Through its correspondents Prudential lent millions for the purpose of providing homes. A comparatively small amount was provided for large housing projects and multiple-dwelling units of various sorts. By far the larger portion went into individual homes in the form of small loans. The average home-loan mortgage was for only $4,708. From 1923 to 1931 almost $800,000,000 of Prudential funds was invested in homes throughout the United States and Canada.

Some of the loans didn't work out, but foreclosures on homes were rare. However, in spite of the fact that business was active and jobs plentiful, there were, among the thousands of mortgages in the Prudential portfolio, certain problem properties. In July 1928 the mortgage loan department established in Newark a foreclosure and property section, later known as the service division of the department. It was designed mainly to assist in the handling of foreclosed properties, on the theory that in good times or bad there would always be some foreclosures. Many of the correspondents in the field were not adequately equipped to handle the numerous details involved in such cases.

The service division in those early months was described by one official of the mortgage loan department as "a stepchild who wandered in and couldn't find its way out." For Prudential it was an extremely lucky chance that it was decided in that summer of 1928 to establish the "stepchild" on a permanent basis. For a little more than a year later, when the crash of the stock market spread economic ruin across the nation, that division was to be one of the busiest and most effective in servicing and salvaging mortgages.

In 1928 the possibility of any major financial crisis was to most people inconceivable. In the opinion of the experts, prices had reached new plateaus, new levels from which they could not and would not descend.

But they could—and they did. On the memorable day of October 24, 1929, prices broke on the market and billions in paper profits were wiped out. The riot continued, and on Tuesday, October 29, came the *coup de grâce* as more than 16,000,000 shares were dumped in the most disastrous day in the history of the exchange.

When that day was over and harried brokers tried to pick up the debris, the fantastic prosperity of the twenties had been wiped out, and the grim years of deepening depression, by far the worst the United States had ever known, had set in.

For Prudential, as for all America, this was to be a hard period. The record which the company wrote in those years of crisis is a stirring story. Charged with the responsibilities of handling investments of millions of dollars of policy-holders' funds, Prudential could operate only within the strict legal and moral limitations imposed upon an insurance company.

But within the bounds of sound business Prudential in those years developed a reconstruction policy which for scope and range and simple humane dealings ranks high in American business annals. It established a socially conscious program by which it salvaged not merely investments but people—men and women, homes and families, deep in trouble.

The problems which mushroomed up in the months immediately following the crash were sudden and for many overwhelming. In manufacturing industries employment fell 41 per cent from 1929 to 1932. Payrolls in the same period dropped 58 per cent. Factory workers were hit first, and after them white-collar workers. People without jobs couldn't pay rent, and people who had lived on rentals found their properties empty and their pocketbooks the same. Families doubled up where possible, and tens of thousands of young couples went back to live with their parents.

It seemed that everybody was in difficulty in those days. The people of America were in trouble. And when the people had trouble, Prudential had trouble too.

One of the major troubles involved policy loans, granted to ordinary insurance policyholders on the basis of the equity they had built up in their policies. Although Prudential knew from experience that such loans were often the forerunners of lapses, in those critical days the company stood ready, as always, to advance cash to policyholders against their policy reserves. As the months of the depression stretched into years, policy loans rose to unprecedented levels.

On Sunday, March 5, 1933, the day after his inauguration, President Roosevelt declared a national bank holiday. Cash was virtually impossible to obtain during the week from March 5 to 13.

Throughout that week and during the following months policy loans continued to mount. The record of company loans made against policies during the years of the depression is illuminating:

1929	.	.	$42,000,000
1930	.	.	54,325,000
1931	.	.	74,000,000
1932	.	.	94,750,000

One of the major problems Prudential faced during the depression was, of course, delinquencies in mortgage payments, taxes, and interest. The service division in Newark was nearly swamped by the flood. So also were the loan correspondents in the field who normally handled the collections but who now found themselves laboring under the additional burden of hundreds of delinquencies.

As the delinquencies piled higher, the situation from the company's point of view frequently got completely out of hand. To meet the crisis the mortgage loan office sent into different areas "trouble shooters," specialists who opened offices in central locations and set about the business of straightening out records and handling delinquencies. Before the depression was cleaned up, some of these emergency headquarters had become permanent establishments and in time developed into the regional offices which later formed the basis of Prudential's whole national mortgage loan network.

The significant fact about this new effort was that the trouble shooters were sent out not to foreclose but rather to prevent foreclosure wherever possible. Through their efforts a considerable number of delinquent loans were reinstated, either by refunding or modification and extension of the original mortgage. Under the refunding plan a new mortgage was written incorporating the old delinquencies but starting off fresh on new and usually lower rates.

Prudential's investments in city property mortgages followed the pattern of the times. In 1920, at the beginning of the postwar housing shortage, the company had held fewer than 7,500 mortgages with a total investment of just over $90,000,000. By the end of 1929 the holdings had risen to more than 116,000 mortgages with a total of $872,000,000. The number of mortgage loans continued upward until the end of 1931, when the company held 127,581 mortgages amounting to $942,140,000. From that point city loan accounts declined, until by the end of 1936 they stood at 86,784 mortgages totaling $665,808,000.

These are figures. They give no real indication of the human values involved nor of the tremendous efforts of the company to preserve these homes for their owners, to prevent the hardship of lost equities, and to salvage property and personal pride for those in difficulty.

There are case histories of some of these homes and of what happened to them and their owners. They are simple stories of human beings in trouble trying to fight their way out—and of the help they received from a large and "impersonal" financial institution.

A business man and his wife and their three children lived in a home in Columbus, Ohio. They had bought it in 1927 and had a Prudential home loan on it to the amount of $4,800. The owner, a coal dealer, did all right until 1930. After that he began having more and more difficulty meeting his payments to Prudential. From 1930 to 1934 The Prudential on several occasions "revamped" payment schedules to help him liquidate his delinquencies.

Despite these adjustments, the loan continued in arrears. The man had been trying to meet payments when illness struck and cut further into his meager income. In view of the circumstances, Prudential again rescheduled the loan and carried it with no payments whatever until 1937. In that year business conditions began to improve a little, and the payments were resumed.

In 1941, when the war came, the man enlisted, along with two of his children, now grown. In 1945 the father died in the service of his country. The widow continued to live in the same home. By 1950 only a few hundred dollars remained to be paid on their Prudential loan.

Back in 1927 a man and his wife took a $3,000 loan from Prudential, by which they were able to purchase their home in Waterbury, Connecticut. The husband earned a modest income and made his payments regularly until 1930.

In June 1930 the owner died. On that same day his wife gave birth to their eighth child. Upon his death she became a widow with eight children to support and no income except a few dollars a month from the State Widows' Aid Fund. Neighbors offered to take the children, but she refused. Somehow she would handle them and the home and the mortgage.

This loan was in continual delinquency in the years that followed. Prudential made adjustment after adjustment, at last reducing payment to a few dollars a month. But the widow stayed on in her home and brought up her children. By the end of the war the children were grown and able to contribute their share to the support of the family. By 1950 the loan on the home of the widow and her eight children was in current status and plans were under way to make the house debt free within another year or two.

Insurance companies are the traditional targets of those who choose to minimize the achievement of a free business system. They are pictured as cold and impersonal machines without sympathy or understanding. But thousands of people are today living in their own homes because of the policy of forbearance of The Prudential Insurance Company. Their attitude is somewhat different.

In Lakeland, Florida, a railroad engineer with four dependents was laid off. For four years Prudential carried his home without payment and in addition paid the taxes. In the late thirties conditions improved and the owner was able to pay up all arrears. He wrote a simple letter of thanks. "My family and I are certainly grateful to you," he said, "for helping us keep a roof over our heads."

Of all the groups in America, the farmers were hardest hit in the years of the Big Depression.

Prudential's experience with farm mortgages extended back to 1898. It had been different then. Farming had not been the complicated business it was to become. The large majority of farms was small, and whatever financing was necessary could be handled through the local bank. Farm prices had been good and relatively stable.

Prudential's loans to farmers had grown swiftly and steadily in the first decades of the new century. By 1904 Prudential held 2,157 farm mortgages for a total of more than $6,700,000, and for the first time farm loans exceeded the amount involved in city loans. They were to hold that lead for the next two decades.

The obtaining and servicing of these loans to farmers were handled almost exclusively by loan correspondents in the field. Through the decade of the teens, the years of the war, and the land boom which followed immediately thereafter, farm loans kept well ahead of city loans on the company books. Many farmers in the boom right after the war purchased extra properties; a good percentage of the added land and buildings was bought with money obtained through mortgage loans from insurance companies.

The beginning of the farmers' troubles had come in 1920, with a sudden collapse of farm prices. They recovered only a little over the years of the twenties. Prices for manufactured goods of all types were high. Everything the farmer had to buy cost him dearly; everything he had to sell went cheap. With the crash of the early twenties many farmers, particularly in the Midwest states, had gone heavily into debt. Loans which they were able to negotiate with local financial institutions on a three- or five-year basis fell due, and when the farmers were unable to meet them, were extended. Many of these extended loans matured about 1929 or 1930, when the farmer, after nearly ten years of chronic hard times, was plunged into acute economic crisis.

Back in Newark the increasingly pressing problems which arose as a result of the deepening farm crisis occupied much of the time and thought of Prudential's executives. As the deterioration swept from area to area, R. R. Rogers, of the mortgage loan department, and John W. Stedman, vice-president of the company and head of the bond department, Executive Vice-president Franklin D'Olier, and President Duffield geared the company's operation to combat the economic blight which had overwhelmed the country. No company and no group of men could alleviate entirely the basic results of the crisis, but in so far as it was possible Prudential was determined to relieve the pressure on its borrowers.

Foreclosures soon became a commonplace of the times, and indeed thousands of borrowers, unable to meet their obligations, voluntarily surrendered ownership. But foreclosure or abandonment was in no sense a solution to the problem. Prudential realized more than most the significance of lost homes and farms as a social hazard of the day. Very early in the story Rogers sent a dispatch to all branch offices and correspondents: If the owner believed he could somehow pull through, he was to be given his chance. A little later, when this liberality proved too sweeping, the company was forced to revise this scheme somewhat with an announcement that Prudential would not foreclose on any farm where the farmer was making "every effort in his power to meet his obligations." Still later another modification of the order was sent out: Prudential would foreclose on farms only where the borrower was not making every effort to meet his obligations and where there was no reasonable possibilities of his ultimate recovery. Within the bounds of reason and a decent consideration of its other responsibilities, the company made every possible concession to help the farmers and homeowners of the nation to a constructive solution of their problems.

No program, however well planned, could eliminate entirely the hardships of the times. In many instances the situation was hopeless, and failure to take over the property actually would have meant a burden to the farmer, since it would have been piling up more debts, more interest, and more taxes on his shoulders. Often the farmer would come to Prudential and plead with the company to take over his property. In at least one case a farmer wrote an indignant letter to the home office, complaining that the branch office had refused to take his property, but had insisted that he was a good enough farmer to carry on.

With farms as with homes, where foreclosure was the only way out, Prudential always gave the original owner or the members of his family a chance to buy back the property for the amount of the mortgage or for the current market value, whichever was lower. One of the most successful procedures developed by the company at that time was the lease-option plan, in which, in the majority of cases, no initial cash payment was required. The monthly rental was set at one per cent of the purchase price plus taxes, and the tenant had the option to buy the property at any time during the period of the lease or at its expiration. The rental paid was applied to the purchase price. A number of other renegotiation and refunding programs was worked out to fit the individual needs of owners. In most cases of foreclosure—in literally thousands of cases—the company permitted the farmer and his family to remain on the premises and to carry on as tenants, and many of these people eventually were able to reclaim their land.

Severe as this financial sickness was, complicated as it was by drought and crop failure in many areas, Prudential was able, nevertheless, through its all-out program, to save thousands of homes and farms for the original owners. In spite of the fact that more than 40 per cent of the company's farm mortgages was in delinquent status during the depression years, the Prudential approach "solved" nearly two thirds of these cases. During the five-year period ending December 31, 1934, Prudential foreclosed the equivalent of only 22 per cent of the number of farm loans in force December 31, 1929. The percentage of homes was even lower. In a period when many other lenders were forced to take over more than half of their properties, Prudential's achievement was astounding.

Gradually conditions began to improve. In Washington, faced with the staggering problem of the farmers, the Administration had begun to take active steps to lift the prices of commodities. And Prudential, with a heavy load of farm properties, numbering at its peak 8,204 farms, with an aggregate value of $61,642,000, set about the business of rehabilitating these properties. If there was a shadowed side to the farm picture in those dark years, this was at least a bright side, for Prudential's experts in the mortgage loan department bought paint and fence wire and plows and seeds and all the equipment needed to rehabilitate farm land. It was said, in the tail-end days of the depression, that when you saw white farmhouses and well-kept fields, it was probably a farm in the process of rehabilitation by The Prudential. Some of these farms, after rehabilitation, were sold to new owners.

Many of them came back to their old owners in better shape than they were before.

But even as they were pulling out of the critical years of the depression in 1936, new trouble struck in the form of a drought which blighted the fields of the Midwest. Prudential had a double stake in the farm situation now. Many of the farms were being operated under refinanced loans or by tenants or by tenant farmers who were hoping to buy back their land and to make payments from the proceeds of their harvests. With the crops blighted, their situation was once more desperate. Prudential by now had learned something of this farming business and moved into action quickly. If next year's crops were to be saved, the fields had to be fertilized and replanted without delay. Prudential experts scurried about the country buying seed on an unprecedented scale. In the north central area alone the company provided 60,000 bushels of oats, 28,000 bushels of barley, 27,000 bushels of wheat, and 2,500 bushels of flax—a grand total of more than 115,000 bushels of seed. Distribution on the basis of need and the size of the property was made by Prudential seed trains sent out throughout the area. The total amount distributed was roughly estimated at seventy carloads. The crops of the coming year would be good.

Letters came in to Prudential from some of the people it had helped, testimonial letters, unasked for and unsought. John Koistenen, Hamlin County, South Dakota, had a quarter section with a $4,000 loan on it from Prudential, made back in 1923. He put buildings on it and a silo and a house. Prudential pulled him through in those rough years until he was able to pay off all the debt. At seventy-two he wrote in a scrawled letter, "During the drought and depression I had a $4,000 loan and I wasn't able to pay the interest or taxes and the interest was $600 already and they renewed the loan and that gave me a chance to get on my feet and since then I have paid that loan and paid the loan on another quarter and have bought two tracts of land since. I have also improved the place for about $10,000 worth. So The Prudential Insurance Company has treated me right and will recommend them to anyone who needs money."

As soon as possible in the years after 1933 Prudential set about the work of returning lands and homes to the people. The company intended to play its part in getting the country back to normal conditions. During the years 1931 through 1939 The Prudential acquired 46,159 farm and city properties, the number owned at any one time reaching a peak of 30,790 in 1936. By the end of 1945, however, the number had dwindled to a mere 1,783.

It had been a new challenge to Prudential, this depression and the years that followed. Any course of action, any decision, had to be firmly based in the best interests of every group in the country. The times demanded broad social understanding. Prudential's response to the national need was its way of meeting the challenge.

In the history of growth and development through the thirties and the forties, one essential foundation stone was to remain untouched: Prudential was still a company for the small man, for the individual. In 1950 the average size of its city home mortgages was still only $5,402; its farm mortgages only $7,404. Prudential was still primarily concerned with providing help for all the people.

Take Luke Butler, for instance. Luke Butler was a Negro down in Tennessee. His neighbors said he was good and hard-working and smart too. Luke Butler had managed to save up $100 from his earnings and he had, in addition, a few mules and a few hogs and cows and a year's supply of food.

Prudential decided that Luke Butler was a good risk. It let him buy a $4,000 farm for $100 down payment, with small additional sums scheduled to pay off the whole thing in ten years. The company also let him have $115 with which to buy materials for repainting and seeding and setting the place in order. There was a time or two when the crops went bad and Luke Butler couldn't meet his payments and Prudential had to advance his taxes. But by 1945 the loan was in good standing, and Luke Butler worked out a new arrangement with the company, enabling him to buy more land. So Luke Butler sat down and penned a letter of thanks, "I started with you might say nothing and today I have 320 acres of good land, two tractors, a combine, four mules, one horse, and a car and truck. This is my story of how I have come from nothing to be worth what I have today. The Prudential has always been very nice to me."

The individual stories may not seem important. Their significance is apparent only when you add up the totals. By the end of 1949 Prudential had in force over 279,000 mortgage loans for a total of more than $2,300,000,000, representing 27.8 per cent of total assets and reaching into every one of the forty-eight states and into Canada. The great bulk of them was small loans reaching down to the people. The pattern had been set back in 1875—the pattern of service and protection for the individual. That had been the heart of John Dryden's vision, and the concept had not changed in three quarters of a century. On the strength of that philosophy Prudential had grown into a company whose assets totaled into the billions.

In 1947 a young veteran up in Boston telephoned to the Prudential office. His wife, he said, had just lost their third prematurely born infant. Hospital bills and nursing bills and funeral expenses had piled too high. He was sorry, but he couldn't meet the payment due on his Prudential mortgage loan. He wouldn't be able to meet any of the bills for at least some months. Very politely he inquired when the company would begin foreclosure proceedings. He seemed a little surprised when he was told that it wouldn't foreclose. There was a sixty-day period of grace anyway, and when that was over, if he would stop in a rescheduling of the loan payments would be worked out.

The young veteran hung up the phone and hurried off to tell his wife the exciting news: they would keep their home. Later, after the loan was once more made current, he wrote a letter of thanks: "The Prudential Company was informed of our financial difficulty and sickness and came to our aid. . . . We weren't pressed for our monthly payments. . . . Instead, we received such co-operation that it was surprising and hard to explain in writing that a big company like Prudential would care what happened to us."

CHAPTER 13

Group Grows Up

THE Acme Products Company was an important part of Centerville, U.S.A., in 1950. Not that Acme was a big or well-known manufacturing concern. It wasn't. No more than 500 people worked in the sprawling plant down by the river, and they turned out parts which went into the washing machines and the automobiles and the motors which made Detroit and Pittsburgh symbols of industry. Even though it hadn't made Centerville famous, Acme had changed the pattern of life in the town in the twenty-five years it had been operating there. It had built Centerville's past, and in 1950, with a broad employee welfare program, it was building Centerville's future.

The "factory," as everybody called it, put up the plant in Centerville in the early 1920s. The owners were forward-looking people, and in Centerville they found the kind of community they wanted to grow up in. They wanted to be a part of the life of the town and they wanted the people of the community to feel that they had a permanent place in the business as it grew up. They provided opportunities and outlets for their employees in their work and helped them build a future to which they could look forward. And because they wanted these things for their people, and because they knew it was good business to give their people a sense of security, they installed a group life insurance program. That was in 1930. It was the first step, the very beginning of the Acme Welfare Program.

During World War II Acme Products was hard pressed to fill the contracts it had. It needed more and better men than it could get. Wage increases were restricted for the duration. As a way of strengthening employee relations and building its position in the community, Acme decided to expand the Prudential group welfare plan that it had begun years before. To the life insurance coverage it added benefits covering loss of salary owing to sickness and accident, loss of sight or limb owing to accident, and the cost of medical care, hospital confinement, and surgical treatment. In addition, the benefits included hospital expense and surgical expense insurance for dependents. By 1950 Acme had a well-rounded program which insured excellent employee relations. The members of its employees' families had a sense of security that improved their work, and helped them live satisfying lives. What was even more important, there had been developed in Centerville an air of stability and confidence that was reflected in every attitude and activity in the town. This group welfare program was the result of the co-operative efforts of three groups—employer, employee, and an insurance company. Working together, they had established conditions beneficial to all. They had built in the community an atmosphere conducive to the best kind of American life, although elsewhere during these years industrial unrest was prevalent.

In 1950 the people of Centerville were proud of Acme Products and of its part in building the community. To them "welfare" and "security" were not dangerous or frightening words—they were something to be worked for and achieved. They had confidence in the future and in their own ability to meet its problems. In 1950 discussions were under way at Acme for the installation of a Prudential group annuity retirement plan to round out and complete the welfare program begun twenty years before with Prudential.

Group insurance was a major development in the insurance business, the fastest-growing and the most exciting innovation since John F. Dryden launched industrial insurance in America in 1875. It was new in technique and in application rather than in its principles. Actually it was no more than a remarkable adaptation of mass selection and buying to the fundamental principles upon which all insurance was based. Through the application of such methods it was possible to provide for employee groups the benefits of insurance at the lowest possible cost. Premium rates could safely be reduced because under group coverage the costs of servicing the contracts were considerably lessened. No medical examinations were required; the company dealt with one source instead of with many widely scattered individuals; administration and clerical work were centralized and simplified; collection of premiums was limited to a single monthly transaction with one administrative agent. These factors made group insurance feasible in the beginning and later contributed substantially to its phenomenal growth.

Long before the basic techniques of group insurance had been worked out, the need for such coverage had been demonstrated by the almost universal growth of voluntary benefit societies among employees. Workers everywhere banded together in mutual benefit associations in an effort to provide the financial assistance they needed in time of sickness or death. These associations were sometimes poorly organized and ineptly run, so that in most cases the employer was eventually called upon to support the association and to administer its affairs. In one way or another the employer often found himself morally if not legally responsible for the benefit society in his shop or factory. An increasing number of employers suggested that these benefit funds be turned over to established insurance companies for administration. These experiences, to a large extent, pointed the way toward the group insurance welfare programs created by the insurance industry.

The first group life insurance case was written in July 1912 by The Equitable Life Assurance Society and covered employees of Montgomery, Ward and Company. The inquiries which Montgomery, Ward had made throughout the industry and the requests received from other employers soon led a number of companies to offer the same coverage. In August 1916 Prudential announced a group plan for insuring employees of businesses with 100 or more workers. A week later Prudential wrote its first group life case.

In the early stages of group insurance the full cost was borne by the employer. It continued on this "non-contributory" basis until the early twenties when, because of the depression, some employers found it difficult to continue to pay the full cost. At this point, faced with the loss of insurance protection, employees in some cases agreed to share the cost with their employer. These facts were called to the attention of the New York State Insurance Department, and shortly thereafter a ruling permitting the writing of insurance on this "contributory" plan was issued. The recognition of the need for a cost-sharing program marked a major turning point in the history of group insurance. Although the new ruling did not eliminate programs in which the entire cost was assumed by the employer, it did open up large new areas where a division of the cost was the only feasible way in which protection could be provided. In time a large part of the business was set up on the contributory plan with deductions made by the employer on a monthly basis and remitted to the insurance company.

For a long time the general feeling among life insurance actuaries and executives had been that accident and sickness insurance belonged in the casualty field. Ever since the days when insurance broke away from the old friendly societies there had been a reluctance on the part of life companies to enter this field, although some contracts had been written as far back as 1910. When more and more requests for such benefits were received, The Prudential decided to enter the field, issuing its first group accident and sickness policy in 1925.

Early in the development of group welfare programs it was quite natural for both employers and employees to reason that since group life insurance protects the family of the employee who "dies too soon," then some form of protection was needed for the employee who "lives too long." Railroads in particular had for years provided their employees with pensions, but it was not until the early 1920s that an insurance company first offered what are now known as group annuities. The Prudential laid the groundwork for its position in this field by issuing its first group annuity contract to the Cleveland Public Library in September 1928.

Group insurance grew in spite of many obstacles—legislation that failed to keep pace with its rapid development, opposition of companies not writing this form of insurance, and others who were skeptical of this vigorous and sometimes rambunctious newcomer.

It grew because it admirably filled a specific need and purpose. It was adapted to the requirements of an age characterized by the spread of industrialization and financial insecurity. A time when millions of employees were feeling ever more acutely the need for some measure of security for themselves and their families, when those needs were being recognized by government, business, and trade unions alike—such a critical time demanded the broad coverage which only group insurance could supply inexpensively to millions of employees.

On into the 1930s the development of group insurance was actively opposed by those whose thinking was centered entirely on the conventional methods of providing insurance protection. But the advocates of group insurance had also grown stronger. They were now able to show a respectable area of achievement. Group insurance, they pointed out, was never intended as a complete insurance program. They agreed that only level-premium insurance with cash values could adequately serve the basic lifetime needs of the individual. But they also stressed the fact that a very large part of the population was quite unable to afford the coverage which it needed. This was particularly true of the young married man with children who could not in many instances afford anything like the protection he needed. As it developed increasingly wide coverage, group insurance made it possible for the average individual to assure himself and his family of minimum standards of living in the face of unpredictable contingencies. It made available to him a welfare program based upon his own foresight and efforts.

That group insurance was able to progress from its beginnings in life insurance to the broad scope it reached later was owing in great part to the creative thinking of a number of outstanding actuaries. Among these was James F. Little. During the critical formative years of group insurance he applied his extraordinary genius to the solution of the scores of problems which arose in the application of sound actuarial methods to new fields. It was basically his thinking upon which Prudential's success in this new field was built.

In 1928 Little made it possible for Prudential to introduce group creditors life insurance, an entirely new departure in the field. The purpose of this new form of coverage was to enable a bank or similar creditor to make installment loans which were covered by insurance, so that if the borrower died before the loan had been completely repaid, the lender would be protected. This form of insurance, first written for the National City Bank of New York, expanded with astonishing rapidity and was soon applied in scores of other fields. In time installment buyers of almost every possible type were covered—from buyers of automobiles to buyers of toasters, oil burners, and cemetery plots. By the middle of 1950 more than 2,500,000 individuals were covered by Prudential group creditors life insurance, with more than $1,000,000,000 in force. Installment buying, which has become an important factor in our economy, was made safer for the creditor because his security was better. And it was safer for the borrower too—he left a car or refrigerator or washer all paid for —not debts.

The growth of group insurance was not only a growth in the number of workers covered. It was also a record of expanding service, of new types of protection brought to new groups of people across America, and of new benefits developed and maintained for these groups.

Prudential's coverage continued to expand in response to changing economic conditions and social needs. The greatest development in the services offered came during the 1930s and 1940s. Plans for group hospital, group medical, and group surgical expense benefits were added to the program already available and, when they had been established, were extended to include employees' dependents as well as employees themselves. Designed to provide funds to meet doctors' bills, hospital charges for room, board, and other services, and surgical fees, these added benefits soon became an important and integral part of the broadening Prudential welfare program.

The growth of Prudential's group coverage during and after World War II was made possible by the decision of President Franklin D'Olier to reorganize the department completely in 1943. In 1942 the activities of the group branch had been distributed in various departments of the company, and the dispersal of functions had resulted in a failure to realize the potentialities of the market to the fullest extent. Anticipating the increase in the demand for a program of broad coverage, Edmund B. Whittaker, at that time associate actuary in charge of group underwriting, was chosen to carry through the reorganization of group activities. In May 1943 Mr. Whittaker was made a second vice-president and, under the direction of Vice-president Valentine Howell, put in charge of the reconstituted group department. Three years later the business had expanded to such an extent that a separate group insurance department was formed with Mr. Whittaker in charge as vice-president.

Convinced that group insurance was only on the threshold of its development, Mr. Whittaker in 1943 immediately set about preparing the department for a period of rapid expansion. The sales organization was set up to utilize fully facilities of the existing agencies. At the same time the group insurance department operated field sales offices of its own which by 1950 had reached a total of twenty-eight in the

United States and the Territory of Hawaii. These offices were supervised by four regional headquarters located at key points. From these offices salaried group sales representatives were sent out to assist the agents in selling and installing group insurance cases.

To facilitate payments and to promote better relations between employers and employees, Prudential originated an entirely new procedure under which companies with more than 300 enrolled workers were authorized to pay most of their own claims. The company furnished the employer with blank drafts for this purpose and provided advice and help through both the home office and by means of roving specialists from the group claim division. So successful was this new system and so generally was it adopted that by 1949 more than 100,000 claims a year were being handled entirely by employers.

The great development of group insurance in the forties was owing to causes related to the war. Because of the acute labor shortage, employers were increasingly anxious to install group programs which already had proved their popularity with the workers. Because wages were controlled within certain limits for the duration, an expanded program of health and insurance benefits became one of the most popular methods of satisfying labor demands. Somewhat later a ruling of the National Labor Board, which was confirmed by the Supreme Court decision in the Inland Steel case, made pensions a proper subject for collective bargaining and involved the trade unions directly in the movement for increased welfare benefits. More than any other single factor, the participation of the union movement was responsible for the great development of group insurance after the war.

The entrance of the trade unions into the field in force posed a number of problems. Funds for the increased welfare programs came usually in the form of percentage-of-pay increases won by the unions in collective bargaining. As the employees represented by a union often are dispersed among many small employers, it became necessary to set up trust funds to implement the program. Under the Taft-Hartley Act these funds were jointly administered by representatives of the employees and the employers. This system was elaborated still further to include non-union as well as union members in industry programs.

While the trade unions were securing group insurance benefits for their members, it became apparent that a further extension of the methods of coverage was necessary if group benefits were to be made as available to the workers in small industrial and business enterprises as they were to the employees of larger firms. In this field Prudential pioneered with "association" group insurance. This method, while holding to sound principles of group insurance, made it possible to extend group coverage to members of various types of associations even though the individual employee units might be small and widely separated. The most conspicuously successful application of this system was in the automobile dealers' associations which, enrolled on a state-wide basis, were thus enabled to install group insurance programs in shops employing as few as three persons and averaging about eight.

Prudential's group insurance department in 1945—as the war ended—was at the beginning of a great period of expansion. Broad new avenues of coverage had already been developed, and the department had been newly reorganized to meet the demands of the postwar years.

By 1950 Prudential's group insurance program was at the strongest point in its history. The trend of group insurance continued upward. Prudential was ready to face the looming challenge of the future—whether it would be private industry or government which provided the answer to the growing demand of the people for a broad welfare program.

In 1876 John F. Dryden prepared a little brochure setting forth the aims and purposes of a new kind of insurance being issued in Newark, New Jersey. It was a simple, direct statement written so plainly that anyone could understand it:

The
Prudential Friendly Society
✕812 Broad St., Newark
(State Bank Building)

Has ample cash funds and promises to its members, male and female, from infancy to old age, aid when sick, a pension when old, and a burial fund at death. No medical examination is required.

The Prudential from its adaptation to all the various conditions in life, from its provident character, from the benefits it affords to ourselves and those dependent upon our exertions, from the considerations of prudence, and the incentive to duty which it presents, commends itself to all classes.

When the brochures were delivered by the printer, John F. Dryden spread one out on the desk before him and read it through several times carefully. It seemed right to him—right because it offered the great mass of people the security and protection they needed.

That afternoon Dryden stood on the steps leading up from the basement office and watched a group of boys start down Broad Street to hand out the prospectuses to passers-by and place little stacks on the counters of the stores where the people went to buy calico and kerosene.

Dryden was proud of that first statement of aims and purposes, of the program that his company was offering to the people. More than he knew he had a right to be proud. Sit-

ting in that cramped little basement office, he had done more
than write a prospectus for the people of Newark in that day.
He had also drawn up the first rough plans of the Prudential
welfare program which was not to be fully realized until the
advent of group insurance had made it possible almost a half
century later.

CHAPTER 14

Millions of Claims—and Mike Mulloy

I n a cramped hole-in-the-wall speakeasy in New York, back in the twenties, a bewildered old Bowery tramp known as Mike Mulloy smiled with infinite if slightly incredulous pleasure at the large tumbler of whisky his three new friends had kindly provided for him. Mike didn't bother to ask why these three men whom he had met only a few days before were so interested in his welfare. It was enough for him that they were providing him with the liquor he craved. And not only that: they even supplied him with food—tasty little bits that a man could keep on his stomach. In Mike's foggy mind it didn't seem important that his friends had had him scrawl his name on a form one of them spread before him on the table. Some sort of policy to protect him, the men had explained. His glass was empty again, so Mike signed.

Mike's new-found friends had a real interest in his welfare —in a negative kind of way. The three men—one the son of an undertaker, the second a proprietor of the drinking establishment, and the third his bartender—had selected Mike as a candidate for murder. By fraud and forgery they were able to convert Mike's scrawled signature into two policies on his life, one for $800 with a New York firm and one for $988 with The Prudential. Mike was their first victim, and they planned the details of his case carefully. If it worked out profitably, they had a list of other possible subjects already drawn up. There were plenty of derelicts available.

For the amount of thought that had gone into its preparation the plan proved disappointing. The trouble came because of the seeming indestructibility of Mike Mulloy. Hopefully the plotters poured into him huge quantities of the worst "rotgut" bootleg liquor in the city. For days Mike gulped it down and asked for more. His impatient friends then decided to speed things up. They served Mike a new delicacy—oysters soaked in wood alcohol. Mike found the bivalves most palatable, and asked for another plate. Somewhat annoyed at this juncture, the conspirators introduced an even more drastic diet—sardines sprinkled with bits of the can itself cut up into tiny pieces. The day after he ate those, there were signs of success. Mike complained briefly of mild indigestion.

In the weeks that followed the three would-be murderers made half-a-dozen further attempts on Mike's life. They poured buckets of water over him, left him out all night on a park bench in freezing temperature. But Mike showed up the next day without even a cold. In desperation they finally brought a cabdriver into the conspiracy for a promise of $150. Having first been reduced to a state of complete helplessness, Mike was thrown out of the cab one night on a deserted street and run over by the taxi not once but several times.

Back in the bar the killers congratulated themselves on this new inspiration. They assumed the police would call it a hit-run accident. This would mean double-indemnity payments on the policies. The next morning they searched the papers carefully. There was no mention that Mike's body had been found. For a time it seemed that their whole investment had been lost. But a few weeks later Mike came into the bar limping a little. He explained that he had been in a minor accident. Nothing serious, he assured his friends. How about some more of that good liquor?

They succeeded finally, these killers. But it was an awkward job. They took the inebriated Mike to a furnished room they had rented and forced a tube from a gas jet into his mouth. After fifteen minutes of this, Mike at last succumbed.

When the claim was presented to Prudential, the claim department people grew suspicious. The papers indicated that the man might be some sort of Bowery tramp. Then why was he carrying that large a policy? And why had he been buried within twenty-four hours of death, according to the undertaker's report?

Prudential's claim representatives at once launched a quiet investigation into the case, working in conjunction with the New York police. The body was exhumed and evidence of gas poisoning uncovered. Eventually the little band of killers, including the doctor they had brought in to certify that death was caused by pneumonia, was brought to the bar of justice. The doctor received a long term in prison. The other plotters were sent to the electric chair.

The case of the "Durable Mulloy" was a classic in the annals of attempted insurance frauds. There were many such sensational cases on the records of every insurance company. One of the most famous of recent years was the Philadelphia Arsenic Ring, which resulted in the death of more than fifty individuals—widows and lonely old men, husbands and wives and stepchildren. Prudential paid out more than $35,000 on nine lives taken by this malevolent gang before the truth was uncovered and Prudential representatives, working with police and representatives from other companies, finally solved the case and sent twenty-two of the criminals to prison or to death in the electric chair.

And there were other cases—seamy, sordid crimes which were paraded through the sensational press. The infamous "Goodman Ring" in New York—broken finally with the arrest and conviction of thirty-eight persons on various fraud charges. The Brooklyn insurance murders, carried on by men on the fringes of the notorious "Murder, Inc.," gang. And the lurid Snyder-Gray case of the 1920s.

It was inevitable that the tragicomical murder of a Mike Mulloy, or the super-sensationalism of a murder ring's mass homicide, should be spread in headlines across the newspapers. It was inevitable also that companies dispensing millions of dollars each year in claims should be the target of criminals intent on fraud or worse.

But it was unfortunate that many people had only these sensational stories in their headline or motion-picture versions as a basis on which to judge the work done by the claim department of an insurance company. Too few realized that such cases, however interesting, constituted only a fragment of the real story of the claim department.

The Prudential had risen to world recognition on a credo of paying all just claims swiftly, without lengthy questioning or red tape. In 1950 The Prudential was paying claims at the rate of over $1,500,000 for every working day of the year on thousands of claims of all sizes coming in with each day's mail. Many of these claims were paid in less than twenty-four hours after receipt of proof of death. By this mid-century point Prudential was paying nearly one million claims a year, and the remarkable fact was that only a handful of these was ever even brought into question or suspicion, and of these even a smaller percentage proved to have been attempts at fraud.

In the very inception of the company the principles which were to govern the payments of claims were firmly established: to pay all just claims in the shortest possible time and to resist payment in the small number of cases that were plainly fraudulent. This principle had persisted unchanged through the whole history of the company—and in the claim department it was almost the only thing that had remained unaltered.

In May 1876 the directors noted with some consternation the appearance of the company's first death claim—on a two-year-old boy by the name of Joe Smith. Total claims for that first year amounted to the rather alarming sum of $1,958. Those were the days when the necessity to meet claim payments was a pressing, ever-present problem, when Dr. Ward would sit up all night to keep a policyholder alive, and when John F. Dryden sent out the office boys to collect premiums in order to meet an urgent need.

By 1885, at the end of the first decade of operation, the claim department had paid 16,109 claims for the sizable total of $1,331,000. At the turn of the century the staff had grown to twenty employees who, together with the limited help of the field, disbursed the claim funds to policyholders. Calculations were still made without the help of adding machines and the checks were all drawn in longhand.

In 1949 alone The Prudential Insurance Company of America approved claim payments amounting to more than $365,000,000. In the accumulation and processing of the records the claim department used a battery of complicated punched-card machines, calculating devices, electronic dictating recorders, automatic check writers, and other business aids, all smoothly co-ordinated in the business of transferring policies to dollars for the millions of policy-holders and their beneficiaries.

The problems of paying claims multiplied with the growth of the company. From the earliest days, it was the chief concern of The Prudential to pay all claims with a minimum of delay. In 1898, to improve still further the dispatch of funds when most needed, Prudential had permitted payment of many industrial claims by superintendents in the field. There were many stories of feats accomplished by fieldmen in settling claims. One of the best of these stories—perhaps exaggerated in its detail—concerned a fieldman who witnessed an accident in which a man was drowned. He quickly found the man's brother, filled out the necessary forms, and made the death benefit payment, all in a matter of thirty-two minutes—in fact, before the coroner arrived to pronounce the man dead.

The problem of meeting claims quickly did not grow easier as the company expanded into ever-widening areas and remote communities. Gradually, as experience proved it safe, Prudential permitted field agencies and agents to pay more and more of the claims direct, when the sums involved were moderate. Whether it was within the shadow of the home office—or in some adobe hut in the desert—a family could count on funds arriving swiftly in the moment of loss and need.

Meeting the claims arising in a great national disaster was always a challenge to the efficiency of a claim department. Prudential had been tested in the first decades of the century, and throughout the thirties and forties continued to perfect procedures designed to ease the shock of catastrophes which periodically struck the nation. In 1937 floods inundated a half million homes in the Ohio basin, causing an estimated

900 deaths. The following year a hurricane whipped the East coast, leaving in its wake 453 dead and 100,000 homeless. A train wreck on Long Island, an explosion in South Amboy, a plane crash in Washington, D.C.—in every such instance Prudential's claim department moved into action, helping at least somewhat to ease the burden of the families of some of these victims.

An example of the technique employed in the handling of such disasters was shown in the case of the S.S. *Noronic*, Lake Ontario pleasure steamer which burned at the dock in Toronto, Canada. Of the 119 persons who perished in this fire, thirty-seven held Prudential policies. As the news of the tragedy broke, members of the claim divisions of Prudential joined forces to bring financial aid to the families of these victims as quickly as possible.

Recovery and identification of the dead were slow and difficult. But as the names were reported in the press, they were immediately checked through the policyholders' index. When a similar name appeared in the index, the application was secured from the file division. If it appeared probable that Prudential had insured the life of the victim, that information was wired to the local Prudential office where the policy was in force, with a request to verify the death and wire back. Prudential offices in the Great Lakes area were requested to report by telegraph the names of any victims known to have carried insurance with the company. Payment to the beneficiaries of those victims—including accidental death benefits—was authorized at once.

When World War II plunged the United States into a global holocaust, the claim department faced the most serious testing of the machinery it had developed to handle the problems of a great calamity. Special war claim sections were formed so that war claims could be paid with dispatch without delaying the processing of civilian claims. It was clear that the reports of casualties would necessarily be delayed by the nature of the war and, to prevent additional waiting, Prudential instructed its field offices to accept as proof of death letters or telegrams from the armed forces. Only after the payments had been made did the company obtain official death certificates from the Canadian or American authorities. Invaluable was the co-operation of governmental agencies, which made available information essential to the proper settlement of claims on war casualties. In only a small number of instances were deaths erroneously reported under this system, and in all but a few of these cases the families happily refunded claim payments in full.

After the war the search for those who had been reported as "missing" or "missing in action" continued, and as rapidly as possible all claim settlements were made. These cases were individually reviewed by governmental authorities and, upon assumption of death and the forwarding of the certificate to the company, the claims were paid. By June 30, 1946, The Prudential had paid claims of more than $70,000,000 on nearly 100,000 policies in which death was in some degree the result of war.

Though every effort was made in peacetime, as in war, to facilitate and simplify payments, it was inevitable that certain types of recurrent problems should arise. The people —and the machines—of the claim department had to be prepared to process not only the daily routine of thousands of uncomplicated claim payments, but also to meet the demands of those few difficult cases which, for one reason or another, required special attention. It was recognized at an early stage in the Prudential claim history that the prompt solution of these problem cases required that a claim representative of the company actually be sent to the scene to gather

the facts about them. By 1950 more than 100 claim representatives operated from coast to coast and from Florida
to Canada.

These men were of necessity resourceful and adaptable.
Their work might take them to a coal town in Pennsylvania
or a honky-tonk in Harlem, to a resort hotel in Miami or a
crossroads in Minnesota. They had to handle themselves
equally well in water-front dives or in supper clubs; they had
to be able to glean the kernel of truth from the gossip of the
neighborhood busybody and extract the necessary facts from
the reluctant witness. Above all they needed intelligence
and imagination to reconstruct a situation and to see the inevitable flaw that marks a fraud.

The prevention of frauds against the company—and against
the policyholders—was obviously one of the major problems
of the claim representative. From the very beginning attempts to mulct the company had been a matter of concern.
At the initial meeting of the stockholders of The Prudential
Friendly Society, the first question put to John F. Dryden
was a request that he explain precisely how the company
proposed to protect itself against those attempting to cheat
it through false declarations. Dryden had carefully explained
the procedures to be used at that time, but in the years that
followed the techniques were to be infinitely improved.

Experience taught claim representatives that attempted
frauds almost invariably fell into certain well-defined cate-
gories. Not that every case was so patently criminal as that
involving the sad and sodden Mike Mulloy. But though they
might be greatly varied in detail and subtle in concept and
execution, the basic pattern remained unchanged.

Disappearances made up a large number of the cases which
claim men had to hunt down, but very few of these were
actual attempts at fraud. In most instances it was merely a

last desperate attempt of a person to escape a situation which had become intolerable. Claims were rarely paid on the missing husband or missing wife until a thorough investigation and search through its widespread facilities had been made. These cases were so common that a standard technique had been developed. A man went on a vacation and didn't return. Later the wife tried to collect on his life insurance. The claim representative located the man, found he had remarried, and was living in another city or state or country. The wife was told that her husband was still alive and no payment on the policy was due. This was the normal pattern. In one such case the husband had left home to go swimming and had never returned. Prudential's representatives looked into the case and eventually found the man. He was living under another name in Canada. He had intended to kill himself, he told them, by swimming out until he grew tired. But when he got there, he changed his mind and started to swim back. A fishing boat picked him up and eventually landed him in British Columbia. He told the Prudential representative he had wanted to die because of the quarrels he and his wife had been having. Now he wanted to return to her. Whether he did or not was not included in the Prudential records.

A large proportion of the disappearance cases in which the company was involved were handled by the bureau known as the unclaimed equities division. This division was established in 1931 for the purpose of attempting to locate individuals to whom Prudential owed claims. Some of these people were included in the class of the husbands who walked out never to return. Others were merely individuals who did not realize that money was coming to them on paid-up policies or endowments or dividends.

In disappearance cases the job of finding the unwilling

subject was sometimes long and tedious. The division corre-
sponded with relatives, employers, unions, fraternal organizations, government agencies, and scores of other sources.
In addition the representatives searched their own vast
library of 2,500 city directories, telephone books, and guides,
as well as the available records in public libraries.

The search for those to whom money was due was no less
difficult than that for the person deliberately in hiding. In
the matter of unclaimed endowments, the individual was not
usually averse to being found, but here there was another
difficulty. The last known address of the insured was—on
the average—thirteen years old. Nevertheless, in spite of the
lack of useful information, in approximately 90 per cent of
these cases the insured was located within one year after the
search was launched.

One of the major problems of the claim department involved the handling of disability claims. The finality of death
brought with it an abrupt climax to the insurance contract—
it was seldom that complexities were involved. However, in
the case of a disability claim, the inquiry as to the existence
of the disability of necessity had to be broader. Decisions
in such instances required specialized insurance knowledge
and a thorough foundation in such diverse fields as human
relations, economics, medicine, and law. Disability clauses
applied to virtually all Prudential ordinary, intermediate, and
weekly premium policies. The benefits consisted of two main
types—waiver of premiums and waiver plus payment of sums
to the policyholder periodically.

Perhaps the most heartrending story of this branch of
claims concerned a little band of men who came home to
America after the end of World War II from the Pacific area—
the men who were made prisoners of the Japanese after the
fall of Bataan. Many of these men were permanently dis-

abled as the result of the conditions under which they had
been forced to live.

One case of record concerned an army officer captured on
Bataan who subsequently suffered from arteriosclerosis and
chronic myocarditis. In the camp where he was imprisoned
a group of fellow American Army doctors established themselves as a board of officers and adjudged him physically
unfit. A record of this action was written down on a scrap
of paper. The officer concealed this paper in his shoe. Later
this scrap of paper was accepted as bona-fide evidence of
total disability.

Disability insurance made its Prudential debut in 1912.
One year later the first two claims were presented and approved. By the beginning of 1950 this small total had increased to more than 375,000 approved claims of all types.

The Prudential claim department exercised remarkable
ingenuity in serving the policyholders. In 1947, for example,
a man living in Angus, Scotland, had a small endowment
which matured. When asked to complete the necessary claim-
ant's statement, he returned it with a note: "Instead of a
check to me, buy an alarm clock. I know it is a rather strange
request to make, but it is almost impossible to get one in this
country. As you know, money cannot be sent abroad, and
this is the only way I can think of getting one."

Though the clock shortage in the United States in early
1947 was not so acute as it was in Scotland, it took nearly a
month to locate a clock and ship it, with a check for the balance of the claim, to the man in Scotland.

In due time, however, The Prudential Insurance Company
of America received proper acknowledgment. Wrote the man
in Angus, "It is with the greatest pleasure I now write to
thank you—for the alarm clock. It arrived safely. Everyone
who has seen it has been amazed. It has been so long since

we've seen anything of that kind, after all these years of austerity here in Britain."

Unfortunately the claim department could not satisfy all demands made on it. But even the impossible requests were not always without value. Some of them could be added to the amusement file. One such case concerned a policy for $5,000 which was issued without a disability clause. Some time later the insured's son wrote in part as follows:

> Dear Sir:
> Would like very much for an inquiry to be held about my father ——— who, I assume, is a policyholder. I think he is mentally insane. Is there anything you can do?

It was explained that the policy involved did not provide for disability benefits, therefore it was necessary to continue premium payments if the contract was to remain in full force. The following letter was then received from the insured's son:

> Dear Sirs:
> If there is any way in which I can accomplish my father's demise and this, in a very short time, I promise to let you take $100 out of his insurance policy.
> Hoping we may meet, I remain,
> Very truly yours,

Needless to say the company did not see fit to co-operate in this connection.

As the number of policies had climbed over the years since 1875, the claims, too, had climbed, the figures mounting steadily from a few thousand to many millions. By the end of 1949 benefits paid under these claims totaled $5,708,310,-934.

People sometimes found it hard to understand the philosophy of the claim department. They saw a vast organization of men and machines. They saw one group of men whose sole job it was to find people to whom a few dollars might be owing. And another group devoting their efforts to the prevention of fraud. To the casual observer it somehow seemed a contradiction.

And yet it wasn't. It was not obscure or difficult, this philosophy of "Claim." This whole complex operation was designed for a single simple job: the payment of all just claims as promptly as possible. This was the chief purpose of any insurance company. It was when a claim was paid—as one Prudential district agent expressed it—that the benefits of insurance ceased to be theory and became, instead, heartwarming reality in time of need.

CHAPTER 15

D'Olier Takes Command

COLONEL Franklin D'Olier had the knack of making others succeed brilliantly. From his first days at Prudential, when he was appointed executive vice-president, the colonel liked to describe himself as the coach or captain of the Prudential team. Always in his mind he saw this company as a great team of thousands of individuals, with success depending on how fully and faithfully each man, from the agent on the debit to the president himself, played his part. The approach was frankly sentimental. It might even have seemed a little shopworn, if it had been set forward by a less dynamic character. But it had genuine meaning and reality as expressed by this tall colonel whose ideas and humor and adventures were to play a large role in shaping the destinies and development of Prudential through the tumultuous thirties and forties and on into the postwar era.

A company takes its shape and its direction from the individuals who set its policies. Prudential from its founding had been fortunate in bringing together a remarkable group of individual leaders—Dryden and Ward, Duffield and Linda-

bury. In 1925 the board of directors, on the recommendation of President Duffield, invited Colonel D'Olier, the
president's friend and fellow Princetonian, to become a
member of Prudential's top executive family. In vain the
colonel protested that he didn't want the job. He had
made plans to retire from active business life. He also
stressed the fact that he knew very little about insurance,
its problems and procedures. It would take time to learn
the business. Duffield was not impressed by Colonel
D'Olier's insistence on his negative qualities. He pointed out
that the colonel's career demonstrated that he knew how to
handle men and that it was that skill which was needed. In
the end Duffield prevailed. Colonel D'Olier set up shop in
the office next to that of the president and entered a part-
nership in the business of running one of the great companies
of the world.

Franklin D'Olier had always been a man of unusual traits.
He had a tremendous love for people, of being with them.
He enjoyed gatherings and sitting down with a group of
friends and telling stories, mostly on himself. He liked the
business of organizing, of getting people to work. And he
had a deep and abiding sense of public responsibility which
resulted in his becoming the directing force of dozens of
committees performing an innumerable array of public services—everything from selling bonds in wartime to providing
milk for hungry children abroad.

D'Olier's family had lived in Burlington, New Jersey, a
city which proudly considered itself the mother of Philadelphia. On his father's side he was descended from a line that
went back through Ireland to France, and on his mother's
from colonial settlers. In 1869 his father had founded William D'Olier and Company, a thriving textile business, in
Philadelphia, but young Franklin was not raised in the tra-

dition of the rich man's son. During the winter he tended the furnace for $2.00 a month, and in the summer he mowed the grass for the same standard fee. Later Franklin started into the cotton business with summertime jobs in the mills. He began at $3.00 a week, but when his experience qualified him for full-time employment his wages soared to $12. For that salary he began his working day at seven in the morning, took thirty minutes off for lunch and a full hour for supper, and was through work at 10 P.M. His career at Princeton was modestly distinguished by academic achievement, by light-weight boxing—in which his nose was thrice broken—and by track competition in which he also ran. After his graduation D'Olier joined his father's business in Philadelphia and during the early 1900s gradually assumed its management.

At the time he joined Prudential, D'Olier already had several careers behind him. World War I had been responsible for two of them. A trip to Europe in 1914 convinced him that sooner or later the United States would be in the war, and when he returned he took a commission as a captain in the quartermaster corps. When Congress declared war, he gave up his job of running the cotton business and reported for duty. The Army shipped him to France on a vague assignment to organize a new salvage service. At the start he was given four officers, two enlisted men, and an empty yard to fill with whatever discarded and useless material he could collect. Before the end of the war that salvage service grew to an organization of 7,000 men and women, enlisted personnel, refugees, and an assorted group of attached officers. At one salvage depot alone D'Olier turned out in less than a year $23,000,000 worth of usable equipment. For his work he was awarded the Distinguished Service Medal by the United States, and the French Legion of Honor by France.

In February 1919 D'Olier was in Paris with a group of officers General Pershing had called together to consider the problems of getting the boys back home. Colonel William, "Wild Bill," Donovan of the Fighting 69th and D'Olier were particularly outspoken about the treatment the men were getting—sitting in camps, working and drilling as though the war was still on, waiting to go home. Everybody wanted to get out of France, and D'Olier's and Donovan's statements were enough to start a movement to do something about it. A group of officers and men launched into a three-day session to lay the foundations of a new soldiers' organization and called a full organizational meeting for a month later in Paris. There were about a thousand delegates from every division in France at that meeting. After a blustery first session they hit on a name for the new organization: the American Legion.

Colonel Theodore Roosevelt, Jr., and D'Olier were assigned the job of organizing in the States, and as soon as he was back home D'Olier found himself in the middle of the drive to set up the new Legion on a nationwide basis. The first national convention was held in Minneapolis in November 1919. When it was over, D'Olier had been elected first national commander.

The Legion's commander spent a strenuous year visiting almost every state in the Union. He worked so hard at the job that a strong movement to re-elect him for a second term got under way. But D'Olier had other plans. He called some of the leaders of the movement together and asked them for their help. "If you want to do something for me," he said, "I would like your support for my suggestion that the Legion's constitution be amended to provide that no national commander can ever succeed himself." That amendment was made at the next convention.

In 1925, when Prudential invited him to become executive vice-president, D'Olier was planning to retire. He had been thinking about it for quite a while, in fact, but somehow he never seemed to have the time to do it. He throve on activity and responsibility. A strenuous routine seemed to be the only thing that kept his weight up to its normal one hundred and thirty-six pounds. The offer from Prudential seemed to promise enough work. The full title was "Vice-president in Charge of Administration." D'Olier thought it over for a while, and then decided that perhaps it was something he could handle. He started to work on January 2, 1926—and, as it turned out, he was rather good at that sort of job.

D'Olier was more than a new executive at Prudential, he was a new spirit of organization. The company had grown and expanded in its technical operations, the coverage it was providing, the protection it was offering to the people. But the great need was for a similar development in organization and management to keep pace with this progress in volume and size.

Organization to D'Olier was a matter of people. It was getting others to realize that every individual in the company was important; it was getting every individual to realize that his job was a necessary and important part of the operation of the company. D'Olier put it simply, so that everyone could understand: it was building a team. This concept of teamwork wasn't a new or impressive abstraction, but it was a useful idea, and to Prudential it was invaluable. It was, perhaps, the greatest of D'Olier's contributions, and in his years as vice-president and later as president it became the foundation stone of a great business enterprise.

As a person D'Olier was friendly, warm, and genuinely interested in people. As an executive he was impatient with red tape, protocol, and sham. To him the important thing was to get the job done. It wasn't long before the people at Prudential began to understand how D'Olier operated. His idea of teamwork started with himself. He did not hesitate to go about the home office calling on men of high and low positions, to get at the realities of problems, and to impress his own views directly upon others. He was a master in consultation. While president, it was almost his daily practice to consult with General Counsel Charles B. Bradley upon every over-all problem of the company. In this respect the relations between D'Olier and Bradley were very similar to those that had existed between Duffield and Lindabury.

D'Olier, Prudential's officials began to realize, was a man who believed in spreading authority downward, getting the responsibility into the hands of the people who did the work. He would encourage a man to tell him what was wrong with his job and then give him the authority to correct it. "All right," he would say, "go ahead and straighten it out. That's the new job I've just assigned to you. Forget the red tape. Let's have a report in a week. Let's see what you and I can do to get this thing working right."

The thing that impressed people most about D'Olier was his understanding of men and his ability to put his finger on the person who could best do the big job at hand—or the job that would be big tomorrow. To the colonel, handling the problems of the present and preparing for the future were actually two aspects of a single situation. It was all part of D'Olier's philosophy of organization. It was the people of Prudential who faced the problems and made the decisions, and upon them depended the future of the company. Constantly and diligently the colonel sought out the men best equipped to do the job as it existed. And just as diligently he insisted that they find and train and develop the men who were to make the decisions in the years ahead.

The business life of any individual was limited, but in the continuity of a well-directed organization there lay a way of shaping the future. As always with D'Olier, it was a problem of people rather than things—and the colonel knew people.

The colonel had a way of adding a man to a problem and getting a success. And in the years after 1929 there was no lack of problems. The bond department alone had a whole rash of them. To handle some of the difficult ones D'Olier, on the recommendation of Vice-president Stedman and Bradley, then general solicitor, brought in a young lawyer who had made something of a reputation in the field of investment law with the firm of Root, Clark, Buckner, and Ballantine over in New York. Stedman had heard about his work and one day, after he had discussed it with D'Olier and Bradley, he called on the lawyer. A few weeks later he was working for The Prudential in Newark.

So began the insurance career of Carrol M. Shanks who by 1946 was to become the president of Prudential.

Throughout all the years of his service with Prudential, D'Olier's abiding interest lay in the development of a staff for leadership. In all phases of the work and in every department of the company he insisted that the authority be delegated to those who were willing to use it. He wanted men of the type who were dissatisfied in a comfortable situation, men who were less impressed by the achievements of the past than the improvements yet to be made. He didn't create leaders. What he could and did do was to provide an atmosphere in which leadership flourished and to put into it men who could use it advantageously.

During the grim years of the thirties the over-all responsibility for the direction of this vast enterprise was in the hands of President Duffield. It had been a tremendous burden, and the years had taken their toll. In September 1938 the president, with D'Olier, went to Toronto to address a gathering of the field staff. Duffield talked to the men about the life insurance they sold and of some of the qualities it had which weren't always apparent on the surface. His theme was the value of qualities unseen. "The things which are seen are temporal," he quoted, "but the things which are not seen are eternal."

Duffield returned to Newark on the morning of Friday, September 16, apparently in high spirits and good health. But later that morning the president collapsed at his desk. He was taken home, suffering from cerebral hemorrhage, and died the following evening.

The loss of President Duffield was a tremendous shock to the company—to his associates who had known him and admired him over so many years of his term of office and to the thousands of employees who had learned to think of him as a friend.

By direction of the board of directors Colonel D'Olier became acting head of Prudential immediately following the loss of Duffield. At the November 14 meeting of the board he was named to succeed Duffield in the president's chair.

It was natural for the colonel to tackle a series of problems which were a challenge to administrative and executive abilities. A number of these thorn-in-the-side problems had plagued the company, some of them for a number of years. The administration of Colonel D'Olier was to become noted for removal of several of the most prominent of the thorns. One of these was the achievement of complete mutualization.

Since 1915, when all but technical mutualization had been achieved, an anomalous and annoying situation had persisted. The fact that there were at that time some 2,700 shares of stock outstanding—2,400 of which were held by various members of the Blanchard family—had prevented the company from realizing the full benefits of mutualization. In spite of the background of hostility and dissent which existed over the years, various blocks of the Blanchard stock had from time to time been tendered to the company at the appraisal price of $455. In 1933, with the purchase of the largest of these blocks—900 shares owned by the estate of Milton E. Blanchard—the company had reduced the number of outstanding shares to 508.76. In addition there were twenty-eight shares in other hands and forty-eight shares—afterward reduced to thirty-two—held by the directors under a trust agreement for legal reasons, making a total of 584.76 shares. At this point there had been a stalemate, the company being unwilling to go above the appraisal price and the owners refusing to part with the stock at that figure.

In 1937 the estate of Leon F. Blanchard filed a bill in chancery to compel an accounting and distribution of the so-called stockholders' fund, held to meet contingent requirements of the company. Shortly thereafter another bill, attacking nearly every act of the company with relation to its capital stock over a period of more than twenty-five years, was filed by the estate of Milton E. Blanchard. Thus began a bewildering complexity of pleadings, motions, and arguments.

These suits dragged on for years in a welter of litigation. In 1940, however, a bill was introduced in the New Jersey Legislature—prepared, it was thought, by the Blanchard interests—which, in effect, provided that Prudential might negotiate for and acquire all outstanding stock at a price in excess of that originally fixed back in 1914. The company did not oppose the bill, and it was enacted with minor amendments.

Negotiations began in January 1941. General Counsel Charles B. Bradley, Special Counsel Josiah Stryker, both directors of the company, and the colonel on one side of the table; the Blanchard interests, the principal holders of the outstanding stock, on the other. Bradley had been associated with Prudential since 1923. As general solicitor he had for a number of years specialized in problems arising in connection with the operations of the bond department. In time, however, his activities had extended widely throughout the company, and upon the death of Alfred Hurrell in 1938 he had assumed the broader duties of general counsel. Bradley's influence reached far beyond the sphere of his legal work. His undeviating integrity, his insight and extraordinary scholarship, his guiding sense of social responsibility were felt wherever he moved. He had a brilliantly thorough and supple legal mind, and during the months of litigation and negotiation on the complex problems of mutualization he contributed enormously to the success of the outcome.

Both the colonel and Bradley were agreed to resist all demands which seemed extravagant, with the result that a tedious and unfruitful series of meetings continued throughout the entire year of 1941. Just as the situation appeared hopeless, Stryker, to whom Bradley with the approval of Colonel D'Olier had delegated the task of rescuing the negotiations from utter breakdown in February 1942, happened to have an informal conversation with counsel for the Blanchards. Out of this meeting came a compromise—a tentative arrangement which the colonel agreed was sufficiently reasonable for him to submit to the board of directors.

The terms of this tentative agreement provided that stockholders should be paid $1,500 per share on condition that all stock outstanding would be subject to the agreement and that the two suits still pending in chancery would be dismissed without counsel fees or costs to either party against the other. The terms were approved by the board, and on February 17, 1942, the company accepted the offer of the stockholders.

At the subsequent hearing before the chancellor, who, under the statute, had to approve the transaction, the colonel outlined his reasons for approving the $1,500 price. He was convinced, he explained, that this was the Blanchards' rock-bottom price of sale. Further, the cost of carrying the pending lawsuits through to conclusion would have been tremendous. The elimination of the necessity to qualify public statements on the company's mutual character and the effect of complete and outright mutualization in the field of public opinion were perhaps the most compelling factors. These facts and others presented by the colonel were full and ample justification for the action taken.

There were a few further minor legal details to be taken care of in the course of the proceedings, but on July 29, 1942, the chancellor approved the arrangement, and on September 1 the outstanding shares were delivered to the company in exchange for $1,500 per share.

Full mutualization, however, was still one step ahead. Before it could be accomplished, special legislation had to be passed regarding the government of a mutual life insurance corporation in New Jersey. Strangely, no such legislation existed, since other mutual companies in the state operated under special charters. Bradley and his aides labored intensely over a comprehensive plan of legislation which resulted in three acts, one setting up the method of election of directors, another providing for the amendment of the charter of a mutual life insurance company, and a third providing for an amendment to the mutualization act defin-

ing the legal position of the company after complete mutualization.

These acts were approved by the Legislature, and on
March 30, 1943, the board of directors at a special meeting
ordered the transfer of their thirty-two shares which had
been held under a trust agreement to the trustee for policyholders. With that transfer The Prudential became in fact
and in law a mutual company.

With the mutualization issue settled, the colonel and his
aides turned to another problem which had been growing
in dimensions in recent years: the question of taxation by the
city of Newark and the state of New Jersey.

For many years The Prudential, together with other New
Jersey life insurance companies, had been paying certain
heavy taxes which they felt were discriminatory. These
special taxes, levied in addition to the usual tax on real estate, were of two kinds: a local personal property tax on
essentially 100 per cent of the company's surplus (less New
Jersey real estate); and a state "franchise tax" also on surplus
as well as on gross insurance premiums collected anywhere.
Both of these taxes were assessed against New Jersey life
insurance companies only and not against "foreign" or out-
of-state companies. Moreover, they were applicable only to
life insurance companies and not to other businesses.

Not only were the taxes onerous in principle, but they
were becoming increasingly oppressive. During the ten years
from 1935 to 1945 alone they had more than doubled. In
1944 The Prudential paid the state $1,554,314 in franchise tax
and paid Newark $2,058,944 in personal property tax. This
in addition to a real estate tax of $1,385,507 paid to Newark.
The total amounted to more than $5,000,000.

This peculiar system of taxation placed an unusual dual
burden on Prudential. In the first place, it put the company

at a distinct disadvantage in relation to out-of-state companies. Whereas outside companies paid less than 1¾ per cent tax on their New Jersey premiums, The Prudential paid more than 9 per cent—more than five and a half times as much. In the second place, the New Jersey taxes were far heavier than those imposed on life insurance companies domiciled in other states. In no other state would Prudential have been so heavily assessed, and in many states the savings would have been enormous. In 1944, had the company been chartered in New York, for example, the tax saving would have been $2,300,000. In Illinois the reduction would have amounted to $2,700,000, and in Pennsylvania to $2,900,000.

At D'Olier's behest Prudential's experts had gone over the figures carefully. Supported by a phalanx of irrefutable facts, the colonel had gone to the city and state authorities and asked for tax relief. He didn't indulge in threats or heroics. He began by speaking of the wonderful years of growth they had had together, Prudential and Newark. And of the years of growth ahead for both the great city and the company. Certainly the company wanted to remain in the city where it had grown and developed. But the company did not consider it proper to subject itself to unjust taxation. He was not, he pointed out, asking for preferential treatment; he was merely asking for fair treatment. In the interests of 22,000,000 policyholders he could accept no less. The Prudential wanted to be placed on a par with out-of-state companies—with aggregate taxes of 2 per cent of annual premiums collected in the state.

"We must consider the interests of our 22,000,000 policyholders," the colonel declared, "and be motivated by what will be best for them."

D'Olier turned next to the possibility that Prudential might be forced to leave Newark. The colonel wanted to avoid any misunderstanding on that important question. He spoke as seriously as he knew how. "In all fairness to you, let me say that we have studied this entire problem with great care. There is more than a tax advantage in such a removal. The difficulties are not half so great as may appear on the surface. Some of our buildings are old and obsolete; new modern office buildings in a different location would have certain definite advantages. I make this statement because we believe you gentlemen and the public are entitled to know the true facts. We all hope that the necessity for removal will never arise. We hope that a solution to the mutual advantage of all will be found and that the city and The Prudential in the coming postwar period will continue to work together in meeting the many problems that will be faced by this community."

When the colonel had finished speaking it was clear that a decision important to New Jersey and to Newark, as well as to Prudential, was to be made.

D'Olier's statements produced a minor tempest. There were a number of state and city officials who served notice that they would oppose any revision of the tax law. The colonel, however, was not prepared to back down. With the help of Executive Vice-president Shanks, General Solicitor Smith, Secretary Groel, Comptroller Menagh, and Vice-president and Actuary Howell, the president proposed to fight it out on that line. D'Olier and Shanks were responsible for the strategy of the campaign that followed, but plenty of the day-to-day work fell on their associates.

Mr. Shanks and his colleagues spent days and weeks in meetings with state and city officials working out a formula which would be fair to all parties. After a tentative basis for agreement had been worked out, a special meeting of the

Newark Board of Commissioners was called to consider the question. The compromise effected provided for the gradual revision of the tax structure to grant parity between New Jersey life insurance companies and their out-of-state competitors. A bill calling for tax reductions spaced over the years until 1954 was introduced in the New Jersey Legislature, was unanimously passed by both the Assembly and the Senate, and upon signature by the governor became effective April 10, 1945. In its final form the bill was widely praised by city and state officials as an excellent example of "moderation on the part of all concerned."

D'Olier believed always in the simple human approach: get people working together and understanding each other's problems, and you have the basis for efficient organization. The colonel applied that principle with fine impartiality from top to bottom in the company, from the newest agent in the field to the board of directors. And if any of the 20,000 agents did not fully understand the workings of D'Olier's system it is certain that every director was intimately acquainted with its operation.

D'Olier had a high regard for the members of the board of directors. From the founding days when John Dryden and his associates had gathered together the best business minds of the community, the caliber of the membership had been maintained.

The colonel was anxious to utilize to the utmost the enormous reservoir of ability and experience available to Prudential in its board. Characteristically, he felt that the way to do that was to bring the members of the board into more direct contact with the men actually responsible for the operation of the various departments of the company. He revised the old policy of having the president summarize

FRANKLIN D'OLIER

in the annual report to the board the chief events of the year. Instead, he had the head of each major department write for the directors a factual report covering his own phase of the company's activity. These reports were presented to the board with a brief covering statement by the president. Thereafter a special committee of seven directors, empowered to increase its membership by inviting other directors to its meetings, met with the head of each department and his principal assistants to discuss his work in detail.

Prudential's board of directors responded as D'Olier knew it would. As it was familiarized with the details of the operation, it took an increasingly active hand in the direction of the company. The attendance record of the directors—only one of whom was an officer of the company—rose sharply until it stood at more than 80 per cent over a period of ten years. The attendance at the weekly committee meetings was even higher because of the practice of having another director fill the place of an absent member. The important executive committee and finance committee, for example, both recorded 100 per cent attendance for several consecutive years.

In 1940 Prudential had a strong and smoothly operating organization. The strength of any organization can be fully gauged only under test conditions, and in 1940 Prudential faced those conditions under the spotlight of the TNEC investigation.

The Temporary National Economic Committee was born of the depression, of political and social dislocations and the desire to ascertain the causes responsible for the debacle that had overwhelmed the country. Since the days of the first Roosevelt, and before, "monopoly" and "concentrated economic power" had been built in the public mind as symbols of danger. In an atmosphere of economic distress and insecurity Congress needed little urging to launch an investigation which eventually reached into nearly every phase of American business activity. Actually the letter which President Roosevelt wrote to Congress in April 1938, outlining the scope of the investigation, had been particularly mild in its mention of life insurance companies:

> The tremendous investment funds controlled by our great insurance companies have a certain kinship to investment trusts in that these companies invest as trustees the savings of millions of our people. The Securities and Exchange Commission should be authorized to make an investigation of the facts relating to these investments with particular relation to their use as an instrument of economic power.

Once organized, however, the congressional inquiry chose to go far beyond the area of investments and directed the major part of its efforts to delving into numerous unrelated activities of insurance companies. Moreover, the hearings were sometimes conducted in a manner apparently calculated to convey the impression that the activities of the insurance business were at best suspicious and probably entirely reprehensible.

Throughout the investigation Prudential endeavored to supply the committee with the enormous number of records, charts, and graphs they required, and in February 1940 Colonel D'Olier and a group of company executives went to Washington to testify before the committee. One by one the members of the team D'Olier had developed were subjected to the harsh and probing examination of the committee's counsel. And one by one they demonstrated to the committee the constructive role the company had played in the national economy. R. R. Rogers outlined Prudential's program for salvaging farms and farmers during the depression—and backed his statements with the amazing figures that proved them. John Stedman, in many ways the most effective witness who appeared, described the meticulous methods of the bond department and sketched in for the members the constructive and vital part played in the national economy by wise investment. Henry Sutphen explained the place of agency forces not only in the sales of insurance but also in providing continuing service which clearly increased the value and usefulness of the protection to the policyholder. Hendon Chubb, a director for many years, told the committee of the work of the board of directors and of the concept of public service underlying the assumption of its duties.

Witnesses of this caliber were not to be shaken under grilling by committee counsel. The simple fact was that they had no cause to be afraid of the most searching examination because they had nothing whatever to hide. Rather, they were proud of the company's record of achievement.

Colonel D'Olier was available to the committee throughout the hearings, but he was never called. There had been no need to question him. The straightforward testimony of the Prudential witnesses had given the committee the information it needed.

The colonel could be justly proud of these men of Prudential. They had represented the company handsomely. But he had expected that. What was really important to Franklin D'Olier that day in 1940 was the proof that he had built a team—a strong Prudential team ready for the future.

CHAPTER 16

A Colonel Returns to the Front

The advent of total war brought many changes to the routines of Prudential, as it did to every home and business and individual in the country. Agents who had tramped the debits in Newark or Wichita or Elkton were soon to be tramping over roads in North Africa or lugging mortars through the steam of island jungles in the Pacific. Typists from debit valuation and group actuarial in the Newark home office were joining the Wacs or the Waves or signing up for training courses to become army or navy nurses. Shipping clerks and executives were going into the Air Corps, the Marines, the Navy, or the Army. Before the war was to end nearly 6,500 men and women of Prudential were to serve in the armed forces and 111 were to give their lives in that service.

On the home front in Newark The Prudential, like every other American industry, also had its role to play. The company announced its readiness to lend its specialized skills, its plant and equipment, and its highly trained staff for work that in any way would hasten victory. There were jobs to be done. Over those years of world conflict the organization that Prudential had designed and built specifically for serving the policyholders was frequently engaged in new wartime assignments utterly remote from the business of processing policies.

Prudential undertook a variety of jobs, some of a top-secret character, for the War Department and the armed forces. There was, for example, the assignment to help assemble the tiny parts of the "cage" for a peanut-size radio tube used in the new "walkie-talkie." More than a half million tubes for this important gadget of war were put together by several hundred stenographers and clerks of Prudential, working part of the day in space set up for this project in the Gibraltar Building.

While the "walkie-talkie" project was going on in the Gibraltar Building, another important and highly confidential war activity was being carried on a few hundred yards away in the company's eight-story printing building. Prudential presses, normally engaged in the printing of policies and insurance forms, letterheads and pamphlets for the company, turned to printing multicolored maps on squares of rayon acetate, escape maps of enemy-held territory in the Pacific, for use by American pilots and bomber crews shot down behind enemy lines. These maps—precision-printed on smooth, durable material in colors that wouldn't run, even if submerged in salt water for hours—were responsible for the saving of hundreds of American lives.

Still another of these wartime assignments involved the packaging of thousands of insecticide "aerosols"—bulblike containers which, when uncapped, released a spray of DDT solution. Volunteer Prudential employees, working on this project after hours, packaged more than 4,000,000 of these DDT "shells" for our armed forces. In the crawling jungles of the Pacific these "bombs" were an important weapon against disease—a menace often more deadly than enemy bullets.

In 1944 there was the matter of the absentee vote of New Jersey's soldiers overseas. The absentee voting law required that correct and verified lists of voters be furnished by the Army to county clerks throughout the states. In practice, however, it was impossible for the Adjutant General to keep his records sufficiently up to date for the purpose, and other methods had to be found. The job of assembling the list of New Jersey soldiers overseas, of verifying addresses and mailing out ballots, was a staggering one which had all but stumped the state officials. Asked for assistance by New Jersey's Governor Walter E. Edge, Colonel D'Olier agreed to let Prudential take on the complicated job of assembling and putting in order the information required.

The colonel called in Vice-presidents Harry J. Volk and Albert F. Jaques. Both of these men were expert in the handling and collating of statistics on a vast scale. Under their direction volunteer civilian defense workers were organized, a door-to-door canvass was conducted throughout the state, and 400,000 correct names and APO addresses of New Jersey service personnel overseas were obtained. After this information had been checked and verified against partial records in the Adjutant General's office, Prudential's lists were photographed and copies sent to every county clerk. These lists made it possible for the state to mail absentee ballots to New Jersey's fighting forces overseas. As a result of Prudential's effort, New Jersey's absentee vote in the 1944 presidential election ranked among the highest of all the states in the Union. Governor Edge later officially commended the company and its employees for this patriotic service.

The record of service carried on in this time of war was one of which the company could be justly proud. Like many other communities in America, it was playing an important role in the war—in a number of unusual ways.

The Prudential not only carried on its own projects with its own personnel, it also provided space for essential government activities. Upon its completion in 1942 the new Washington Street Building was taken over by the Government for the Office of Dependency Benefits. This office, responsible for all payments to dependents of men and women in the Army, continued to occupy the Washington Street Building until 1947. When it moved out, Colonel R. R. Bradshaw, commanding, sent a letter of appreciation to the landlord— The Prudential Insurance Company of America:

> Your building has a place in history as the home of the agency which served as fiscal agent for soldiers and their families throughout the critical years of World War II. The building at 213 Washington Street became famous as the best-known mailing address in the country.

From the beginning of the war Colonel D'Olier himself had been involved in a half-dozen different aspects of the war effort. There was a saying at Prudential that one or two major occupations were never enough for the colonel. He was always ready to take on another assignment, always willing to assume the responsibility of directing another important committee. And not only did he find the time to devote to these voluntary activities, somehow he also found the program and the people that made the job outstanding.

D'Olier's wartime activities actually began months before Pearl Harbor. In the spring of 1941 D'Olier had gone with a group of experts on a government mission to England to study British methods of civilian defense against air attack. On his return he had been pressed into service to help plan and organize America's belated civilian defense program. Later he had served as civilian defense director of the Second Civilian Defense Area, under the late Mayor Fiorello H. LaGuardia of New York.

In 1943 the Secretary of the Treasury, the Honorable Henry Morgenthau, Jr., asked D'Olier to become chairman of the War Finance Committee of New Jersey. The colonel promptly accepted the chairmanship and headed the Third War Loan Drive.

As in many of D'Olier's assignments, the problem was largely one of organization. As his vice-chairmen he chose Horace K. Corbin, president of the Fidelity Union Trust Company, and Prudential Vice-president George E. Potter. He also induced John E. Manning, Collector of Internal Revenue, to continue as state administrator. D'Olier, with their assistance, rallied to the drive's cause leading citizens in every county in the state, and the organization formed at that time continued to function throughout the entire period of the war.

D'Olier, notwithstanding his necessary absences from the country on other war assignments, kept in close touch with all War Loan activities. New Jersey rolled up an all-impressive record, attributable, as D'Olier so often stated, to the untiring efforts and leadership of his state, county, and municipal organizations.

Even before he had finished one task, there were other calls he could not refuse. Would the colonel take over the chairmanship of the state drive to raise USO funds? The colonel would, gladly. He was an executive and an organizer. These were the jobs he could best do, this was his place in the war.

But the colonel's biggest and most important assignment began with a phone call from Washington late in 1944. The

Secretary of War, Mr. Henry L. Stimson, and General H. H. "Hap" Arnold of the Air Forces were anxious to see him. Would the colonel come to Washington in the morning?

The Secretary of War and General Arnold presented the problem to him the following day in the Pentagon Building in Washington. The Air Force was spending $20,000,000,000, much of it on a program of strategic bombing. They believed this to be the surest way of smashing the power of the enemy —by precision bombing of essential factories, plants, and facilities.

But this whole concept of strategic bombing was new in warfare. President Roosevelt had suggested the organization of a committee to investigate and find out just how effective it was.

The job which D'Olier had just assumed was an incredible undertaking. There was no precedent for this study, the first statistically detailed analysis of the total direct and indirect effect of a sustained air attack against the economy and morale of a nation. The task of collecting, sorting, arranging, and evaluating the mountain of information necessary to reach a valid conclusion taxed even D'Olier's organizing genius. There seemed no way to encompass the material, and yet there had to be some place to begin. "After the first frustrating look, the job began to assume some shape," D'Olier said later. "I finally thought of this whole survey in terms of our Prudential organization. Prudential worked efficiently through departments. We would do the same in this war job. We decided on ten classifications, oil and rubber, chemicals, iron and steel, ball bearings, submarines, and so on. We even had a morale division to study the effect of strategic bombing on troop and civilian morale."

Having broken the problem down into manageable parts, D'Olier enlisted the help of outstanding experts as directors of each section. Each time he found a qualified man, D'Olier asked him to give sixty to ninety days to the work. When they objected, as they often did, that the work could not be accomplished in that time, D'Olier blandly answered, "Of course it can't. But if you aren't interested enough at the end of ninety days to go on and finish the job, you can go home." It was a shrewd guess. The survey was not completed until many months after the ninety days had passed— and the men stayed on.

D'Olier asked that Colonel Guido Perrara, who was familiar with the origins of the project, be assigned as an aide immediately. As vice-chairman he selected Henry Alexander, a member of the firm of J. P. Morgan and Company. One by one in the days and weeks that followed they were able to find the men to take charge of the various phases of the project and thus formed the nucleus of the organization.

The next step was to establish on-the-scene headquarters in Europe. D'Olier first flew to England with a small group of his experts and set up offices in Grosvenor Square in London. From there the group fanned out to look at the situation in France and Italy. On one of these trips D'Olier met General Eisenhower. The general recognized the difficulty of D'Olier's project and offered a word of advice. "If you can organize so that you have your own transportation, so your men won't be a burden to the units they travel with, you'll find you get along much easier."

D'Olier was an old hand at organization, and he took the advice seriously. Moreover, he had a letter from President Roosevelt authorizing this survey. Photostatic copies of this letter were always on hand, giving White House standing to the survey and thereby easing a number of their organizational problems. Before the survey in Europe was finished, the group had grown to a force of 1,600 men. They had 600 vehicles for transportation, and every man had his own bedroll and rations. They could move anywhere they wanted with the troops, sending experts into the field right behind the advance combat units taking over the wrecked cities and factories of Germany as the Nazis fell back.

As on-the-spot reports were furnished they were rushed back to headquarters for correlation and analysis. Each of the ten department heads was responsible for breaking down

his work into subsections and for assembling the information he needed to draw up a report on his particular phase of the work. These reports were in turn consolidated into an over-all report. The survey was begun in October 1944 and by the fall of 1945 the German report was completed. From Europe the staff moved to the Pacific theater, and by the spring of 1946 had completed the Japanese report. The two reports were backed up by 208 volumes of detailed studies and by tons of unpublished documents.

In the processing of vast quantities of information assembled for these reports Prudential had been able to demonstrate once again how the company's unique experience and equipment could be turned to the service of the nation. In Washington were filed hundreds of thousands of reports on every American flight over enemy territory. These reports included such valuable data as the types of aircraft used, targets, bomb loads, altitudes from which bombing was done, time over target, amount of flak and fighter interception, and losses suffered. Unfortunately, it was almost impossible to utilize this accumulated information until it had been tabulated and arranged in more available form.

To solve this problem D'Olier again called in Prudential's Vice-president Harry Volk. Under Volk's supervision a staff of 250 volunteer Prudential workers transferred the data to punched cards and thus made the information on the weapons, methods, targets, and other details of our bombings statistically available. Two complete sets of more than a million cards were prepared and the second set turned over to the Air Force.

The reports prepared by the Strategic Bombing Survey had a profound effect on the conduct of the last years of the war. Graphically, clearly, and completely they told the story of the part the air offensive played in the destruction of the power of the enemy during World War II. In large part they were responsible for the continuation of the strategic bombing which crippled the German offensive and reduced Japanese industrial production by more than 80 per cent by VJ Day. More important, perhaps, they provided a full, usable record upon which to base the strategy and training of the peacetime military forces.

Two days before his retirement Secretary of War Patterson called D'Olier to his office. "For some time," he said, "I have wanted to tell you this, but before I did I wanted to be positive that I was right. In the hearings on the Hill your strategic bombing report has been referred to more often than any other document because of the strong stand you took toward unification of the armed forces. I want you to know that because of its impartiality your report was a very substantial contribution toward that unification."

By the end of 1945 the colonel, past his sixty-fifth year, was ready to retire. A younger man, he believed, should take over the heavy duties and responsibilities of the president of Prudential—a younger man to cope with the new problems of the postwar era just ahead.

To the colonel the vast organization of The Prudential was still "the team." He had built it well over the years. At the head of each department was a skilled and seasoned executive, and under him there was not one assistant but several carefully picked, highly trained assistants, thoroughly prepared to take over when their superior moved up or retired. This was the colonel's technique of organization, his way of planning for the future. Nor had he neglected to provide a successor for himself.

The colonel's "replacement" for the high office of president of The Prudential was an attorney who had risen to become the company's executive vice-president—Carrol M. Shanks.

Carrol Shanks at that time was only forty-seven years old. He was born in 1898 in Fairmont, Minnesota, where his father had been the local postmaster. When Carrol was fourteen the Shanks family moved to a farm near Payette, Idaho. In the summers he worked in a brickyard. After Shanks finished high school in Payette he entered the University of Washington. The only way to meet expenses was to work, so Shanks took on a job as a shoe clerk—five afternoons a week and all day Saturday. The rest of the time he was making A grades in his courses in business administration.

World War I interrupted his education. He enlisted in the Army, was shifted from camp to camp, and by the war's end was in officers' training school in Waco, Texas. Discharged after the armistice, young Shanks went to New York and briefly tried his hand at bond selling. Later he decided to go back home and finish up his college career. Quitting his job, he traveled back across the continent, riding coaches and boxcars, back to the University of Washington and the shoe-clerking job.

He was graduated in 1921 with high honors. A few weeks later he married Martha Taylor, his college sweetheart, and with his bride came East once more. A little older now, Shanks was better prepared to try his fortunes in New York City. For a year or so he worked in the office of an oil company and then entered Columbia Law School. His scholastic achievements won him a scholarship and a job as assistant to one of his professors.

A close friend of his during this period was a classmate named William O. Douglas, subsequently an associate justice of the United States Supreme Court. Later Douglas and Shanks collaborated on several textbooks on corporation and business law, which were widely used at Yale, Columbia, Northwestern, and other universities.

After graduation Shanks went to work for the firm of Root, Clark, Buckner, and Ballantine and at the same time taught law at Columbia at night. In 1929 he went to Yale as associate law professor, but after a short professorial interlude decided to return to the more demanding but more exciting field of active practice. He went back to the same law firm where he had started out and specialized in cases of railroad bankruptcies and receiverships.

Shanks had joined the legal staff of The Prudential, as assistant solicitor, in 1932. Step by step he rose in the company. In 1938 he became general solicitor. He was advanced to be vice-president and general solicitor in 1939. In 1944 he was named executive vice-president. In the latter capacity, during the colonel's frequent absences on wartime missions, Executive Vice-president Shanks served ably as acting president. As a matter of fact, Colonel D'Olier had long considered Shanks as his potential successor. With that idea in mind he had placed upon him ever-increasing executive responsibility, so that Shanks was well fitted not only to perform the duties of president in the colonel's absences, but finally to assume the office itself.

The people with whom Carrol Shanks worked found him a man of contradictions and divergent interests, a man who loved books and scholarship and quiet—and also big-game hunting in the Canadian Rockies. Retiring and soft-spoken, he was also warm and easily approachable and entirely democratic and liberal in his thinking. Shortly after Shanks's promotion, a newspaper reporter's interview with him appeared under the headline, "New President of Prudential Takes Trolley Car to Office . . . Likes to Read on the Way to Work." A man who loved people and got on well with them, he was also adept at handling abstract ideas, at piecing them together into broad concepts for practical action.

In January 1946 Colonel D'Olier retired as president and was elected chairman of the board by the directors. It was a fitting job for a man like the colonel, a job without cramping limitations. It could be as big as the man who filled it.

At the same time the board elected Carrol M. Shanks to be the company's new chief executive. Hardly had he assumed his duties when the challenging problems of the postwar economy were upon him.

CHAPTER 17

Salesmen of Security

In 1853, some twenty years before the founding of The Prudential Friendly Society in Newark, New Jersey, the New York *Times* cast a searching editorial eye at the subject of life insurance. It was a matter of some public interest. A dozen or more companies had recently been founded to transact such business, and it was estimated that in all there were perhaps as many as 30,000 policies in force in the United States. After a lengthy consideration of the theories and purposes behind life insurance the *Times* stated its position succinctly: "He who insures his own life or health must be indeed a victim of his own folly or others' knavery."

Less than a century later, in 1950, 80,000,000 Americans owned 190,000,000 individual policies totaling more than $200,000,000,000. While between these two points there was almost a space of one hundred years, time alone did not account for the extraordinary growth of the insurance industry in the United States. The development of the understanding of the purposes of life insurance had in great part been the work of one individual—the agent.

HOME OFFICE BUILDINGS, NEWARK

Back in 1875, when John F. Dryden organized The Prudential Friendly Society and announced his intention of providing protection for the masses of the people, life insurance in any form was still comparatively new, and industrial insurance in the United States was unheard of. Few knew just what an "industrial insurance man" was and still fewer cared to find out.

The new company had its troubles finding agents able to sell this new kind of insurance to a suspicious and reluctant public. The job called for a special kind of person—a man who knew and understood the problems of the people, who had enough fortitude and patience to carry on the work day after day in the face of ridicule and abuse, who had enough confidence in the future of the business to keep on at a thankless task when the returns were meager. These were uncommon qualifications, and not all who were tried measured up. In the files of early records at the Newark office are still preserved the brief comments of an unidentified supervisor written beside the names of some of those first agents who didn't make the grade. The explanations are terse:

"Wanted the earth—not mine to give."
"Too bashful to call on strangers."
"Formed his own company and busted."
"Skipped."
"Too lazy—born tired."

The wonder was not that some failed, but that so many succeeded.

They were men of varied types, these early agents. There was the aggressive salesman pushing ahead to open up new territory and the friendly fellow riding his bicycle year after year over the same debit. There was the scholar who had given up his books and the miner who had left his trade. But one thing they had in common: they knew and understood the people with whom they had to deal. More than anything else it was that understanding which made it possible for Prudential to reach out, along the streets and the highways, to all of America.

Those were the pioneering days in insurance, when an agent was sent out with a rate book and a slap on the shoulder. Those were the days, too, when a bucket of water or a housewife's descending broom was a normal hazard of the job. The agents who survived took everything in stride. Afoot or riding their bicycles, in heat or blizzard or flood, these men of Prudential told the story of insurance in tenements and on farms, in good sections and poor, across the land. In the years that followed they sold hundreds of thousands and millions of policies in every town in the country. They did more—they sold the *idea* of insurance to the people of America.

The agents themselves were the heart of Prudential's business, but almost as important was the agency system, the branch office organization by which their efforts were directed and correlated by the home office. With weekly premium insurance, the agent's job was not merely to sell the policy, but also to service the continuing insurance needs of the policyholder. An agent's duties were many and varied. Each week he called at the home of the insured to collect the premium due, to make sure that the payments were kept up to date, and that the policy was prevented from lapsing. It was he who watched the changing circumstances of the policyholder and suggested the proper changes in coverage to fit the new situation. He advised the insured on the rights and choices available to him under the terms of his policy. He discussed with the policyholder the kind and amount of insurance which would best fit his needs and showed him how the same insurance could be used to provide several different kinds of protection. Throughout the life of the policy and up to and including the payment of the claim the agent assumed the duty of providing the service which the policyholder needed and expected.

The district agencies were developed as an efficient means of making it possible for the agent to carry out his dual function in sales and service. In the early days the problem was relatively simple. The operation was at first a local one easily directed from the Newark office, and the territory covered was broken down into simple geographical areas. As the company's business increased in size and complexity, however, and as the district agencies spread out across the country, it became necessary to set up a carefully integrated district agencies department to direct the enormously complicated job of supplying the services required by the policyholders.

By 1950 the district agencies had grown to a vast field force of more than 25,000 people engaged in supplying the insurance needs of millions of families throughout the United States and Canada. There were 467 districts, organized in eighteen regions supervised by regional directors. Each region was made up of a number of districts and each district was further divided into a number of sections, depending on the size of the district and the density of the population. Each district agent serviced one of these sections—his debit. Within this debit territory he made his regular rounds to provide total insurance coverage for the people in an area he had made his own.

With the growth of the business and with the introduction of new types of policies the agent's job had increased in scope and complexity. It was no longer a simple matter of making regular calls at the homes of the policyholders and handling the details of weekly premium insurance. Within his area he was equipped to provide the full, rounded protection which the company had made available—debit insurance, both weekly and monthly premium, and ordinary and group insurance. It was his job now to fill, so far as possible, the insurance requirements of every person on his debit—in factory, store, office, or home—suiting the kind of insurance and the method of payment to each individual case.

The district offices had changed with the agent in the years since they were first established. The typical office was no longer the bare little upstairs room with a roll-top desk, a hatrack in the corner, and a few straight chairs along the wall. Offices were larger now, and were located in modern office buildings convenient to the districts they served and staffed and equipped to carry on the complex operations required to provide insurance service to the whole community.

The district agency was in charge of a district manager who was assisted by several staff managers. All were experienced men who had risen from the ranks and knew from years of experience the problems of the staffs they directed. They were responsible for the over-all planning of the work in the district and for the total operation of the office and its integration with the whole field force of the company. The staff managers—five or six men in the average agency—were in direct charge of the agents working in the district. Normally each of these staff managers directed the work of six or seven agents, supervising their activities, training new men as they came into the business, and spending much of his time in the field guiding and instructing the agent in developing new and more effective methods.

The district office was responsible for the efficient handling of the vast amount of detail connected with the selling and servicing of the insurance in force in the district. This work was carried on by a clerical staff which, in the average office, was made up of an office supervisor, an assistant supervisor, and five other clerical employees. These members of the staff competently took over the important and never-ending job of quickly handling the problems of receipts and accounting, file cards and change forms, claims and home office communications—all the essential processing of insurance on the local level—and thus enabled the agents to perform their sales and service functions more effectively.

To make it possible for him to carry on his varied duties regularly and efficiently, the agent necessarily husbanded his time and arranged his schedule carefully. He usually devoted a good share of his effort during the early part of the week to the collection of premiums. Some agents preferred to spread collections over a longer period in order to have more time throughout the week for the development of new business. As a rule the agent called at the district office on Tuesday and Thursday mornings to deposit the premiums he had collected on the preceding days. Friday mornings were given over to his accounts and finishing off the routine details of the week's work. On Friday morning also the district manager met with the agents to discuss general problems of the business, and the staff managers discussed with their men plans for the following week.

The story of the growth of the field agencies was one of continued and gradual expansion under the guidance of a number of outstanding personalities. In the early years Dr. Ward was in charge—one of the most-loved and respected men in the history of the company, his influence reached to every district. George W. Munsick was another who left his impress on the agency system. Beginning as a clerk in the audit section when the company was only seven years old, Mr. Munsick had established a service record of more than half a century at his retirement in 1935. Later there was Henry B. Sutphen who joined Prudential as a clerk in 1900, rose to be vice-president, and at his retirement in 1944 had served with Prudential for more than four decades. Hearty, direct, and indefatigable, Mr. Sutphen was a firm believer in establishing close personal contact with every part of the field. Nobody ever counted how many thousands of miles Sutphen traveled across the continent and through Canada visiting the agencies and directing the opening of new districts.

Under the leadership of these men and later of Harold M. Stewart, the place of the agent in the company's operation was greatly enhanced. Stewart, who began his Prudential career as a clerk in a New York City district office in 1920, had by the end of 1944 advanced to the position of vice-president in charge of the district agencies. His thorough firsthand understanding of the agent and his problems and needs made it possible for him to contribute much to the modernization of the agency forces. To keep pace with the trend, Prudential enlarged and improved its selection and training program. In 1947 President Shanks declared that it was the aim of Prudential to have the best selected, trained, and equipped fieldmen in the business. Under the direction of Vice-president Orville E. Beal, who succeeded Stewart in 1947 when the latter was promoted to executive vice-president, the program was rapidly put into operation. By 1950 the Prudential district agent had gained new stature as a career professional with a vital job to do and with expanding possibilities for promotion both in the field and in the home office.

In the thirties, encouraged by the passage of the National Labor Relations Act, labor organizers and others turned their attention toward bringing industrial insurance agents into labor unions. The first attempts to unionize Prudential agents in the United States began about 1937. Over the course of several years three unions entered into negotiations with the company—International Union of Life Insurance Agents (Independent), United Office and Professional Workers of America (CIO), and National Federation of Insurance Agents' Council (AFL).

In 1950 in the United States the company had contracts with the International and the AFL unions, the UOPWA having been defeated in a run-off election held by the National Labor Relations Board in July 1949.

Even though there were certain misgivings among some of the officers at Prudential, John Lunger had been able to convince Dryden in 1886 that the company had grown to the point where it could handle ordinary insurance profitably. Whether life insurance was big or little, Lunger argued, whether the premiums were paid annually or weekly, made little difference. Essentially all life insurance was a method of providing protection for the individual. Protection was Prudential's business, and certainly it should be able to provide more than a single type.

Lunger won his point and the district agents began to sell ordinary. A number of experienced underwriters—among them Fred W. Tasney who was later to become a vice-president—were hired and sent into the field to instruct the industrial agents and to make calls with them to demonstrate methods for selling ordinary insurance.

As it became apparent that the volume of ordinary insurance could be further expanded, Lunger and Dr. Ward actively set about the business of obtaining agents who would confine their activities to the sale of ordinary insurance. By 1897 these representatives, together with the debit men, had written a little more than 50,000 policies for slightly less than $60,000,000.

That year John Lunger left Prudential, George Speer was placed in command, and within three years had more than 100 general agents working for the company in various parts of the country. The advertising campaigns featuring the Rock of Gibraltar were beginning to show results everywhere. Businessmen and executives began to accept the company which they had once identified solely with weekly premium insurance. Prudential's ordinary business began to move upward. The ordinary agencies' first "big case" was closed in 1900 when General Agent Dutcher of New York wrote four policies of $100,000 each on the lives of Richard, August, and Albert Hahne and William H. Kellner, four members of the firm of Hahne and Company, Newark department store. These policies were solely for the protection of the business, and it was the largest case of its kind on record at that time. The writing of this insurance caused quite a stir in the press of the nation. The Rock of Gibraltar was making big news.

Perhaps the most famous policy of that time was written that same year when Prudential General Agent Edward A. Reilly of Philadelphia got word that L. Rodman Wanamaker, the son of John Wanamaker, intended to take out a large insurance policy on his life. Reilly's motto had always been that the big ones are easier than the small ones. He filled out an application blank in Wanamaker's name for the largest sum ever written on a single life. Through a mutual friend he obtained an interview with Wanamaker, put the application blank in front of his prospect, showed him a specimen policy—whole life on the five-year dividend plan—explained how the policy operated, and an hour later walked out with the signed application for the first $1,000,000 single life policy on the books. Twenty-eight years later, when this policy became a claim, Prudential sent out a check for $1,066,525—including dividends—on the same day that proofs of death were received.

These sales served a purpose for Prudential in those days. They put over in graphic terms a story the company wanted the world to understand: The Prudential was selling not only five-and-ten-cent insurance but policies of every size to serve every need.

Throughout the first decades of the twentieth century the position of Prudential improved in relation to other companies in the ordinary field. From slightly more than 2 per cent of the ordinary in force in 1900, Prudential's share rose to more than 7 per cent in 1925, and of the policies issued that year the company wrote just more than 11 per cent. Ordinary finished the year with 2,673,706 policies in force for a total of $4,006,509,000.

During the late thirties and the early war years the production of the ordinary agencies declined in relation to the total amount of ordinary insurance being written by the company. By 1943 the number of agencies had been reduced to sixty-three. There were 106 assistant managers, and full-time special agents numbered only 403. The amount of new business paid for that year by the ordinary agencies had reached a low point of $135,000,000.

Colonel D'Olier assigned Executive Vice-president Shanks the job of looking into the whole problem. Actually the survey was part of a broader program looking toward the postwar years.

Shanks set about the business briskly. In 1947 Sayre Mac-Leod, a former special agent, was made vice-president in charge of the ordinary agencies department. A complete reorganization was well under way.

Although the over-all program for the ordinary agencies called for a rapid increase in the field force, the standards on which applicants were to be selected were kept high. The managers and assistant managers, who were expected to do most of the recruiting, were urged to look for men with the qualifications for a career in underwriting—men with the background, education, imagination, and intelligence to achieve more than average success in the field.

Before and after an agent went into the field he was trained for the work. He familiarized himself with the basic facts of life insurance—what it is and what it does, the types of policies and their particular uses, techniques of selling—using a course prepared at the home office. Later he went into the field for his first actual interviews with clients, accompanied by an assistant manager or staff manager, who guided and watched his progress.

A series of courses covering the broader aspects of taxation and business insurance also were part of the training program. For many district and ordinary agencies' men this led to the course given by the American College of Life Underwriters and to the Chartered Life Underwriter (C.L.U.) designation —a mark of distinction in the insurance field.

The specific knowledge and skills developed through the comprehensive Prudential training program were not, however, an end in themselves. They merely equipped the agent to understand and apply the over-all philosophy of service to the policyholder which was the fundamental concept guiding the revitalized field force. This philosophy, the "total needs approach," was based on the company's belief that the client himself was the best judge of his own insurance needs and that the agent's primary job was to help the prospect select the program which most fully served his purposes. The agent had become more than a salesman: he was an expert guide and counselor.

The Prudential approach to the problems of supplying proper coverage to the broadest possible public was not in itself a new departure. That philosophy had been inherent in the whole development of the company from the day it was founded. New policies, new benefits, new methods had been constantly devised to broaden the scope of the service. In the postwar forties, however, with the company-wide re-

alignment of methods and objectives, new stress was laid on the general principles underlying the duties of the whole field force. With the support and help of President Shanks and Executive Vice-president Stewart, a new program involving a broader outlook and purpose was presented to all agents, district and ordinary. The field training division was given the task of preparing suitable sales material for use by the agents in this new program. The agent was selling in every field; not only in ordinary, weekly premium, and monthly premium insurance, but also in the broadening field of group insurance.

Two special tools were designed to help the agent provide more proficient service—the "Dollar Guide" and the "Prudential Planned Program." The Dollar Guide was planned to enable the underwriter to base his approach on the prospect's own estimate of his insurance needs. Through a series of graphs the client and the agent together were able to work out a program which fitted the exact requirements of the prospect. The Prudential Planned Program was designed for use with more comprehensive cases and enabled the agent to make a complete survey of the client's financial situation as a service, and to furnish a detailed analysis when necessary.

The selection techniques, the elaborate training program, the tools provided for the use of the agent and the client—all were merely the physical aspects of the new attitude, the new understanding of the role life insurance was to play in the social structure. They were the equipment designed to help the agent find his proper place in providing continuing service to the individual and the community.

The new agents carried on the old traditions and built the new techniques for the future. But the direction of the agency forces was still shaped in large part by the leadership of experienced men who had been with the company over many years. These men of the district and ordinary agencies had learned the business of insurance long before scientific techniques of selling had been developed. They had learned by doing; and the understanding they had gained was available to supplement the training program for the new agents, who were the new models of a long line of successful representatives.

The tremendous expansion of Prudential, the growth in its size and service and importance in the American way of life would never have been possible without these seasoned veterans who year after year continued to produce a major portion of the company's business.

There was more to selling insurance than writing policies. Prudential found, as it always had, the men it wanted—men who responded to the challenge and the opportunity. In 1950 the company was well on its way with these men to the objective President Shanks had set for it: to have the best-selected, the best-trained, and the best-equipped fieldmen in the business.

CHAPTER 18

Investing in America

IN SEPTEMBER 1945 Japan accepted defeat aboard a battleship in Tokyo Bay, and a war-battered world began to clear
away the wreckage and rebuild after six years of blood, tears,
and destruction. Physically, the United States had been un-
marked by bombs or shells. But it had not gone unscathed.
Its whole way of life had been disrupted. On that September
morning the United States faced a problem in many ways
more difficult than the war itself—the task of reshaping to the
ways of peace an economy that had been geared completely
to the purposes of destruction.

For half a decade America's vast industrial plants had been
pouring out the tools of mechanized warfare, weapons and
ammunition, planes and tanks and torpedoes, with which
the Allied armies had crushed the Axis. Since 1941 the country
had operated under the restrictions and curtailments of total
war. Whatever was not directly connected with the job of
destroying the enemy was put aside for another day. Peacetime industry converted or closed down for the duration. All
but the most essential construction stopped. Home building,

other than housing for war workers, was drastically curtailed, and repairs on existing dwellings and business properties were postponed. The dislocation of the economy of America was deep and serious.

By war's end the need for normal, large-scale production was urgent. Business and industry scrambled to return to peacetime pursuits, to meet the tremendous dammed-up demands for everything from new automobiles to fresh paint for the barn. The potential for expansion in the postwar years seemed almost limitless.

But the realization of this potential required financing on an unprecedented scale. Funds were necessary to start again the flow of goods and services—to resume factory operation, to enlarge and develop and increase the services of industry; funds for small as well as large business, for individual home builders, and for contractors who would bring housing for millions across the nation.

Prudential was prepared to make a substantial contribution to the great need for postwar financing. During the war the needs of industry were reduced, and mortgages were being paid off with money that would normally have gone into consumer goods. For every one hundred dollars Prudential received in repayments on existing mortgages, the company was able to reinvest in new mortgages only $61.

For Prudential the postwar demand for investment funds was both a challenge and an opportunity. Prudential quickly responded by reshaping its mortgage loan organization in the field to meet the needs of borrowers of all types and to render all financing services possible within the limits imposed upon insurance companies by statute. Early in 1946 the company began the realignment of regional lending territories for more effective coverage. These moves were made to implement the concept of all-purpose investment.

The mortgage loan and real estate department functioned through a system of branch offices set up throughout the country. The beginnings of the network of branch offices went back as far as 1923, when an office was opened in Montreal and, in 1924, in Toronto. These had been followed by branches in Newark, in 1927, and in Lakeland, Florida, and Richmond, Virginia, in 1929. The major development of the system, however, had taken place during the depression when it became necessary to have company experts in the field to service large numbers of delinquent mortgages. These branch offices were a direct answer to the needs of the time. Originally, though the operations of the mortgage loan department continued to expand in the years after the depression, each branch office confined its activities primarily either to farm mortgages or to city mortgages.

But the needs of the postwar forties were far different from those of the desperate thirties. Farmers and manufacturers and builders and private individuals were seeking funds for a variety of purposes, often involving various types of investments. The needs of these borrowers required the establishment of offices capable of handling every type of investment service, large or small, in the community.

The unique all-purpose program was designed to fill that need. The branch offices, now called regional offices, were reorganized to make it possible for them to serve the needs of all types of borrowers—the homeowner, the industrialist, the businessman, the farmer, the builder. They reached more than 5,000 communities, and there was literally no part of America where Prudential funds were not available for investments in the soil, in the buildings, and the industry of the country.

The Ohio Valley regional office in Cincinnati, Ohio, was a typical example of these new field headquarters. A large modern office with a staff of more than fifty, it was located in quarters on the thirty-third floor of the Carew Tower Building. In charge of the office was the regional manager, who had complete responsibility for the operation of the office, the "production" of new loans throughout the Ohio Valley territory, the servicing of these loans, as well as the handling of all office administration.

Assisting the regional manager were two production managers, each in charge of a sub-part of the Ohio-Kentucky-West Virginia area along the Ohio which the office served. These production managers were assisted by supervising appraisers, and the areas were in turn broken down into "production zones," each with its own inspector or appraiser working under direction of the supervising appraiser. The zones ranged in size from a section of a city to a dozen or more counties in rural sections.

Through offices such as this one in Cincinnati, Prudential's investment activities blanketed the United States and Canada. Each office was staffed by legal and administrative specialists thoroughly familiar with the needs of the community and prepared to provide financing for every purpose —from helping to make a hog farm more productive to building a skyscraper. Much of the business handled by these offices was referred to Prudential by real estate brokers or bankers or other financial institutions in the community. Some came through direct contact with the borrower. To every group and element in the community the company offered an all-inclusive financial service that was quick, convenient, and as available as the nearest Prudential branch office.

The greatest immediate need in the years following the war was for housing. Paul Bestor, vice-president of the mortgage loan and real estate investment department, early realized that millions of GI's returning from service had to have living space for themselves and their families. Many were forced to double up with in-laws or to live in Quonset hut villages and converted army barracks. The demand for housing, particularly housing within the reach of the average individual, was acute. Bestor and his successor, Vice-president Charles Fleetwood, and their associates were convinced that Prudential could make the best contribution toward relieving the housing shortage through the medium of mortgage financing. Others, they argued, could more efficiently do the actual building and renting and operating of housing. Prudential's job was to provide the funds.

Prudential did provide those funds. It was not a story which made the headlines. But in hundreds of communities across the land houses were going up and people were able to purchase their own homes or move into new apartments because of financing provided by this insurance company. Sometimes it was a new house on a farm, sometimes a home on the outskirts of a quiet country town. Or perhaps it was ten or fifty or a hundred homes in a suburban development or an apartment building in the more crowded section of a city. Prudential was not the builder, and Prudential's name seldom appeared on the construction signs. But Prudential funds had made these homes possible. The year-end figures told the story more emphatically. In 1949 about one million family units were started throughout the United States. That year The Prudential approved loans to finance new and proposed construction containing approximately 50,000 family units. It was a record unmatched by any other private lending organization in the nation.

A substantial part of Prudential's housing investment was made in the form of construction loans granted to contractors and builders. By this method funds were made available at specific stages in the work—so much when the roof went on, further payment when the plaster was on the walls, and full payment when the house was finally completed. When the house was sold to the individual owner, Prudential continued to hold the mortgage. The loan thus served the dual purpose of aiding in the construction of the house and enabling the individual family to purchase it.

By the end of 1949 Prudential had in force more than 279,-000 mortgage loans for a total of more than $2,313,000,000. The greater part of these were loans to small borrowers, and the average of all loans was still under $8,300.

Homes, however, were only part of this story. Types of

loans made under the all-purpose program included commercial, industrial, residential, farm, ranch, grove, and suburban. The range, especially as the all-purpose program developed in the late forties, was as wide as America itself. There were loans on city homes and farms, on cattle and sheep ranches, tobacco farms and citrus groves, wheat and corn and dairy farms, cotton plantations and rice fields. There were loans on suburban bungalows and country homes; on hotels and apartments and motels; on office buildings and factories; on warehouses and country clubs. Wherever there was a legitimate need for financing, Prudential was prepared to supply it.

The company financed a wide variety of business, farm, and manufacturing ventures, from the roadside filling station to the modern integrated farm. An example of the latter was the Lee Wilson plantation down in Arkansas, a rich territory of 30,000 cultivated acres of cotton and diversified farm products, stretching into two counties and including a whole town. A $2,000,000 Prudential loan aided in the development of this property, known as the "largest cotton plantation in the world."

Loans of this nature—and Prudential had a number of such investments in its portfolio—illustrated the versatility of the all-purpose program. The property could be large or small, all farm, all industrial, all residential, or a combination of any of these. Prudential tailored its loans to fit the needs.

Another phase of the all-purpose program involved the outright purchase of income-producing real estate. A section of the mortgage department was organized to develop and handle the purchases made. Investments of this type included apartment houses, well-located shopping buildings, and industrial buildings. The majority of these investments was in small or moderate-size commercial properties in the business districts of cities and towns across the country.

In the early days bonds had been the rock on which Prudential built for security. At the mid-point of the twentieth century they were still the most important single element in Prudential's investment picture. The bond department was charged with the investment of more than $5,000,000,000.

For many years after the founding of the company John Dryden personally had handled most of the bond purchases, first with the assistance of Edgar B. Ward, and later with the aid of the latter's brother, Jacob E. Ward. The funds had not been great and the problems of investment had not been too complex.

At that time the United States was in the final stages of filling out its present-day boundaries. Among the first tasks of the newly enlarged country were those of binding itself together with railroads and developing its growing towns and cities. The demands for funds were largely in the fields of the railroads, public utility gas and traction companies, and municipalities desiring improvements. The Prudential's security investments prior to World War I were largely concentrated in these fields.

When Dryden died in 1911, Jacob Ward, as vice-president in charge of investments, continued to conduct this phase of the business. After Ward's death, Forrest Dryden, with the advice of the finance committee, brought John W. Stedman into the company in 1915, to establish the bond department as a separate organizational unit. For a number of years Stedman had been associated with a New York investment house specializing in railroad bonds. He was to become a potent factor in the affairs of The Prudential, where his integrity won him the respect of his associates. His approach to any problem was based on a rigid code of ethics, and he was as keen a judge of men as of markets. He became vice-president of the bond department in 1918. To build the department, he assembled a small but highly trained group of specialists, including a number of men with engineering training, who understood the technical aspects of railroad, utility, and industrial operations. Stedman picked these technicians carefully for their knowledge and background. It was not necessary, he found, to employ an extensive staff. Bond purchases, although relatively larger in size, were far fewer in number than mortgage loans.

One of the first policy changes Stedman made was to curtail the heavy purchases which the company had been making up to that time in railroad bonds. As early as 1915 the unique position the railroads had occupied for many years was being challenged by the developing automotive industry. Trucks and automobiles were beginning to be important in transportation. Throughout the late teens and into the twenties Stedman's guiding rule became: make only small investments in rails and then only the cream of the crop.

During World War I Prudential bought large amounts of government bonds. Following the end of the war came the intensive development of electric lights, appliances, and machinery, and the increasing demand for electrical power. The Prudential invested in public utility electric companies. The peak of this type of financing was reached in the twenties. The funds were used for steam-generating plants, hydroelectric stations, and transmission systems. Somewhat later the mass distribution of manufactured products created a large-scale need for industrial financing. Prudential again was in a position to supply funds, and did so, on through the thirties.

With the deepening of depression in the thirties many railroads were thrown into bankruptcy. Stedman, with his knowledge and skill in the field of railroad finance, played an important part in the reorganization of a number of these roads and helped restore many of them to a sound operating basis. With the end of war, in 1945, Stedman retired after more than thirty years of service to the company. Vice-president Caleb Stone, who had joined Prudential in 1931 after ten years of investment experience, assumed charge of the department.

The joint endeavor program developed by Prudential after the war greatly increased the scope and effectiveness of the investment services provided through the regional loan offices. Under this plan, when it appeared that a borrower would be better served by a security issue than by a mortgage loan, the case was turned over to a bond department expert. In some instances the necessary financing was provided through bonds alone and in others by a combination of mortgage loan and security issue. This method made the technical skills of one of the nation's largest investors conveniently available to small and medium-sized enterprises. The businessman on Main Street and the small-town manufacturer for the first time were able to get in their own home town an investment service comparable to the best to be found in the great financial centers of the country.

The "direct placement" method of financing was used in the direct handling of securities between the issuer and the investor. No intermediary was required, although an agent might be, and often was, present in the transaction. Prudential purchased securities in substantial volume by this method. Each case was considered on its own merits. Prudential negotiated large loans of this type, but it also made many comparatively small ones. For smaller amounts, however, a mortgage loan on specific real estate was usually more practical, since it was cheaper, standardized, and more easily administered. As an economical method of channeling some of the savings of more than 26,000,000 policyholders into the hands of those who used the funds for productive enterprises, this type of financing performed a new and important service to the public as a whole.

Security investments of all types, of course, were carefully investigated. Members of the bond department's staff of experts went over every minute detail of the business operation, including on-the-scene examination of the plant facilities, a complete study of the product and its reception by the public, and diligent investigation of the individuals operating the business. The question of continuity of management was important. Prudential insisted that a firm must have a record of continuing operations, with the management so organized that the successful conduct of the business did not depend on any single individual. So long as the history and prospects of an enterprise insured the necessary stability, however, Prudential was prepared to invest in any sound business venture.

As a result of the development of new techniques and the expansion of its lending program, Prudential's bond department was venturing into ever-widening fields of industry, into everything from "the stockyards to the cosmetic industry," as President Shanks told a congressional committee in Washington. By 1950 the company had investments in construction companies, clock factories and steel mills, in concerns manufacturing automobiles or iceboxes, in chemical works and department stores, in firms making paper cups or dungarees or pianos. The company's industrial investments in 1950 were a very real cross section of the country's expanding business and industrial economy. They ranged from a few thousand dollars in the corner grocery to more than $166,000,000 in bonds in the American Telephone and Telegraph system.

It was an impressive story—this record of Prudential investment funds helping to build great enterprises. The variety of investments was remarkable. Out in Chicago a $12,000,000 loan was made to the International Minerals and Chemical Corporation, whose Florida mines ranked high among the world's great producers of phosphates. More than 3,000,000 tons were produced annually by these mines, their modernized methods and equipment made possible in large part through Prudential funds.

Down in the South, Prudential funds were helping in the

expansion of the great Burlington Mills, producers of textiles. Since the early twenties "Bur-Mil," under the management of Spencer Love, had grown from a single plant with a few hundred workers to a decentralized operation of eighty-three plants in fifty-five communities, employing nearly 30,000 workers. By 1950 Prudential's investment in this company to provide for the development of these modern mills had reached $35,000,000.

Prudential also had a part in the remarkable achievements of the Port of New York Authority in building and operating harbor and traffic facilities in the New York–New Jersey area. In 1929 the company purchased bonds for the George Washington Bridge; in 1931 for the Holland Tunnel; in 1934 for the Lincoln Tunnel; in 1948 further purchases contributed to the development of the city's integrated system of air terminals, including the vast new International Airport.

In its investment activities the role of Prudential—as of all life insurance companies—was solely that of a lender. The company did not participate in the management or direction of the enterprises in which its funds were invested, nor did it seek such participation. What it could do as a lender was to provide funds for the development of existing enterprises and to make those funds available to borrowers of every class everywhere in the United States and Canada.

Prudential did not and could not create the demand for investment funds; it could only respond to that demand. But through its national network of regional offices Prudential was able to fill a wide variety of needs, large and small. In meeting these demands the company also provided another extremely important service. Prudential's investments played a valuable role in channeling funds from areas where there was a surplus of capital—as in New England, for example— into newer and younger areas such as the West and Southwest, where financing of all types was needed to meet the demands for the rapid expansion of industry.

This flow of funds to areas in which there was a demand for investment finance was graphically illustrated in Texas, Oklahoma, Arkansas, and Louisiana.

Texas, in the years following the war, was enjoying one of the greatest periods of development in its history. New housing was going up. New factories. New industries of all types were moving to Texas cities. And in this swift and exciting growth Prudential funds were helping to raise new buildings, new homes, to bring in new machinery, to provide the financial support which would sustain this growth. In 1949 President Shanks was able to report that Prudential's investments in the four-state region totaled almost five and a half times the company's policy reserves for that area.

Texas is a state of vast resources. Chief among them are oil and natural gas. It was logical that a large share of Prudential's investments should go into companies whose job was to utilize and develop these resources. A $65,000,000 loan, in the form of bonds, was made to the Lone Star Gas Company, for example. This company, a producer and distributor of natural gas, served 306 communities in Texas and twenty-six in Oklahoma. A loan of $12,500,000 was made to an independent Texas oil producer, R. Lacy, Inc., for the development of rich oil- and gas-producing holdings in Panola County. There was a $3,000,000 loan to the Schlumberger Well Surveying Corporation for general expansion, and a loan of $3,300,000 to the Warren Petroleum Company for the purchase of five hundred tank cars. And another of $450,000 to Oil Drilling, Inc., a small oil and gas producer in the Texas Gulf coast country.

Closely tied to the story of the expansion of industries concerned with the production and distribution of Texas's oil resources were the famous "Big Inch" and "Little Inch" pipe lines stretching almost 1,500 miles from the oil fields in Texas to New Jersey. Built by the Government during the war to carry desperately needed fuel oil to the East coast, the lines were later sold to private interests and converted to the transportation of natural gas. The bulk of the funds necessary for the purchase and conversion of the lines was obtained in the form of loans, part of which was provided by Prudential.

It was an exciting, stirring record of growth, this story in Texas. It was more than merely factories or oil companies, vital as these were. It was also mortgage loans on small business, on homes, on cattle ranches. It was investment in small companies and large. In the state of Texas, Prudential loans in force on business properties, factories, farms, ranches, and homes totaled more than $140,000,000, money which had gone to work not only for the policyholders of Prudential but also for the people of Texas.

The story of what happened in Texas could be told about many other parts of the country. The differences would be mainly in the details. Carried to the people through the normal business channels of the mortgage loan and bond departments, these funds of an insurance company, reaching into every state and section of this country and Canada, were helping America to build a stronger and freer economy.

In November 1949 President Shanks received an invitation to attend another congressional hearing in Washington. This one was conducted by the Celler Committee, named for its chairman, Representative Emanuel Celler of New York. The committee's legal name was The Special Subcommittee on the Study of Monopoly Power of the Committee of the Judiciary of the United States House of Representatives.

President Shanks arrived to tell the committee about The

Prudential. Would Mr. Shanks sit down? No, Mr. Shanks preferred to stand. Had he a prepared statement? Yes. Would he read it? He would be pleased to. But hardly had he begun when the committee members interrupted him.

The questions appeared to have little relationship to the main subject of the investigation—monopoly. How many policyholders were there in Prudential? Was Prudential a mutual company? What was the average size of policies? How many were weekly premium? How many ordinary? What was the percentage of lapses? These were familiar questions—the questions that Prudential people had been asked through a long series of governmental investigations. They had all been answered before, fully and without equivocation, and Shanks answered them once more in the same way. The figures had changed, of course, but the substance was the same.

The chairman broke in several times to ask about Prudential's assets. There had been expert testimony, he said, expressing concern over the growing assets of the legal reserve life insurance companies. Would Mr. Shanks care to comment on that?

Mr. Shanks would. The amount of insurance in force, he said, had remained less than one year's national income for the past twenty-five years. If the national income doubled, insurance in force would presumably double. If the national income should run along level, insurance would level off too. "We have figures also showing that, year after year, somewhere between 3 and 4 per cent of the national income is spent for insurance premiums. . . . Assets of the companies run along just about 25 per cent of the amount of insurance in force."

But it was on the matter of investments and loans that the chairman was most persistent, probing sharply with a number of questions. Shanks answered to the point. "Funds provided from premium payments can be and are being invested throughout the United States and Canada wherever there is a demand for such funds with reasonable safety. . . ." Later, speaking of Prudential's all-purpose program, he added, "We are not limited by any particular geographical area. We provide capital in a variety of forms for expansion and modernization of business and industry. We enable families to buy and build homes and to own and operate farms.

"The Prudential has more than 265,000 mortgage loans. More than 95 per cent of them are on homes and farms scattered throughout every state and Canada, and their average is less than $8,000." President Shanks paused, then repeated deliberately, "That average, including all of our big loans, is less than $8,000.

"The businesses which we have helped finance are a complete cross section of our economy. They include practically every type of business in every part of the country. . . ."

It was clear and concise, the testimony of this man standing before the committee. He had nothing to hide and no apologies to make. He was the president of a big insurance company which was doing a big job for millions of people, not only in insurance protection, but in its wide investment program as well.

Over the years since the founding of the company the list of governmental hearings on insurance had become rather lengthy. But Prudential always seemed to do well at these investigations. Perhaps this was not only because of the high caliber of the men who testified; perhaps it was also because the story Prudential had to tell was a record of service and constructive achievement in an enterprise of importance to the people.

CHAPTER 19

Operation Newark

T HE Prudential sprang from a very small beginning. It was organized in a room not as large as the one we are now in, and the business has progressed from year to year until they have been forced to break through one wall to another, and go upstairs and downstairs, so that I got lost there one day and had to inquire my way out . . ."

That was John Dryden, addressing the board of directors in 1877, on his return from England. He had been somewhat overawed by the buildings of the British Prudential.

In 1950 the visitor to the Newark home office of The Prudential Insurance Company of America was often as overwhelmed as John Dryden had been seventy-five years before in London. The American Prudential had not grown upstairs and downstairs, through a random collection of buildings, as had its counterpart in England. But through the years new building after new building had been added, until by 1950 the Newark home office had become almost a small city of insurance.

As part of its seventy-fifth anniversary celebration the company began a series of conducted tours of these buildings. The visitors who went on these tours were shown the working apparatus of the company. The guides were familiar with the details of the company's operation and were carefully trained to explain the meaning and purpose of the activities the visitors saw. Nevertheless, the sightseer was often bewildered by the intricacy of the organization and the magnitude of the plant itself. Here was an eight-story building devoted solely to printing the company's 15,000 forms, policies, reports, and magazines. Near by was the building for storage of records—six floors of huge filing cabinets, row after row, from floor to ceiling, where records of policies and payments going back to the earliest days, hundreds of millions—were kept. Over in the Gibraltar Building were the punched-card machines, a tremendous installation for handling the routine details of servicing more than 30,000,000 policies.

The tour through these clustered buildings in Newark presented a picture of a whole city of operations. The telephone exchange handled 35,000 calls each day. The mail division each day processed a ton of incoming and two-and-a-half tons of outgoing mail. There were libraries, a gymnasium, recreation rooms, employment and personnel offices.

Over the years, as Prudential grew, the problems of organization had multiplied and the business had to become more and more departmentalized in order to handle with maximum efficiency the mounting details and to fulfill the ideals of service and swift payment of claims to the policyholders. As the number of policyholders increased and the variety of services expanded, the direction and control of the organization became more complex.

In 1950 the co-ordination of all home office activities was under the direction of the general office administration de-

308 THE PRUDENTIAL

partment, headed by Vice-president F. Bruce Gerhard. This
department was charged with direction of personnel administration and personnel research. It was also charged with
the responsibility of furnishing advice on the development of
all office procedures.

Through its methods division this department was very
active in applying modern machinery to the ever-increasing
volume of detail required in Prudential work.

The story of this mechanization of Prudential was more
than a story of machines. It was also a record of inventive
genius. When John K. Gore was the company's actuary, he
helped to meet the problem of handling records by inventing
a "perforated card sorter" capable of classifying and sorting
cards at a rate of 15,000 per hour. Gore's machines served the
company for many years but their uses were limited in scope.
As the problems of maintaining accurate records grew, owing
both to volume and complexity, the need for more powerful
tools was sorely felt.

Vice-president Valentine Howell and Harry Volk, at that
time a supervisor, undertook to make application of the
newer punched-card machines to Prudential work. At first
these machines were used primarily for statistical and
actuarial work. But as machines were developed which could
write names and make possible sorting cards by name,
methods of using them for the life and lapse register preparation in the weekly premium department were devised.

Creation of the punched cards required to install the new
system was an enormous undertaking. It involved the trans-
lation into punched-card form of the details of more than
25,000,000 policies. All these cards were verified and the new
listing compared with the old. The main job of installation
was completed late in 1940, nearly five years after the first
testing of the new system was inaugurated.

This system attracted a great deal of attention from other companies and organizations.

The use of punched-card equipment for aiding in the clerical work of The Prudential was extended after 1940. By 1950 a very large installation in the ordinary department was completed for the purpose of preparing premium notices and receipts and performing premium accounting. This installation required the punching of nearly 10,000,000 cards to start with, and was even more complex than the system in the weekly premium department. It was expected to result in substantially reduced costs as well as an increase in accuracy.

The activities of the general office administration department were by no means confined to problems of mechanization, however. One of the department's most important responsibilities involved the selection and training of thousands of employees. Its personnel division handled the placement of home office personnel and developed policies governing promotion, job evaluation, training, and the general direction of personnel activities and personnel research.

Finding the right man for the right job was one way of keeping office morale high and thereby improving service to Prudential's policyholders. But it was also important to test office procedures and policies with a view to determining how these affected the worker in his job. In 1947, in conjunction with the Survey Research Center of the University of Michigan, Prudential launched several projects in the field of group relations. The surveys at Prudential were particularly concerned with the effect of office management and procedures on the employee's personal satisfaction and productivity.

Through the Prudential Athletic Association, Prudential men and women joined in scores of varied extracurricular activities which included everything from playing soccer to

singing grand-opera arias. An abridged list of some of these
activities included: tennis tournaments for men and women;
rifle-range practice for men and women—with women out-
numbering the men; golf tournaments in the spring and fall;
a fishing committee which conducted week-end fishing trips;
bowling teams; soccer teams; baseball; basketball; a motion-
picture club; a camera club; a swimming team; barn dances;
moonlight sails, and fashion shows.

During the war Prudential home office employees staged a
number of musical revues. Some of these productions were
presented for war relief, and several companies of highly professional Prudential performers toured the army camps and
hospitals, playing to audiences totaling nearly 200,000
servicemen and women.

The primary functions of the medical department were
the medical selection of applicants for insurance, the supervision of approximately 10,000 examining physicians, and the
administration of the employee health service.

In the course of serving Prudential policyholders and employees, the medical department made valuable contributions to medical science itself, particularly in connection
with electrocardiographic and diabetic research. In the field
of electrocardiographic research the Prudential's scientific
exhibits received wide acclaim by national and state medical societies. Prudential scientists evolved a technique for
determining whether or not certain types of sugar in the
blood or urine are or are not suggestive of diabetes.

The company had always stressed the importance of each
individual's contribution to the business. Prudential was one
of the first large corporations to inaugurate an effective employee suggestion system. As far back as 1890 all employees
were urged to submit ideas or plans for improvements in

working methods and practices. Declared John Dryden in his rather formal phrasing, "The executive department, at its leisure, will have each scheme impartially considered."

The idea took hold. Over the years many employees contributed significant and fruitful suggestions, and were paid by the company for these ideas. This suggestion program became an accepted part of office routine. In 1948 and 1949 alone a total of nearly 20,000 suggestions from members of the home office and field staffs was submitted. Thousands of these suggestions were accepted and put into practice. Prudential paid out to the employees who made these suggestions many thousands of dollars in cash awards, ranging from $5.00 to $2,500.

In hundreds of ways the constant search for improvements went on—the search for new methods to save time and reduce costs. It was important to give care and thought even to seemingly small details. In 1936, for example, the company authorized a forms control section of the methods division—a group to pass on the wording, color, grade of paper, and printing for all forms used by the company. The control section saved hundreds of thousands of dollars—and hours of labor for Prudential's staff—by determining proper size and shape and arrangement of printed matter on the forms.

The actuarial department was the gyroscope which held the company on a safe course over long years. This department, through its underwriting division, working with the medical department, accepted, modified, or declined applications for ordinary insurance, and issued new policies. It calculated rates and values and dividend scales and prepared rate books for use by the agents. Often it had been the actuarial mind of a John Gore or a James Little, or, in later days, Valentine Howell, which had devised new ways of providing coverage when the need for that coverage appeared. The actuarial department was concerned with far more than mere figures. It required a broad comprehension of the whole purpose and philosophy of insurance. This department, because of its key position, had produced many of the outstanding executives of the company.

A large share of the responsibility of handling the detailed work of the company was shouldered in the home office by the debit policy department and the ordinary policy department, both under the direction of Vice-president Gerhard. Most of the essential servicing of Prudential's millions of policies was handled by the skilled workers in these two departments.

The ordinary policy department was charged with handling the records of all ordinary policies—the job of premium billing and accounting and dividend calculations; changes in addresses and status; the recording of lapses and reinstatements, loans and surrenders and withdrawals; the preparation of all checks for payments under such policies, except for claim payments.

The debit policy department's job was to issue policies for weekly premium and intermediate-ordinary applications; to process lapses, transfers, and reinstatements; to act on requests for duplicate policies and changes of beneficiaries; to maintain the basic policy accounting record; to keep the weekly premium register card file on which were recorded all payments made by Prudential's approximately 15,000,000 weekly premium policyholders.

Each department in this interlocking organization had its own specific role to play. The law department, which in 1950 was under the direction of General Counsel Sylvester C. Smith, Jr., provided advice and assistance on legal questions and acted on legal matters, from patents to criminal law, from keeping track of current or impending congressional investigations to handling all matters of litigation. Perhaps the most important aspect of the law department's activities centered on investments, which occupied the full time of 75 per cent of the staff of lawyers.

Concerned with the administration of company finances was the comptroller's department, under the direction of Vice-president and Comptroller Louis R. Menagh, Jr., who also headed the claim department. The comptroller was charged with the establishing and maintaining of the accounting and auditing procedures for the entire company. His department audited all financial transactions and maintained records of those transactions in the company's account books. It prepared budgets for the home office and field offices and made general cost analyses of the company's operations. It assembled the data for the company's annual statement. The department also had the duty of arranging for payment of rents and licenses, and administered all tax matters. This was the department which established and administered the financial controls guiding the over-all operations of the company.

The treasurer's department, headed in 1950 by H. Woodruff Tatlock, had custody of all bonds, stocks, mortgages, and policy loan certificates. It had charge of all company bank accounts, and the deposit and transfer of funds. Its pay-roll division prepared salary and disability payments to company employees and maintained records of pay-roll deductions for the welfare program, taxes, and similar items. The department also approved and disbursed policy loans, cash surrenders, and dividends.

The advertising and publications department, under the supervision of Vice-president George E. Potter, was responsible for the company's national and local advertising, trade-journal advertising, special campaigns, and radio programs. It prepared and published the company's home office and field publications. It created promotional material and visual selling aids for the company's group insurance and mortgage loan activities, and health booklets, posters, and other material.

Serving the needs of this city of 12,000 men and women was an enormous housekeeping arrangement, performed by the home office buildings and plant department. Somewhat more than 1,500 employees were required to maintain these buildings and their services. Elevator service had to be provided for some 70,000 passengers daily. Inventories of more than 100,000 pieces of office furniture and equipment had to be kept up to date. More than 2,500,000 gallons of fuel oil were used yearly for heat and power. Paper consumption totaled nearly 1,500 tons annually.

This was a big job, and a number of special divisions were set up to handle it. A supply division stocked all forms and office supplies; an office equipment service division maintained and repaired office machines; a purchasing division was charged with the job of buying all supplies needed by the home office. There was a printing division equipped with job presses, cylinder presses, and offset, and a bindery division; a commissary division of more than 400 people furnishing cafeteria and dining-room service for home office personnel and guests; and even an architects' and engineers' division, which prepared sketches and drawings for building alterations and supervised the work of the various building programs.

The visitor making a tour of this city within a city might well be excused for being somewhat overwhelmed by the scope and extent of its activities, covering such a wide range of diverse operations.

Yet the magnitude and complexity were not the significant factors. More important was the single undeviating purpose behind all of this operation with its intricate workings—swift and accurate service for American families and homes, for businesses and factories and farms.

CHAPTER 20

Decentralization—
A Mid-century Milestone

THE DC-6, coming in for its landing, circled high above the lights of Los Angeles. Through one of the plane's windows the hostess pointed to a sight which had attracted the attention of some of the passengers—a blaze of light from a building which seemed a little way off from the heart of the city, light from a thousand windows glittering against the darkness.

The spectacular display which the passengers had seen came from a new office building on Wilshire Boulevard, the hostess explained. A modern edifice of glass and concrete and aluminum, it was completed in 1948 and was one of the most unusual structures in the city. While still thirty miles from their destination, passengers on night flights into Los Angeles saw the building's striking lines bathed in light. This new landmark of Los Angeles was the western home office of The Prudential Insurance Company of America.

The new office, charged with responsibility for supervising Prudential's insurance business in eleven western states and the Territory of Hawaii, was more than a gleaming, ultra-modern new building, more than a step in the development of managerial organization. For Prudential it was a stride into the future—the age of decentralization.

The western home office was only the start, the pilot operation. If it was successful, there would be other regional home offices established to serve the needs of other wide areas, in Canada, in the Southwest, in other great regions.

Decentralization as conceived by The Prudential was new to large insurance companies. From the outset, however, there was no intention or plan to "break up" The Prudential. The Rock of Gibraltar was not being split into a hundred pieces. Basic policymaking decisions for the direction of the company's activities would continue to be made by the president and board of directors in Newark. But broad authority would be granted, sufficient to allow a regional home office free and independent action by which to bring swifter service—custom-made to fit the needs of a specific area of the nation.

From time to time prior to 1946 the executives of The Prudential had considered the possibility of some degree of decentralization as a means of improving the company's service. Such discussions, however, had not proceeded much further than talk of a branch office in Canada. The company had begun in Newark, and the early development of the business, in the natural course of events, had been in the East, in areas not far distant from the home office. But with the development of remote areas of the country the business became a national one, and Prudential's local offices had been established throughout the length and breadth of the land. Supervision of all these offices, no matter where situated, came from Newark, New Jersey.

There were some in the company, however, who believed that Prudential could do a better job in providing life insurance services of all classifications and in making local investments through establishment of regional home offices. One of the strongest advocates of this plan to decentralize authority and control had been Executive Vice-president Carrol Shanks.

During 1946, Mr. Shanks's first year as president of the company, these plans began to take definite shape. The president concentrated a large part of his efforts on the formulation of policies, on selection of the location for the first regional office, on the complicated details of organization. Late in 1946 he was able to present to the board the rough blueprint of a new plan for The Prudential: establishment of a second home office—on the Pacific coast.

Choice of the West coast was logical. The eleven states and the Territory of Hawaii which would form the territory embraced by the western home office were the most remote from Newark. It was an area of assorted needs, where problems differed widely from those of the highly industrialized East. It covered a territory varying from the cattle ranges of Wyoming to the pineapple plantations of the Hawaiian Islands. In this area The Prudential had more than two and a half billion dollars of life insurance in force on the lives of 1,750,000 individuals. Payments to policyholders and beneficiaries annually averaged $45,000,000. The new home office would be taking over about 10 per cent of Prudential's total business.

Each step in the new project, however, was made only after the most careful deliberation and examination of all possible contingencies. The president and the board were setting out on a new course and they moved forward with caution. A committee of executives was appointed by the president and was assigned to study the question of a site for the new venture and its general organization. The detailed arrangements, cost schedules, and all other matters required to carry out the plan without interrupting or delaying the day-to-day services of the company were to be the concern of Vice-president Harry Volk, who had been assigned by the president to head up the first regional home office.

There were many advantages in the new program. Decentralization meant that Prudential would be closer to the people it served, and would be able to provide a more efficient and uniform service throughout the United States and Canada. It would be possible to make quicker decisions, based on more complete information because of close regional knowledge. The very distances which mail, notices, inquiries, and premiums had to travel would be appreciably cut down.

The change was also important to the personnel of Prudential. It would provide new training grounds for general executives and broadened opportunities for individuals within the company to rise to positions of high leadership. Working in smaller regional units, employees would have greater incentives; new opportunities for employment would be created in many cities; new methods and techniques would have a chance for development and testing—and the results could be measured against the performance of other regional offices.

At the company's annual conference held at the Hotel Commodore, New York City, in March 1947, President Shanks announced the plan and disclosed that the first regional office would be established in Los Angeles. The announcement of this pioneering project in decentralization received wide attention in the press of America and throughout insurance circles.

Much of the preliminary work had already been accomplished. The eleven-acre tract on Wilshire Boulevard had been purchased and architects were already drawing up plans. Vice-president Volk himself was on the Coast making his own announcement of the plan to a group of western business and civic leaders at the California Club. Throughout the West the announcement was greeted enthusiastically by businessmen, labor organizations, and the general public. Immediately following his announcement Volk also disclosed the formation of an advisory board composed of western business and professional leaders whose advice would be invaluable to Prudential officials. The five members of this board were Chairman Norman Chandler, president and publisher of the Los Angeles *Times;* Justin W. Dart, president of Rexall Drugs, Inc.; LeRoy M. Edwards, vice-president and general manager of Pacific Lighting Corporation; James E. Shelton, president of Security-First National Bank of Los Angeles, and P. G. Winnett, chairman of the board of Bullock's, Inc.

The states in the new territory included California, Oregon, and Washington along the coast; Montana, Utah, Idaho, Wyoming, Nevada, Arizona, New Mexico, Colorado, and the Territory of Hawaii. President Shanks announced that the new home office would have the responsibility of administering all Prudential affairs in these areas, within a broad framework of company policy established by the board and the president in Newark.

It had been decided to clothe the new office with the highest degree of autonomy possible within this framework. The western home office would have full responsibility in the organization, co-ordination, and direction of Prudential matters in the western area, both in the providing of insurance service and investment service.

Preparations for the move west produced intense activity both on the Coast and back in the Newark home office. In

Los Angeles it was a matter of approving final plans, letting contracts, obtaining material and labor for construction of the new building.

When the original home office was built, John Dryden had insisted on the heaviest material available. It was a massive structure, proudly described as "an iron-and-steel building enclosed in brick and stone." The blue granite flagstones around the Newark home office were the largest ever quarried, weighing up to eighty tons.

The Prudential western home office reflected the spirit of a later day. It was lighter in construction than almost any other building of its kind and size in the world. The concrete in its walls and floors was made with a pumice aggregate instead of gravel. Fire-proofing was of lightweight vermiculite. With less weight to support, the beams of the steel frame itself could be lighter than usual without sacrificing strength. It was a building extending over two whole city blocks—a modern structure of glass and gleaming aluminum contrasting with a concrete windowless block forming the core or center section and housing elevators and utilities. This was a new home office for a new age.

Virtually all materials used in this structure were of western origin—marble from Wyoming, wood from California forests, and aluminum from new industrial mills of the West. Only local labor was employed in the construction.

President Shanks and Vice-president Volk had discussed at length the matter of obtaining the staff. They had agreed that personnel for the new office would be predominantly local people. They would be trained by experts sent out from the Newark home office, some for a temporary period and others who would go out with their families on a permanent basis. When this plan was announced, more than 400 Prudential employees from various departments signified their willingness to join the western migration—with their wives and their children. It would be a sizable moving day.

But more difficult than the movement of individuals were the monumental preparations preliminary to this transcontinental adventure—the segregating of literally millions of records from various departments, the keeping of those records in perfect order and in active use except during actual transportation across the continent. To solve these complicated problems of organization and to train personnel for the special conditions they would meet out West, Volk —who spent a large part of his time commuting from East to West—set up a unique department on the seventh and eighth floors of the North Building. This department was known officially as the Western Home Office—in Newark!

Those who were to establish the various departments on the West coast, and their assistants, aides, and secretaries, set up offices precisely as if they were already in Los Angeles. It was more than mere play-acting. Day after day the records which would be shipped West were transferred to this test operation in Newark, and the skeletonized departments took over the handling of all matters concerned with these records. These trainees for the western trek carried their realism to the point of installing their own switchboard system. Written memoranda to other departments in the Newark home office were sent through the mail department, precisely as if they were being sent from the West. Phone calls were limited to those which would be important enough to warrant transcontinental charges. A story is told about Vice-president and Associate Actuary Pearce Shepherd, who received a call from Volk. The Prudential operator informed him, "Vice-president Volk is calling you from the Western home office." "This modern age!" the actuary exclaimed. "I had lunch with him only an hour ago—here in Newark!"

The job of moving began in January 1948, when the first contingent of experts and personnel workers who would be responsible for much of the hiring on the Coast set out by train. They numbered thirty-one individuals, including eight small children. By May of that year 157 permanent employees and their families, totaling more than 400 people, had been moved by train or plane or car from Newark to California. Also moved by that time were ninety tons of records—and 200 tons of employees' furniture. The company was pleased to report that in this transfer it had not lost a single record or done any irreparable damage to household goods. There had been a few cases of mumps among the children en route.

The situation in Los Angeles at that stage of the operation called for hair-trigger decisions on the spot, and for a great deal of improvising. The new building, which would provide 500,000 square feet of space, was still under construction. In the meantime, Prudential had rented a building containing only a fraction of the space it needed, and there it temporarily stored the records and set up offices for the employees. Groups arriving later from Newark found themselves working in lofts of assorted shapes and sizes and offices over cakeshops and candy stores. Conditions were crowded in Los Angeles, and until the new building was completed, Prudential's western home office had to carry on under rather extraordinary conditions.

Further contingents of temporary employees sent out to set up departments and train staff personnel were arriving from Newark. And hundreds of clerks and stenographers were being hired in preparation for the opening of the building. The training of these new people, the attempts to find room for records and supplies, the job of keeping this organization functioning under these difficulties, became one of the classic stories of the insurance world.

The framework of the new building was reaching higher and the structure was beginning to emerge. In March a gift arrived for the new western home office, a gift weighing two tons. This was a piece of the Rock of Gibraltar, sent as a good-will gesture from the British Government to be used as a cornerstone. On June 17 Vice-president Volk officiated at the laying of this cornerstone of the new building. A number of the distinguished citizens of the city were there, as well as C. G. Kemball, British Acting Consul General. Mayor Fletcher L. Bowron welcomed the western home office on behalf of the community. The vice-president placed a number of historic documents in a stainless-steel box inside the cornerstone. Included was a letter from President Shanks addressed to the president of The Prudential in the year 2021, when the company would be just twice as old as when the letter was written. Declared President Shanks to that future unknown leader:

> The establishment of this Western Home Office is the first step to decentralize the activities of The Prudential. Commencing in 1875, the company has expanded its operations throughout the United States and Canada with all lines of control and direction running directly to Newark. The growth and maturity of the nation, together with the advantages of regional handling of affairs and the disadvantages of continued piling up of work and control in one locality, have made the time ripe for this first step toward regional control of our large business.

On November 15 the Prudential western home office was opened. The ceremonies were attended by prominent businessmen and state and local officials and by more than 1,400 Prudential employees from the home office and from the field. The greater number of these latter were native Californians. President Shanks was there and made a brief talk

WESTERN HOME OFFICE BUILDING, LOS ANGELES

about the important job these people could do for their community and their nation in this new building. President Shanks and Vice-president Volk together pushed open the doors—and decentralization of The Prudential had begun to function.

The year 1949 marked the first full year of decentralization in the West. A completely integrated organization had been established. The western home office boasted its own actuarial and law and medical departments; its own departments of ordinary and group and weekly premium insurance; its own mortgage loan and real estate investment and bond departments; a department of insurance services and another for information and research.

It was an achievement of consequence. But even more important than the physical job of organizing this new venture, of shipping millions of records by the carload without the loss of a premium payment slip, were the results achieved in this first year of operation. This new office had been set up for specific purposes, to increase the service to policyholders, to extend service to people in areas not previously covered adequately, to strengthen the company's relationship with the public by providing it with a fuller understanding of the operations, to increase investment services, and to accomplish these numerous and diversified objectives within reasonable limits of expense.

The records for the end of 1949 told the story. The Prudential western home office had produced $304,717,000 of paid-for new business—an increase of 20 per cent over the previous year. In the field of investments more than 24,044 mortgage loans were approved in the western home office territory in 1949, for a total of $181,161,000—an increase of 38 per cent in number of mortgage loans approved in the western states. Loans in force at the end of 1949 amounted to

$449,348,243—a gain of 40 per cent over the figures of the previous year.

The western home office was employing 1,266 individuals at the end of 1949. Of these 324 were permanent transferees from the Newark home office. They and their families were already solidly established in this new world of the West.

The success of this pilot operation on the West coast was the signal for immediate further steps to extend the decentralization program into other areas. On December 9, 1949, President Shanks announced the plan to establish a Canadian head office, to be located in the new Bank of Nova Scotia Building in the heart of the business section of Toronto, Ontario. This Canadian head office, occupying eight floors of the new building, was ready for operations by the fall of 1950.

The company had been operating in Canada for more than forty years. Since the beginning days of 1909, when it had opened its first district agencies in Montreal and Toronto and Quebec, the company's Canadian agencies and representatives had been an integrated part of the growth and the story of The Prudential Insurance Company of America. The flags of both nations flew side by side at annual meetings and conventions. Personnel moved freely between offices in the United States and Canada. In the business of providing protection to the public through the medium of private insurance, Canada and the States had gone forward together. Growth of the company's agencies and coverage and investment in Canada had continued steadily over these forty uninterrupted years.

By 1950, Prudential had a million and a half policies for more than a $1,000,000,000 in Canada, making the company the fourth largest in that country. Investments totaled $385,000,000, including a mortgage account of $85,000,000.

The company had thirty-one agencies, 900 agents, in all 1,400 full-time Prudential people. This force wrote an average of about $100,000,000 of new business from 1943 through 1949.

As with the western home office, Prudential set up a testing and training organization—on the two floors of the North Building in Newark, formerly occupied by the western office contingent. There was one major variation, however. Instead of organizing teams and shipping them to the new head office to train Canadian employees, Prudential this time, during the summer of 1950, brought employees hired in

Toronto down to Newark for their basic training in insurance operations.

Of the trainees, 225 were young women who had just been graduated from Canadian high schools and 125 were experienced personnel who were coming to Newark to familiarize themselves with the specialized operations to be established in the Toronto office. For the eleven weeks' course in Newark, trainees from Canada had quarters in two nearby colleges. Several Canadian women who had been engaged as counselors accompanied the girls from Toronto.

Named to take charge of the new Canadian office was Prudential Vice-president Robert M. Green. Vice-president Green was born in Cincinnati but his people had come originally from Canada. The vice-president, in fact, owned a home at Pointe au Baril on Georgian Bay. When Green made a preliminary report on the progress of the Canadian operation at the seventy-fifth anniversary conference in Newark in March of 1950, it was noted that he referred repeatedly to the objectives and goals which "we of Canada" would achieve. "We have a population of thirteen and a half million," he declared, "the finest people you could find anywhere, people who are proud of their heritage and proud of the challenge of the future. We of The Prudential are part of the Canadian scene, and an ever-increasing part of it. You people here in the States have a thirty-four-year start on us in the insurance business. The Prudential did not go into Canada until 1909. Our objective is to overcome our thirty-four-year handicap. With a field organization and the new head office you will be hearing a good deal more from across the border."

In January 1950 President Shanks announced the appointment of Vice-president Valentine Howell as executive vice-president in charge of the decentralization program. In

April of 1950, months before the new Canadian office had even opened its doors, President Shanks announced a still further move in decentralization—the beginning of plans to establish a third regional home office in Houston, Texas. The new building to house this southwestern office would not be completed until 1951. Vice-president Charles Fleetwood

of the mortgage loan and real estate investment department would be in charge, and the area embraced by the new southwestern home office would include seven states—Texas, Arkansas, Kansas, Louisiana, Oklahoma, Mississippi, and Missouri.

The program of decentralization moved forward. There would be other regional home offices established in the years ahead—wherever the need was demonstrated for a regional center of operations, serving the special wants and problems of an area.

As decentralization progressed, hundreds of employees in

the Newark home office volunteered to move into these new territories across America. They were part of an unusual migration, a new development in the story of modern business enterprise. At the same time Prudential's traditional policy of job security remained unchanged. Newark would continue to be the policymaking headquarters of the entire operation, and in addition would be the home office for a very extensive and populous territory. Thousands of employees would still be needed to service the increasing hundreds of millions of insurance in force and to carry on the duties of the home office in Newark.

"Co-ordination of the work of the regional home offices," President Shanks informed the board of directors late in 1949, "will be accomplished through the general headquarters in Newark. Control to see that there is no important deviation from company policy will be maintained through a system of inspection. Our organization will not be unlike that of the Army, where there is a general headquarters staff determining over-all strategy and a group of field generals with complete responsibility for operations within their area. . . . This kind of operation . . . will result in a substantial strengthening of our company personnel-wise, public-relationwise, and in the service of the people of the nation. . . ."

Such was the blueprint for the future as presented by President Shanks. Years before he made this statement, before anyone had heard of this concept of decentralization, another Prudential president had made another statement— on the question of change and growth. President John Dryden had sounded a far-off warning that a company would die unless it was prepared to adapt and readapt its policies and operations to the changing social and political structure of society.

Prudential had not forgotten this warning. Throughout the company's history it had hewed to this philosophy of adaptability and change to serve the needs of society— through concessions of the eighties and nineties, through mutualization, through expanding horizons in investments, through the rise and development of group insurance, and finally through this new concept of decentralization.

In 1950 The Prudential stood again—as it had when the company first opened the doors of its basement office in Newark—on the threshold of a new age, of a new adventure in service to the people of America.

CHAPTER 21

Carrol Shanks Talks about Tomorrow

You felt the space and the quiet first. You felt them as you walked with the secretary through the wide-open sliding doors of the connecting rooms into the president's office. It was the last and largest of the rooms—square, with a high ceiling, blue walls, and no portraits.

Strange that it should look so modern here, this office in a fifty-year-old building. Perhaps it was the simplicity of the arrangement—the dominant broad mahogany desk on the right, the grouped chairs across the room, the subdued pattern of the rugs on the floor.

As you came in Mr. Shanks was talking on the phone. A low voice that came to you in a blur. The secretary waited with you by the door. "Yes," she was telling you, "it does seem modern. The rooms have been done over, of course. But the desk was Mr. Dryden's and that sofa was here when Mr. Duffield was president."

When he finished with his phone call, Mr. Shanks came around the desk to greet you. A man of medium height, a little thinner than you'd expected, a little more muscular. You noticed the high forehead, the receding hairline, the deep-set blue eyes behind rimless glasses. "I'm sorry to keep you waiting," he said. "Could we sit over here? I like to get out from behind this desk. Desks can get in your way."

This was the hard one, the talk you'd saved until the last. You had the statistics, a file of facts, months of work behind you, on this history you were writing of The Prudential. They'd given you free access to all the sources, the masses of material, and people to help you sift it. You had all the pieces. What you wanted now was to know the directions, the aims, the plans for the future.

It wasn't any social call. Mr. Shanks was one of the outstanding men in life insurance in this year 1950. It was important for you to understand his way of thinking. You had the questions lined up in your mind.

You watched him as he made his answers. His manner seemed to you significant. He was deliberate, somewhat sparing of words. You had the feeling that he wanted to say exactly what he meant, wanted what he said to mean the same thing to you that it did to him. Not that he was holding back his ideas; it was simply that he had a logical and ordered mind. Words that said almost what he meant weren't good enough. Yet beneath this control you seemed to sense an almost boyish quality of enthusiasm.

What impressed you most was the voltage behind the words. You had expected that this would be an old story to him, one he had told many times before. And yet there was excitement in his words, a freshness in his ideas, an intensity in the way he expressed them as he talked. It was fresh because as he talked with you he seemed to be re-examining concepts he knew well, seeking ways to say them more clearly and more fully.

Above all there was his feeling for people. That was the

way he began answering your questions, talking about people. "The thing I've insisted on," he said, "the thing we've all got to bear in mind constantly, is that insurance is a business of people. It is a mistake to explain this business in terms of dollars and cents. In our system of economy, insurance has to provide the answer to certain basic human needs. That's the only reason for its existence. That was the basis of Dryden's idea when he founded industrial insurance for the common man back in the seventies, and it is just as true today."

The common man. That had come to be a much-abused phrase. It meant a lot of things to a number of people, to politicians and pundits. But Shanks used it frequently. He used it in its basic sense. To him the common man was the ordinary citizen, the average American and his family, men and women seeking some measure of security and happiness from life.

He had a great respect for this common man of America—a respect for his needs and his ability to get what he wanted. And today, Shanks told you, the common man needed and wanted more things than ever before in history. His needs and wants were basic things that Americans had always considered their right. A good house to live in. A chance to work and pay his way. Good food on the table. And security. Life filled with the old uncertainties was not good enough. More than ever before the common man wanted and needed security—protection against poverty, against sickness and accident, against an empty old age.

"But it's an evil thing that these wholesome honest needs, these basic promises of the American life, should have gotten mixed up with a thing called the Welfare State. What a misnomer that is—the Welfare State!" He didn't raise his voice, but a new intensity came into it, an indignation. His fist hit the arm of the chair. "And that isn't all. Because a few people have been able to identify the welfare state with these honest needs, too many of us have been frightened into denying the needs themselves. We've got to stop that. We've got to recognize that these are things people want and should have. Americans are asking for widened security. They have a right to it and will get it. The only question to-day is how."

This was no stand-pat attitude. It was no denial of the wants of people, no searching for reasons why the job couldn't be done. It was a denial of the method of state operation, but an affirmation of the legitimate rights of people to obtain for themselves these benefits.

"We've got to stop thinking in clichés," he was saying. "This is a time for fresh ideas and most of all for clear and honest reasoning about our problems. None of these problems is simple and none of them has any clear-cut black-and-white answer. We have to begin with the fact that these are justified needs which in some way or other have to be met."

It was foolish, he told you, to hold that there is no place at all for government in answering some of these demands. "The welfare of its citizens is the first order of business of any government. There are areas in which an extension of government services is desirable and advisable. Few question the propriety of a social security program, for example. It's right and proper for the government to establish a floor—minimum standards below which nobody would be forced to live. The first thing that all of us have to recognize is that services are going to be provided to meet the wants of people —and whether they come through government or through private insurance, they will have to be paid for."

You noticed the directness of his manner, of his words. He wasn't dodging this issue. "If Americans are going to get these benefits," he was saying, "the question is—who is going to provide them, and at what cost? The proponents of the welfare state think the nation is wealthy enough to support such a program. Economically we are a powerful, growing nation. Perhaps we could bear the monetary costs, even though no one seriously questions that providing benefits through government bureaucracy is the most expensive way."

But the cost in dollars and cents, he emphasized, wasn't the most important thing. "Beyond that, there's the question of a man's initiative and self-respect. This country was founded on a concept of self-reliance. We grew to be a strong country on the belief that we could take care of ourselves and our own. A man's desire and need to take care of himself and his family have been the incentive behind most of our great accomplishments. I believe that it would be a dangerous thing to abandon or to weaken that principle."

His voice was still quiet. But his words seemed more intense—more incisive—as this analysis carried to the heart of what he wanted to say. "The worst thing—the very worst thing—we could do," he told you, "would be to buy security at the cost of freedom. This is a price we cannot afford. Government in a nation the size of ours must deal with people in the mass. It can't treat a hundred and fifty million people as individuals. Any attempt by government to provide for every need of each person must result in the complete loss of individuality. We'd no longer be people—we'd be numbers. We'd have lost our identity, our individual freedom." Mr. Shanks paused, then added slowly, "I am an ardent advocate of welfare plans. But loss of freedom is too high a price to pay."

This was a constructive approach, you were thinking. It was going somewhere. It wasn't any glib over-simplification, no reactionary denial of progress. This was a reasoning man's analysis of the problem, a refusal to accept stereotypes. It was a search for new ways. There was an alternative, he was saying. "I think we can give the people—the common man—the things he needs. We can give it to him within the framework of freedom."

Mr. Shanks didn't think that building a satisfactory program would be easy. The evolving of a workable system, he told you, would mean the picking up and shouldering of many responsibilities by business which perhaps it had accepted before only in part. "It will mean providing steady employment, pensions, sickness benefits, business decisions made with a view to the long-range welfare of the community. It will mean assumption of leadership in local community problems, acceptance of responsibility in national problems. We've got to keep our thinking flexible. All of us must be ready to accept necessary changes. It's an urgent job and we've got to face it now."

Mr. Shanks leaned forward. "This is the job to be done, and government and business each can do its part. But the insurance industry must play a big part—a tremendous part—in the doing of it. We have the experience, we have the equipment, we have the organization. We are ready and capable and willing to do what must be done as times and needs and public demands call for action from all of us, without respect to political beliefs."

Times and needs and demands. You remembered the words of John Dryden, something about a company surviving only if it was ready to adapt its methods and ideas to the demands of the times.

American insurance companies already were doing part of the job, Shanks was saying. "They are providing protection and security in many ways to millions of people. This service is being rendered under constant supervision of the various state and provincial insurance departments charged with protecting the public interest. This supervision has been beneficial to the companies. It has kept them sound and alert. It has allowed them to grow and to provide insurance and security services for our ever-expanding economy, and I hope this forward-looking policy will continue." He pointed out that nearly 80 per cent of America's families carried life insurance of some kind, and in addition there was sickness, accident, hospital, medical and surgical expense, mortgage insurance, group pensions, annuities, term insurance, business insurance, creditor insurance.

One by one Mr. Shanks enumerated the protections offered by Prudential and the other insurance companies of America. You caught his sense of pride in the job that his company was doing and the people who were doing it. He began to tell you about the agents. You knew a lot about them already, you thought. But the way he talked about them, they became salesmen not merely of insurance, but of a way of life. "The agent in the field is the best spokesman freedom could have," he told you. "He's an expert in the business of protection. In tens of thousands of communities across the country he is daily talking to people about their own individual problems. He knows what can be done and what can't, and he knows why. He knows the faults and the dangers behind a lot of the schemes that are put forward and he can tell the people about those dangers.

"Self-interest on his part? Of course." He smiled. "Did you ever think of the fate of the salesman in the welfare state? But self-interest is only a part of the story. I know a lot of these agents. I'm proud of them. I often think how little the average person appreciates the job these men are actually doing. No other group in the country works harder or more effectively for the preservation of our American way."

Many of these agents, he told you, had been with the company fifteen or twenty or thirty years. Not only the agents but hundreds of employees—throughout every department of the company—had built long records of service. He began to tell you about the Prudential Old Guard and how it had been founded by John Dryden back in the 1880s. And how it had grown over the years until today more than 28,000 people in the company were members and 6,000 had been with the company for more than twenty years, and 1,500 more than thirty.

You knew a lot about this P.O.G. program he was talking about, but you were interested in the importance he gave to it, the importance he gave to the entire employee policy at Prudential. He talked about the benefits of delegating authority downward, of giving each individual a chance to rise in the company, and the place of decentralization in this policy. "Decentralization of our home office activities is going to give new opportunities to hundreds of our employees. It's going to be a help in developing our executives. I tell you, if decentralization does nothing more than that, in my opinion it will be worth the effort and cost."

He was talking once more about people. He had a way of moving from people to ideas and back again. You began to realize that Mr. Shanks was a man who measured ideas on a basis of their importance to people, on their social service-ability.

There was no mistaking the air of personal feeling and warmth in his words and manner as he talked about Prudential employees. He leaned back in his chair. "I'm afraid I'm off the subject," he told you. "You want to know about the big questions, don't you? The big social implications. Still"—he paused a moment, considering his thoughts carefully—"still, we're a large company. The personal problems our people face are a cross section of the problems of people all over the country. We've tried to work with our employees toward solving as many of them as we can. I think we have something pretty fine now. And what we can do in our group program for our own employees can be done for millions of employees all over America."

It was interesting, listening to him talk about this group welfare program for Prudential's own employees. He was boasting a little, proud of the benefits Prudential people received. They'd had the program for many years, he explained. It now included retirement benefits, group life insurance, medical expense insurance, and disability benefits, as well as hospital and surgical expense insurance for employees and dependents. The program, he explained, supplemented the benefits provided under the Social Security plan of the government. This was as it should be.

What Prudential was doing for its own was being done in many other companies, Mr. Shanks was telling you. There were about 13,000 companies with private retirement plans in operation this year, covering about 7,000,000 workers. Nearly half of the people in the United States were already covered by voluntary sickness, hospitalization, and accident plans. Within a span of fifteen years 75,000,000 people had been enrolled in hospitalization plans. In even less time 40,000,000 had been covered by surgical insurance plans and 20,000,000 by over-all private medical insurance plans. Not only could insurance provide full security for the people of America—it had already provided far broader coverage than most people realized.

You asked more about group insurance. Was there any chance, you wondered, that the individual would eventually be able to transfer his coverage when he left one job for

CARROL M. SHANKS

another? Mr. Shanks nodded. That was happening on a considerable scale already, he told you, through insurance plans and group policies carried by trade associations and national unions. The more universal group insurance became, the easier it would be to arrange this coverage for all American workers. It was entirely conceivable, Mr. Shanks said, that group insurance, sponsored entirely by private companies, might provide a universal blanket of coverage, within the foreseeable future, for the workers of America during the period when, as active breadwinners, they were supporting and educating their families.

Mr. Shanks told you this quietly, not as a prediction of what was going to happen so much as a statement of a goal for which Prudential and the other great life insurance companies could aim.

"But what," you asked, "would happen to weekly premium and ordinary insurance in that case? Wouldn't they decline sharply?"

"My guess is," Mr. Shanks said thoughtfully, "they'll be stronger than ever for the reason that people everywhere will be more insurance conscious. Group is only part of the story. It can do a large share of the job, but only while a man is actively at work. Term insurance and group insurance are best used to supplement other forms of coverage. Each man, each family, each home, has its own individual needs. Weekly premium, intermediate, and ordinary insurance covering the whole of life will still be the basic insurance for the individual. There's a place for all types of insurance in providing total protection for a man's family."

Family protection, yes, but how about a man's old age? That led to a discussion of pension funds. The problem here centered around the billions of dollars which would have to be put aside to guarantee future payment if pension funds were extended. The question was, where would they find investments for this money?

Mr. Shanks frowned. "The question of funding pensions is one of the most difficult problems we face today," he told you. "If pensions become universal, the setting aside of huge funds as reserves might seriously affect the investment market."

Was there any way the problem could be handled? "I'm sure the solution will be found," he said quietly. "A number of possibilities have been suggested. Partial funding is one. Or some kind of pay-as-you-go method might be evolved. Certainly here's one of the places government could co-operate with private industry by building a minimum old-age benefits program with broad coverage. Such a program would relieve industry of the burden of funding the entire pension needs of a nation."

His expression was serious. "Frankly," he told you, "I don't know what the answer is today. I don't even know the extent of the problem. The mechanizations of the future will call for huge accretions of capital. Much more capital per man employed. And capital means investments for the insurance companies. Anyway, I know there will be an answer. In the final analysis, the difficulty of solving a financial problem is not going to stop the insurance business from solving the important human problem of providing security for people."

Wasn't what he was talking about actually a private welfare program—a welfare state that wasn't dependent on a central government but was purely private business, private initiative, private enterprise? "Exactly," he told you. "Established social security, group annuities and other private pension programs, sickness and disability insurance, hospitalization and medical insurance—group life insurance and individual life insurance—all of these together point a way to a better and more secure way of life under our traditional American freedom. Here is the effective alternative to the demands of the welfare state with its vast load of taxation on the working generation."

There was someone standing at the door. You turned. Mr. Shanks followed your glance. It was the secretary. "I just wanted to remind you, Mr. Shanks," she said, "those two men are waiting for the appointment they have with you." He would see them in a few minutes, Mr. Shanks told her. He came back quickly to the subject you had been discussing. "Doesn't it seem reasonable to you," he said, "that we should concentrate our efforts on developing the patterns that we already have? They are not yet the perfect solution. But they have been and are being constantly improved and extended. They can never be a danger as state control plans undoubtedly are." Mr. Shanks smiled. "Isn't it amazing," he said, almost as if he were turning the thought over in his own mind, "how far afield we sometimes seek for answers we have so close at hand?"

You talked a bit more. But you remembered the men who were waiting to see Mr. Shanks. You stood up to go. You had had a glimpse of the philosophy behind the company. He had told you how he felt about insurance and what he believed an insurance company ought to be today—a private business answer to a public need.

You shook hands with the president of the company and thanked him. It had been a pleasant, enjoyable talk, there in his office. It was late in the afternoon now and most of the employees had gone home.

You took the elevator down and walked on out to the street, past the statue of John Dryden in the rotunda on the main floor. Mr. Dryden was very much in your thoughts. After all, when he started this company, it had been to help the people, the working people of America, find security they couldn't obtain in any other way. The providing of protection for the poor—security—that had been the goal back in 1875. And now, seventy-five years later, Prudential had many new forms of insurance in force, new types of coverage John Dryden had never dreamed of. Yet the changes were only on the surface, actually. The goal of President Shanks—the goal of total coverage of every family in America through private insurance—differed only in degree from the goal set by the young dreamer from Maine who had a strange idea about a new kind of insurance for America.

Security is a never-ending quest of man, and each new gain only reveals new vistas and new goals to be reached.

PRUDENTIAL CHRONOLOGY

1839   John Fairfield Dryden, who was to become the founder of the first industrial life insurance company in America, was born on August 7 in Temple Mills, Maine.

1875   On October 13 The Prudential Friendly Society was established in the basement of the National State Bank Building at 812 Broad Street, Newark, New Jersey. Allen L. Bassett was elected president and Founder Dryden secretary. The first application for insurance was received on November 10 from William R. Drake, cashier of the German Bank in Newark.

1876   Secretary Dryden sailed for a six-week trip to England on November 28 to investigate the method of conducting industrial insurance operations used by The Prudential Assurance Company, Ltd., in London.

1877   On March 15 the name of the Society was changed to The Prudential Insurance Company of America. The first office outside the city of Newark for the sale of insurance was opened in Paterson, New Jersey, on April 28.

1878   During this year The Prudential began making mortgage loans. The home office was now located in the Centennial Building, 215 Market Street.

1879   Noah F. Blanchard became president of the company on May 27.

1881   John F. Dryden was elected president on May 23, following the death of Mr. Blanchard on May 11.

1883   The Prudential moved, on April 1, to larger quarters in the Jube Building, 880 Broad Street.

1886   The Prudential began selling ordinary life insurance, with Mr. Dryden purchasing the first policy on January 19. On December 9 the first ordinary agency was created in Bay Shore, Long Island.

1888   A suggestion by President Dryden led to the formation, in January, of the Prudential Old Guard, an association of employees with five or more years of service.

1892   The company's new home office at 761 Broad Street, the Prudential Building, was occupied on May 1. Construction of the building had been started in September 1890.

1896   The famous rock with its equally famous slogan, "The Prudential Has the Strength of Gibraltar," was first used in an advertisement in *Leslie's Weekly* on August 20.

1899   Ground was broken in September for the erection of three new home office structures adjoining the Prudential Building.

1900   The Prudential observed its twenty-fifth anniversary. It was now providing its policyholders with more than $600,000,000 of insurance protection.

1909   The Prudential began business operations in Canada on February 1, in Toronto, Ontario.

1911   President John F. Dryden died on November 24.

1912   Forrest F. Dryden, son of the founder, was elected president of the company on January 8.

1914   A plan to mutualize The Prudential was announced on October 17. On December 7 policyholders voted in favor of mutualization, which became, as a practical matter, effective in 1915.

1916   The Prudential issued its first group insurance policy on August 21.

1917–18   1,729 Prudential people served their country in uniform in World War I, fifty losing their lives.

1922   On August 14 the Prudential's board of directors elected Edward D. Duffield president of the company, following the resignation of Forrest F. Dryden. Mr. Duffield had been acting president since February 15.

1923   Prudential's first mortgage loan branch office was established in Montreal on July 16.

1925   The Prudential completed fifty years of service to the insuring public. The company had more than $8,000,-000,000 of life insurance in force.

1926   Another home office structure, the Gibraltar Building, was completed and occupied on July 26.

1928   This year The Prudential issued its first group retirement contract, covering the employees of the Cleveland Public Library.

1938   On November 14 Franklin D'Olier was elected president of The Prudential to succeed Mr. Duffield, who died on September 17.

1941–45   In World War II, 6,412 Prudential men and women were in military service, in which 111 lost their lives.

1942   The United States Army took over the newly completed Washington Street Building, to house the Office of Dependency Benefits.

1943   On March 30, after the purchase from the Blanchards and others of the last remaining stock not already deposited with the company, The Prudential became a fully mutual life insurance company.

1946   Carrol M. Shanks became president of The Prudential on January 1; Franklin D'Olier, chairman of the board.

1947   The Prudential announced, on March 20, the decision to establish a western home office in Los Angeles, California, late in 1948.

1949   On December 12 the company announced that a Canadian head office would be opened in the fall of 1950 in Toronto.

1950   This year The Prudential celebrated its seventy-fifth birthday. More than 26,000,000 Americans and Canadians, owning $31,000,000,000 of insurance protection, were now Prudential policyholders. On March 30 it was announced that the company would establish a southwestern home office in Houston, Texas, in 1951.

MEMBERS OF THE PRUDENTIAL'S BOARD OF DIRECTORS
1875–1950

(The first 26 members comprised the original board of directors)

1. John F. Dryden — 1875–1911
2. Isaac Gaston — 1875–1878
3. Allen L. Bassett — 1875–1879
4. George D. G. Moore — 1875–1884
5. David A. Hayes — 1875–1875
6. William Whitty — 1875–1881
7. Noah F. Blanchard — 1875–1881
8. Leslie D. Ward, M.D. — 1875–1910
9. Elias A. Wilkinson — 1875–1881
10. Charles G. Campbell — 1875–1882, 1885–1898
11. Marcus L. Ward, Jr. — 1875–1876
12. Horace Alling — 1875–1902
13. Charles W. A. Romer — 1875–1879
14. Rev. Andrew Hopper — 1875–1876
15. George Richards — 1875–1884
16. Walter M. Conger — 1875–1875
17. Edgar B. Ward — 1875–1906
18. William R. Drake — 1875–1876
19. James M. Durand — 1875–1878
20. Benjamin Atha — 1875–1879
21. Alfred Lister — 1875–1877
22. William H. Murphy — 1875–1881
23. Aaron Carter, Jr. — 1875–1902
24. Albert O. Headley — 1875–1876
25. Henry J. Yates — 1875–1893
26. William Robotham — 1875–1887

––––

27. James G. Barnet — 1876–1877
28. A. Bishop Baldwin — 1877–1877
29. I. Smith Hyatt — 1877–1878
30. William D. Carter — 1877–1884
31. James E. Bathgate, Jr. — 1877–1877
32. John T. Leverich — 1878–1884
33. Samuel F. Blanchard — 1880–1884
34. Abner C. Keeney — 1880–1884
35. Alfred A. Reeves — 1880–1889
36. Theodore C. E. Blanchard — 1881–1916
37. John L. Roberts — 1882–1884

38. Edward S. Johnson   1883–1892
39. James Perry   1884–1893
40. Elias S. Ward   1885–1896
41. Seth A. Keeney   1887–1908
42. Frederick C. Blanchard
                         1889–1911
43. Edward Kanouse   1889–1922
44. Forrest F. Dryden   1890–1922
45. Jerome Taylor   1894–1915
46. William T. Carter   1894–1923
47. Jacob E. Ward   1897–1913
48. Anthony R. Kuser   1899–1917
49. Uzal H. McCarter   1902–1915
50. Wilbur S. Johnson   1902–1925
51. Thomas N. McCarter
                         1905–1906
52. Richard V. Lindabury
                         1906–1925
53. John K. Gore   1907–1934
54. Edward J. Ill, M.D.
                        *1907–1942
55. Isaac F. Roe   *1907–1927
56. Edwin A. Stevens   *1907–1918
57. William J. Magie   1911–1917
58. Edward Gray   1912–1929
59. Gilbert Collins   1912–1920
60. Bennet Van Syckel   1912–1921
61. Edward D. Duffield   1913–1938
62. James S. Alexander   1915–1932
63. Howard Bayne   1915–1940
64. Samuel S. Dennis   1916–1924
65. Frederic A. Boyle   1917–1929
66. M. Taylor Pyne   1917–1921
67. John A. Campbell   1917–1938
68. George M. LaMonte
                        *1918–1927
69. Chellis A. Austin   1920–1929
70. David F. Houston   1921–1927
71. Andrew F. West   1922–1926
72. Felix Fuld   1923–1929
73. Henry G. Parker   1923–

74. Hendon Chubb   1923–
75. S. Parker Gilbert   1924–1926
76. Albert C. Wall   1925–1945
77. Roy E. Tomlinson   1925–
78. Franklin D'Olier   1926–
79. George W. Munsick
                         1926–1935
80. William E. Green   *1927–1930
81. John T. Dorrance   1927–1930
82. Edward K. Mills   *1928–1938
83. Alfred Hurrell   1929–1938
84. Chester I. Barnard   1929–
85. W. Palen Conway   1930–1947
86. Arthur D. Forst   *1930–1934
87. Douglas G. Thomson
                         1930–1936
88. J. Henry Bacheller   1932–1939
89. Jackson E. Reynolds
                         1932–1943
90. Edward L. Katzenbach
                        *1934–1934
91. Aubrey H. Elder   1934–
92. A. Harry Moore   *1935–
93. Harold W. Dodds   1935–
94. John A. Hartford   1937–
95. Charles P. Messick
                        *1938–1948
96. Josiah Stryker   1938–
97. Charles B. Bradley   1938–
98. Walter Kidde   1939–1943
99. Horace K. Corbin   1940–
100. Franklin Conklin, Jr.
                         1940–
101. Thomas G. Walker   *1942–1949
102. Arthur W. Page   1943–
103. Edward W. Sprague, M.D.
                         1943–
104. Carrol M. Shanks   1945–
105. Alexander C. Nagle 1947–
106. Charles P. Hutchinson
                        *1948–1950

*Appointed state director by Chancellor of New Jersey.

PRESIDENTS—1875–1950

1. Allen L. Bassett   1875–1879
2. Noah F. Blanchard   1879–1881
3. John F. Dryden   1881–1911
4. Forrest F. Dryden   1912–1922

5. Edward D. Duffield   1922–1938
6. Franklin D'Olier   1938–1946
7. Carrol M. Shanks   1946–

SENIOR VICE-PRESIDENTS—1875–1950

1. Noah F. Blanchard   1875–1879
2. William H. Murphy   1879–1881
3. Henry J. Yates   1882–1883
4. Leslie D. Ward, M.D.
                          1884–1910
5. Forrest F. Dryden   1911–1912
6. John K. Gore   1912–1934
7. Wilbur S. Johnson   1917–1925
8. Edward Gray   1917–1929
9. Edward D. Duffield   1917–1922
10. Edward Kanouse   1918–1922
11. Frederic A. Boyle   1918–1929
12. George W. Munsick   1924–1935
13. Alfred Hurrell   1924–1938
14. Willard I. Hamilton   1924–1937
15. John W. Stedman   1924–1945
16. Fred W. Tasney   1924–1925
17. Frederick H. Johnston
                          1924–1932
18. Archibald M. Woodruff
                          1924–1935
19. Franklin D'Olier   1926–1938
20. Robert H. Bradley   1929–1947
21. James F. Little   1934–1938

22. Henry B. Sutphen   1934–1944
23. Lester E. Wurfel   1935–1937
24. Roger R. Rogers   1937–1944
25. Valentine Howell   1938–
26. George H. Chace   1938–1948
27. Robert M. Green   1938–
28. Carrol M. Shanks   1939–1945
29. F. Bruce Gerhard   1942–
30. Caleb Stone   1943–
31. Paul Bestor   1944–1947
32. George E. Potter   1944–
33. Harold M. Stewart   1944–
34. Edmund B. Whittaker
                          1946–
35. Orville E. Beal   1947–
36. Sayre MacLeod   1947–
37. Pearce Shepherd   1947–
38. Louis R. Menagh, Jr.
                          1947–
39. Frederick H. Groel   1947–
40. Harry J. Volk   1947–
41. Charles Fleetwood   1947–
42. James E. Rutherford
                          1949–

ACTUARIES—1875–1950

1. John E. Clark   1875–1877
2. David P. Fackler   1877–1883
3. John B. Lunger   1889–1897
4. John K. Gore   1897–1934

5. Frederick H. Johnston
                          1924–1932
6. James F. Little   1934–1938
7. Valentine Howell   1938–

SECRETARIES—1875–1950

1. John F. Dryden	1875–1881	5. Willard I. Hamilton	1912–1930
2. Edward S. Johnson	1882–1890	6. William W. Van Nalts	
3. Forrest F. Dryden	1890–1903		1931–1942
4. Edward Gray	1903–1912	7. Frederick H. Groel	1941–

TREASURERS—1875–1950

1. Isaac Gaston	1875–1878	7. Robert M. Green	1934–1937
2. Henry J. Yates	1878–1893	8. Clifford W. Brown	1937–1945
3. Horace Alling	1894–1902	9. H. Woodruff Tatlock	
4. Edward Kanouse	1902–1918		1946–1947
5. Frederic A. Boyle	1918–1926	10. Robert M. Green	1947–1949
6. Robert H. Bradley	1926–1933	11. H. Woodruff Tatlock	1949–

GENERAL COUNSELS

1. Cortlandt Parker	1875–1879	5. Alfred Hurrell	1925–1938
2. Edgar B. Ward	1880–1906	6. Charles B. Bradley	1938–1944
3. Jacob E. Ward	1905–1906	7. Donald Cruse	1945–1948
4. Richard V. Lindabury	1906–1925	8. Sylvester C. Smith, Jr.	1948–

PRUDENTIAL OLD GUARD MEMBERSHIP—JULY 1, 1950

The Prudential Old Guard was established on January 12, 1888. In the words of President John F. Dryden, of whose suggestion it was born, it is "... an Association based on long, continuous, and honorable service, having behind it a significance of positive value; to every member a bond of good-fellowship and good-will ..."

On July 1, 1950, a total of 28,508 Prudential men and women in the field and home offices and in retirement had been with the company from five to fifty years. From its inception to July the Prudential Old Guard had had 72,153 members.

YEARS OF SERVICE	5	10	15	20	25	30	35	40	45	50	Totals
CLASS	A	B	C	D	E	F	G	H	I	J	
District Agencies Field	3,108	3,225	3,747	3,507	1,809	604	194	47	6	—	16,247
Ordinary Agencies Field	259	143	129	83	55	18	9	3	—	—	699
Group Field	11	—	1	4	—	—	—	—	—	—	16
Mortgage Loan Field	133	186	274	23	2	—	1	2	—	—	621
Other Field	32	76	139	155	108	35	20	6	—	—	571
Home Offices	1,197	1,054	1,523	1,760	682	279	161	174	37	—	6,867
Retired	32	109	319	560	906	601	540	317	85	18	3,487
Grand Totals	4,772	4,793	6,132	6,092	3,562	1,537	925	549	128	18	28,508

EXPANSION OF P

1875

DENTIAL SERVICE

950

ONTARIO
1909

QUEBEC
1909

NEW BRUNSWICK
1909

NOVA SCOTI
1909

MAINE
1900

N
88

WISC
1887

MICH
1888

VT
1898

NH
1897

MASS. 1894

NEW YORK
1879

CONN
1894

R.I.
1894

IOWA
1893

PENN
1879

NEW JERSEY 1875

ILLINOIS
1886

IND.
1887

OHIO
1885

W.VA
1898

D.C.
1884

DELAWARE 1885

MARYLAND 1883

MISSOURI
1886

KENTUCKY
1887

VIRGINIA
1900

N. CAROLINA
1897
WITHDREW 1899
RE-ENTERED
1901

TENNESSEE
1897

S. CAROLINA
1897

ARK.
1900
WITHDREW
1907
RE-ENTERED
1908

MISS
1900
WITHDREW
1917
RE-ENTERED
1918

ALA.
1897

GEORGIA
1897

LA.
1897

FLA
1898

NEWARK HOME OFFICE

WESTERN HOME OFFICE

SOUTHWESTERN HOME OFFI

CANADIAN HEAD OFFICE

Index

Absentee voting lists, 266
"Acme Products Company," 220–21
Actuarial Department, 105–6, 311–12
Actuarial tables, revision of, 77–78
Actuaries, Prudential, 351
Advertisements, Aetna Life, 31–32
Advertising, Prudential, 119–20, 230, 313
Advisory Board, Western, 320
"Aerosol" project, 265
Aetna Life Insurance Company, 30–32; Dryden advertisements for, 31–32
Agencies, district, 280–81; over-all program for, 286
Agents, 276–83; commissions, 53, 92; duties, 278, 281; pioneer work of, 278; place in Prudential organization, 279; qualifications of, 82; recruiting of, 91; routine, 281; service in World War II, 264; training, 52–53, 81, 286–88; unionization, 283
"Alarm clock" claim, 243–44
Alexander, Henry, 270
Alling, Horace, 40, 45, 65

Alling Brothers, 41
All-purpose program, Prudential's, 305
American College of Life Underwriters, 286
American Federation of Labor, 283
American Legion, founding of, 249
American Telephone and Telegraph Company, Prudential investment in, 300
American Tobacco Company, 145
Anniversaries, Prudential: twenty-fifth, 346; fiftieth, 196–98, 347; seventy-fifth, 306–7, 347
Annuities, group, 224
Ardmore, Oklahoma, 172
Armstrong, William (New York State Senator), 130
Armstrong Investigation, 130–40, 155, 159; effects of Dryden testimony at, 141; results of, 140
Arnold, General H. H., 269
Arsenic Ring, Philadelphia, 234
Association group insurance, 239
Association of Life Insurance Presidents, 194
Astor House, New York, 88, 89

Atha, Benjamin, 41
Atha Steel Company, 41
Atwater and Carter, 4

Babbitt, George, 50, 80; in charge
of Jersey City office, 80
Baby insurance, 84
Bank holiday (1933), 208
Bassett, Captain Allen, 11, 13, 17,
36, 45, 49, 60, 61, 62, 65, 66;
failure as organizer, 38, 86;
with Metropolitan Life, 93; or-
ganization of Paterson Office
by, 79–80; president of Pruden-
tial Friendly Society, 46; re-
moval from presidency, 87
Bates, Charles Austin, 118–19
Bay Shore, Long Island, 346
Beal, Orville E., 282
Bedford, Ohio, 29, 30
Belmont Heights, Brooklyn, 32
Benefit societies, employees', 222–
23
Benefits paid, total (to end of
1949), 244
Berlin, N.H., 172
Bernard, Freddie, 21–22
Bernardsville, N.J., 150
Bestor, Paul, 293
"Big Inch" pipe line, 303
Binghamton, N.Y., 172
Black Friday, 186, 207
Blake, Christopher, 50, 80
Blanchard, Leon, 149, 150, 254
Blanchard, Milton E., 254
Blanchard, Noah, 38, 45, 65, 86,
87, 149, 169; advocacy of in-
dustrial insurance, 41; death,
94; election to presidency of
Prudential, 88; policy of econ-
omy, 93
Blanchard Brothers and Lane, 6
Blanchard family claims against
Prudential, 149–50, 163, 169,
254–56
Blanchard Tannery, 54

Board of directors, first Pruden-
tial, 45; functions of, 260–61;
members of, 349–50
Bond department, Prudential,
252, 297
Bonds, Prudential investments in,
105, 296–303
Boston police strike, 185
Bound Brook, N.J., 144
Bowron, Fletcher L. (mayor of
of Los Angeles), 324
Bradley, Charles B., 195, 252;
association with D'Olier, 251;
work for mutualization, 255
Bradshaw, Colonel R. R., 267
Bradstreet and Sons, J. M., 49
Branch expansion, 79–80, 170–
73, 183
Branch office, first Prudential,
79
Broad Street, Newark, 2, 76, 112
148, 230
Broadway, New York, 88
Brooklyn, New York, 32
Brooklyn Bridge, 99
Brown, G. H., 80
Bruen Street, Newark, 6
Buck, Samuel L., 49
Buffalo, N.Y., 172
Buildings: Gibraltar Building,
347; Jube Building, Newark,
101, 111; Newark head office,
112; Main Building, 174, 178;
North Building, 174, 178;
Northwest Building, 174;
Washington Street Building,
267; West Building, 174; West-
ern home office, 321
Bullock's, Inc., 320
Burials, pauper, 14
Burlington, N.J., 247
Burlington Mills, 300
Burrage, Robert, 147
Butler, Luke, 217–18
Buttle, T. W., 80

Caledonia Park, Newark, 113

California Club, 320

Camden office, Prudential's, 80

Campbell, Charles, 46, 65

Canada, Prudential expansion in, 173, 317, 327–28

Canadian head office, 326–27; training of personnel for, 327–28

Capital surplus, 301–2

Capitalization, increase in, 125–26

Capone, Al, 185

Carter, Aaron, Jr., 41, 46, 86, 114

Carter, William D., 86

Case histories, mortgage-loan, 210–12, 216, 217, 219

Cashier's department, 105

Celler, Representative Emanuel, 303

Celler Committee, 303–5

Centennial Building, Newark, 345

"Centerville, U.S.A.," 220–21

Chandler, Norman (publisher of Los Angeles *Times*), 320

Chapel Street, New Haven, 25, 26

Chartered Life Underwriter degree (C.L.U.), 286

Chicago, Ill., 171

Chicago River, 177

Child mortality, 14

Chillicothe, Ohio, 172

Choate, Joseph H., 144

Chronology, Prudential, 345–48

Chubb, Hendon, 263

Cincinnati, Ohio, 292–93

"Claim Adviser, Floor Walker," 182

Claim department, effect of World War II on, 238–39, 242–43

Claim representatives, 239–40

Claims, 232–45; disability, 243; disaster, 176–77, 237–38; highest paid (to 1903), 149; payment by agents, 228; philosophy of, 245; problems of payment of, 181–83, 235; World War II, 238–39

Clark, Alvah, 143

Clark, Professor John E., 42, 47, 77; bill for services, 44, 47; errors in actuarial tables of, 73; first Prudential actuary, 47; recommendations for industrial insurance, 43

Cleveland, Grover, 99

Cleveland, Ohio, 30

Cleveland Public Library, 347

Colgate, Austen (Prudential stockholders' trustee), 168

Collard, Brice, 91

College of Physicians and Surgeons, New York, 8

Collins, John F., 114; first superintendent, Philadelphia office, 88; mediation in struggle with Metropolitan Life, 97–98

Columbus, Ohio, 31

Colyer and Company, 55

Commissions, agents', 53, 81, 92; upward revision of, 82

Comptroller's department, Prudential, 313

Concessions, to policyholders, 122–25, 150, 163, 168

Conger, Walter, 46

Congress Street, Newark, 6

Consolidated Gas Company, 131

Contributory plan, group insurance, 223

Cooke and Company, Jay, 34

Coolidge, Calvin, 185

Corbin, Horace K. (president of Fidelity Union Trust Company), 268

Correspondents, mortgage-loan, 205–6, 212

Court of Chancery, N.J., 150

Court of Errors and Appeals, N.J., 144, 150, 163, 165

Court Street, Newark, 58
Creditors life insurance, 226
Crimes, insurance, 232–35

Daily Advertiser, Newark, 1–5
Dart, Justin W. (president of Rexall Drugs, Inc.), 320
Dawes, Charles G., 196
Death rate, growth of, 14
Debit policy department, 312
Debits, 81–82
Decentralization, 316–331; advantages of, 319; effect on personnel, 319, 321–23, 330; growing need for, 317; new function of Newark head office in, 330; plans for, further, 329; problems of, 322–23
Delmonico's, New York, 114, 115
Depression, industrial, 3–4, 76, 207–9; farming, 212–13
Detroit, Mich., 171
Dickinson, Jonathan (first president of Princeton University), 187
Digannard, William H., 57
"Direct placement" financing, 299
Disability clauses, 242
Disability insurance, 242–44
Disappearance cases, 240–42
Disaster claims, 176–77, 237–38
District of Columbia office, Prudential, 148
Dividends, 169
D'Olier, Franklin, 213, 227, 246–73; ability as organizer, 266–70; business training, 248; character as executive, 246–47, 250–51; civilian defense work, 367–68; concept of organization, 250; concept of Prudential organization, 250; contribution to Prudential's development, 252; elected president of Prudential, 253; first commander of American Legion, 249; re-

organization of group insurance department, 227; retirement from Prudential presidency, 273; work in World War I, 248–49; World War II assignments, 264–72
D'Olier and Company, William, 247
"Dollar Guide," the, 287
Donovan, Colonel William, 249
Douglas, Stephen, 24
Douglas, William O. (Justice United States Supreme Court). 274
Down Neck, 5, 7
Drake, William R., 46; first policyholder of Prudential, 50
Drake and Cook, 51
Drought, 216
Dryden, Albion, 21
Dryden, Caroline, 20, 23
Dryden, Cynthia Fairchild, 26–29, 31, 33, 34–35, 118, 133, 150
Dryden, Elizabeth, 18–22
Dryden, Forrest Fairchild, 31, 34, 96, 113, 147, 297; association with Lindabury, 161–62; character as executive, 162; elected president of Prudential, 157; letter to field staff, 169; resigned from presidency, 189; work for mutualization, 163–65
Dryden, Hannah, 19, 23, 24, 29
Dryden, John, 18–22
Dryden, John Fairfield, 19, 45, 86, 197, 202, 222, 236, 240, 246, 260, 277, 283, 296–97, 306, 311, 321, 330, 337; with Aetna Life, 30–32; at Armstrong investigation, 132–40; childhood, 21–22; as corporation director, 117–18; country estate of, 150–51; death, 155; education, 23, 25–29; elected president of Prudential, 95; elected to United States Senate,

126; European trip (1895), 118; factory rallies held by, 54–55; first meeting with Dr. Ward, 10–15; lobbying activities, 137–38; marriage, 29; move to New York, 32; move to Newark, 35; move to Ohio, 29–32; popular recognition of abilities, 101–2; presidential elector, 126; recommendations for Prudential's reorganization, 74; report on trip to England, 67–74; speech on Panama Canal, 148; statement of Prudential aims, 230–31; statement on Prudential Fidelity merger, 139–40; training in insurance, 30; trip to England, 61; as United States senator, 148; work as Prudential secretary, 45

Dryden, Mary Elizabeth, 20, 23
Dryden, Susan, 34, 96
Dryden and Huston, insurance agents, 32
Duffield, Edward D., 162, 175, 202, 246, 251; acting president Princeton University, 196; concept of functions of insurance, 192; death, 253; fight against depression, 213; organizer of Prudential law department, 147; personality, 189–90; personalized approach to staff, 189–90; in politics, 187, 196; as president of Prudential, 188–99; relations with Lindabury, 188; speech at fiftieth anniversary of Prudential celebration, 198–99

Duffield, Henry Green, 187
Duffield, Professor John Thomas, 187
Duncker's Celebrated Salve, 6
Durand, James, 46
Dutcher, General Agent, 284

East River, New York, 176
Edge, Walter E. (governor of New Jersey), 197, 266
Edwards, LeRoy M. (vice-president of Pacific Lighting Corporation), 320
Egenolf, Peter, 113
Eight eighty (880) Broad Street, Newark, 101, 103, 104, 109, 346
Eight twelve (812) Broad Street, Newark, 53, 55
Eighth Ward, Newark, 85
Eisenhower, General Dwight, 270
Elizabeth office, Prudential, 75, 80
Ellison Street, Paterson, 79
Elmira, N.Y., 172
Employee benefits program, 339–40
Employee suggestion system, 310–11
Equitable Life Assurance Society, 130, 223
Expansion, industrial, 100; after World War II, 291

Fairchild, Mrs. Abigail, 25–26
Fairchild, Eliza, 26
Fairmont, Minn., 273
Farm loans, Prudential, 212–18
Farm mortgage branch, Prudential, 175
Farm rehabilitation, 215
Farmington, Me., 18
Fidelity-Prudential merger, proposed, 157–61
Fidelity scheme, 127–29; Dryden's explanation of, 139–40
Fidelity Trust Company of Newark, 117, 127; attempt to control Prudential, 157–61; injunction against Prudential, 128; participation in mutualization, 166–69; proposed proxy committee, 157

Fidelity Union Trust Company, 268

Field agencies, growth of, 282–83

Field training division, 287

Fifth Ward, Newark, 5

First National Bank, Paterson, 79

First Presbyterian Church, Newark, 48

Fiske, Haley (president Metropolitan Life), 156, 197

Fleetwood, Charles, 294, 329; work for housing loans, 294

Florham Park, 151

Ford, Henry, 172, 183

Foreclosures, mortgage home loan, 206, 213–14

Fort, John Franklin (governor of New Jersey), 165

Fort Hamilton, 2

Fort Sumter, 24

Fort Wayne, Ind., 171

Frauds, insurance, 240–42

Frelinghuysen, Frederick (president of Mutual Benefit Life Insurance Company), 156

"Friendly" societies, 28

Frisbee, Superintendent L. W., 98

Gallitzin, Pa., 172

Gary, Judge Elbert, 156

Gas and oil industry, 302–3

Gaston, George H. R., 57, 63–65, 72, 156; first Prudential office boy, 49; move to Metropolitan Life, 91; vice-president of Metropolitan Life, 105

Gaston, Isaac, 45, 63

General counsels, Prudential, 352

George Washington Bridge, 301

Gerhard, F. Bruce, 312; co-ordinator of home office activities, 307–8

German Bank, Newark, 345

Gibraltar, 120

Giese, Carl August, 56, 57, 80

Gladstone, William E. (Prime Minister of Great Britain), 27, 32

Glens Falls, N.Y., 172

Globe Mutual Life Insurance Company, 32

Gold Rush, California, 22

Goodman, H. H., 33

Goodman Ring, The, 235

Gore, John, 133, 147, 311; card sorter invented by, 308; new policies introduced by, 190–91; organization of group insurance by, 175

Grasshopper plague, 4

Green, Robert M., 328

Griggs, John W. (governor of New Jersey), 165

Groel, Frederick H., 259

Group annuities, 224

Group creditors life insurance, 226

Group insurance, 175–76, 192, 220–29; advantages of, 222; association, 229; contributory plan, 223; growth of, 227–28; need for, 223–25; regional headquarters for, 228; trade unions' effect on, 228–29; transfer of coverage, 340–41

Group insurance department, reorganization of, 227–28

Group retirement contract, first, 347

Grubb, General, 8

Guardian, Paterson, 86

Guild House of Prayer, 5

Guilds, craft, 28

Gummere, William S. (Chief Justice of New Jersey Supreme Court), 156

Hahne, Albert, 284

Hahne, August, 284

Hahne, Richard, 284

Hahne and Company, 284
Halifax explosion, 177
Hall, Rev. Edward Wheeler, 185
Harben, Henry (president of British Prudential), 72, 118; aid to American Prudential, 67–68
Hardin, John (president Mutual Benefit Life), 150, 197
Harding, Warren G., 183
Hatton Quartet, 114
Havana Harbor, 176
Hawaii, Prudential in, 148, 228, 316, 318, 320
Hayes, David, 45
Haynes, Joseph (mayor of Newark), 113
Headley, Albert, 46
Hegeman, John (vice-president of Metropolitan Life), 92, 97
Hell Gate, 176
Heppenheimer, Ernest C. (president of Colonial Life), 197
Hibben, Dr. John Grier (president of Princeton), 196, 197
Hillery Committee report, 159–160
Hoadley's, New Haven, 25
Hoffman, Frederick, 147
Holden, Mass., 19
Holland Tunnel, 301
Home Life Insurance Company, 32
Home office building, 112
Home office building and plant department, 314
Home office organization (1950), 306–14
Hopper, Rev. Andrew, 46
Hospitalization plans, 340
Hotchkiss, William H., 162
Housing shortage, postwar, 293–95
Houston, Texas, 329
Howell, Valentine, 227, 311; aid to D'Olier in tax fight, 259; in

charge of decentralization program, 328; installations of punched-card machines, 308–9
Hudson County, N.J., 80
Hughes, Charles Evans, 131–40
Hurrell, Alfred, 194, 255; influence on Prudential, 195

Immigration, 3, 203
Industrial exhibit, Newark, 35
Industrial Exposition Building, Newark, 3
Industrial insurance, 12, 32–33, 40, 100; advantages, 37; cost of, 136–37; in England, 12, 15, 27; opposition to, 80–81; problems, 43
Industrialism, rise of, 100
Industry, expansion of, 100; after World War II, 291, 300–3
Influenza epidemic, 179–83; in Philadelphia, 181
Inland Steel case, 228
Installment buying, 226
Insurance, creditors life, 226; disability, 243–44; group, 220–29 (See also Group Insurance); industrial, 136–37 (See also Industrial Insurance); ordinary, 283–88 (See also Ordinary Insurance); social aspects of, 192
Insurance companies. See Aetna Life Insurance Company; Equitable Life Assurance Society; Home Life Insurance Company; Manhattan Life Insurance Company; Metropolitan Life Insurance Company; Mutual Benefit Life Insurance Company; Mutual Life Insurance Company of New York; New York Life Insurance Company; Penn Mutual Life Insurance Company; Prudential Assurance Company of London; Prudential Friendly Society;

Prudential Insurance Company of America; Republic Life of Chicago; Republic Life Assurance and Trust Company; Travelers Insurance Company

Insurance company, functions of, 200, 305; investment policy of, 201–2; social responsibility of, 202–3; taxation of, 257–60

Insurance coverage, growth of, 276, 287; response to changing conditions, 226–27

Insurance Journal, 124

Insurance Monitor, 32, 123

Insurance Times, 32

International Airport, New York, 301

International Minerals and Chemical Corporation, 300

International Union of Life Insurance Agents, 283

Investigation of insurance business, Federal government, 303–5; New York, 130–40; TNEC, 261–63

Investment funds, postwar demand for, 291, 300–3

Investment policy, Prudential, 105, 200–2

Investments, purpose of, 201

Ironbound, 5

Izon, Mrs. Hannah, 57

Jaques, Albert F., 266

Jersey City office, Prudential, 80

John Hancock Mutual Life, 88

Johnson, Wilbur, 147, 198

Johnson, William M., 165

Jube Building, Newark, 101, 111, 346

Judd, Samuel E., 30–31

Kellner, William H., 284

Kemball, C. G. (British Acting Consul General), 324

Knapp, Joseph F. (president of Metropolitan Life), 89–98

LaGuardia, Mayor Fiorello, 268

Lacy, Inc., R., 303

Lafayette Street, Newark, 7

Lakeland, Fla., 211

Lane, Merritt, 165

Lapsed policies, 85, 135

Law department, 105, 147, 175, 194, 312–13

Lease-option plan, mortgage loan, 214

Lee Wilson plantation, 296

Leonard, Harry, 181

Leslie's Weekly, 346

Letter to a future leader, Shanks, 324

Leverich, John T., 86

Levis, Que., 173

Liberty loans, 179

Life insurance, boom in, 130

Life Insurance Association of America, 194

Life-expectancy tables, 42

Lincoln, Abraham, 24

Lincoln Avenue, Newark, 35

Lincoln Tunnel, 301

Lindabury, Richard V., 127–28; 142–54, 156, 198, 202, 246, 251; appointed Prudential general counsel, 146–47; at Armstrong investigation, 132, 133; character, 144, 146; as corporation lawyer, 144; death, 193; education, 143; opposition to Fidelity, 157–61; "prime minister of Prudential," 162; selection of Duffield for Prudential, 188; work for mutualization, 153–55, 162–69

Lindabury, Depue & Faulks, 127, 145

Lindbergh, Colonel Charles A., 185

Lister, Alfred, 41, 46

Little, James F., 175, 311; revision of ordinary policy rates, 191; work for group insurance, 225–26

"Little Inch" pipe line, 303

Liverpool, England, 60, 67

Livery stables, 204

Loans, construction, 294–95; farm, 212–18; industrial, 296; mortgage, 203–7, 291–95; policy, 208

London, England, 67

Lone Star Gas Company, 302

Longevity service, Prudential, 175

Los Angeles regional office, 316–25

Love, Spencer, 300

Lunchtime rallies, 54–55

Lunger, John B., 114, 156, 283; proposals for ordinary insurance, 106–8; vice-president of Equitable Life, 156

Lyle, J. V. N., 80

Machines, increasing use of, 109–10, 308–9

MacLeod, Sayre, 285

Maclure, David, 35, 50

Madison, N.J., 8

Madison, Wis., 173

Magie, William J. (Chancellor of New Jersey), 164

Mailing department, 105, 175

Main Street, Paterson, 79

Maine Cough Cure, 6

Managers, district, 280

Manchester, N.H., 4

Manhattan Life Insurance Company, 33

Manning, John E. (Collector of Internal Revenue), 268

Maps, for military use, 265

Marine Barracks, Quantico, 179

Market Street, Newark, 76, 94

Marshall and Company, 55

Mass production, age of, 100

Massachusetts Bay Colony, 18

Matterhorn, The, 120

McCahey, Lieutenant John, U.S.-M.C., 179

McCarter, Robert H., 150, 188

McCarter, Thomas N. (president of Public Service Corporation), 139, 156

McCarter, Uzal H. (president of Fidelity Trust), 139, 156

McGill, Daniel, 4

Mechanic Street, Newark, 36

Medical department, Prudential, 310

Medical insurance plans, private, 34

Medicines, patent, 6

Menagh, Louis R., Jr., 259, 313

Metropolitan Life Insurance Company, 89–98; change to industrial insurance, 90; importation of British agents, 91; rivalry with Prudential, 90–94

Mexican Insurance Department, 191

Middletown, Conn., 172

Military service, Prudential employees, 347

Million-dollar life policy, first, 284

Mills, Mrs. James, 185

Milton, Ky., 174

Missouri River, 72

"Modified 5" policy, 190

"Modified 3" policy, 191

Monopoly, popular opposition to, 261–62

Montgomery, Ward and Company, 223

Montreal, Que., 173; first mortgage loan branch office in, 347

Moore, George DeGraw, 37–38, 45, 60, 65; candidate for Prudential presidency, 95

Mory's, New Haven, 25

Morgan, J. Pierpont, 156

Morgan and Company, J. P., 270

Morgenthau, Henry, Jr. (Secretary of the Treasury), 268
Morristown, N.J., 8
Mortality, child, 14
Mortgage loan department, Prudential, 206-7, 291-94; first branch office, 347; first inspector, 204; service division, 206-7
Mortgage loans, 203-7; 209-11; Canadian offices for, 292; correspondents, 205-6, 212; foreclosures, 206, 213-14; lease-option plan, 214; loans in force, 206, 208-9; postwar expansion of, 292-94; regional offices for, 292
Mosque Theatre, Newark, 197
Moss, Michael, 79
Mulloy, Mike, 232-35, 240
Munsick, George W., 281
Murder, Inc., 235
Murphy, Franklin (governor of New Jersey), 95, 156
Murphy, William, 46, 65, 86, 87; candidate for Prudential presidency, 95
Mutual Benefit Life Insurance Company, 12, 197
Mutual Life Insurance Company of New York, 33
Mutualization, of Prudential, 153-55, 159; achievement of, 162-69; completion of, 254-57; results of, 169; special legislation for, 256; stockholders' opposition to, 165-66

National City Bank of New York, 226
National Federation of Insurance Agents' Council, 283
National Labor Board, 228
National Labor Relations Act, 282
National State Bank, 36, 45, 53
National War Fund Campaign, 106

New Haven, Conn., 25, 133
New York City Hall, 131
New York Life Insurance Company, 33
New York office, Prudential, 88
New York State Assembly, 129
New York State Insurance Department, 194, 223
New York State Senate, 129
Newark, N.J., 1-5, 67: as industrial center, 5-6, 35; effects of depression on, 4-5
Newark Academy, 8
Newark and New York Railroad, 6, 57
Newark Board of Commissioners, 260
Newark Board of Trade, 45
Newark Gas Light Company, 5
Newark Industrial Exhibit, 35
Newtown, Conn., 25
Ninth Street, New York, 88
Northern Pacific Railroad, 34

Odd Fellows Hall, Paterson, 79
Office administration department, Prudential, 307-8
Office of Dependency Benefits, 267
Offices, district, 279-81, 292-93; early equipment of, 280; regional, first, 319
Offices, Prudential's earliest, See Camden, N.J.; Elizabeth, N.J.; New York, N.Y.; Paterson, N.J.; Trenton, N.J.
Ogden, Utah, 172
Ohio River, 174
Ohio Valley regional office, 292-93
Oil Drilling, Inc., 302
Oil industry, loans to, 302-3; See also Gas and Oil Industry
Ordinary insurance, Prudential, 106-8; first agency, 346; first large policies, 284; growth of,

283–85; opposition to, 106–7; reorganization of department, 285–88

Ordinary policy department, 312

Pacific Lighting Corporation, 320
Panama Canal, 148
Pan-American Exposition, 149
Panic, financial (1873), 34
Panola County, Texas, 302
Paris Exposition (1900), 148
Passaic River, 5
Paterson, first Prudential branch in, 75, 79
Paterson First National Bank, 79
Patterson, Robert (Secretary of War), 272
Pauper burials, 14
Payette, Idaho, 273
Peapack, N.J., 142
Penn Mutual Life Insurance Company, 49
Pennsylvania Railroad, 6
Pension funds, 341–42
Pensions, collective bargaining for, 228
Pentagon Building, 269
Perkins, George, 156
Perrara, Colonel Guido, 270
Perry, James, 9, 41
Pershing, General John J., 249
Personnel division, Prudential, 309
Personnel research, 309
Personnel transfer, to western home office, 322–23
Phelps, Rev. S. D., 29
Philadelphia branch, Prudential, 86, 88
Philosophy of insurance, 286
Phosphate mines, Florida, 300
Pipe lines, gas, 303
Pitney, J. O. H., 187
Pittsburgh riots (1877), 76
Police strike, Boston, 185
Policies, children's, 78, 124; lapsed, 85, 135; "Modified 5,"

190; "Modified 3," 191; new types of, 123–24; revisions in wording of, 123
Policy loans, 208
Policy No. 1,000,000, 98
Port of New York Authority, 301
Post, George (Architect for Prudential home office), 112
Postwar problems, 290–305
Potter, George E., 268, 313
Premium rates, basis for, 201; on children, 78
Premiums, collection of, 281
Presidents, Prudential, 351
Princeton University, 8, 147, 187, 248
Prudential Assurance Company of London, 15, 27, 37, 52, 59, 90; assistance to American Prudential, 67–74; bookkeeping system, 69; differences from American Prudential, 69; forms used by, 70; organization of, 69; success of, 71
Prudential Athletic Association, 309
Prudential Bulletin, 175
Prudential Friendly Society, 37, 42, 90, 240, 276, 277; employee training, 52–53; first advertising, 51; first board of directors, 45; first office, 48; first officers, 46; first policy issued, 50; office equipment, 48–49; organization of, 42–45; progress, 56–59; reorganization of, 73–75; salaries paid by, 49–50
Prudential Insurance Company of America, 35, 75; agencies, district, 280; all-purpose program, 305; awards won by, 148–49; bond department, 252; branch expansion, 79–80, 170–73, 183; capital increase, 125; claims paid in 1949, 236; commissions paid by, 81–82; community

service, 171–74; decentralization, 316–31; departmental expansion, 105, 174–75; disability insurance added, 243; early growth, 80; employee benefits program, 339–40; employees in World War II, 264; expansion to other states, 88–89, 109, 148, 170; farm loans by, 212–218; fiftieth anniversary, 196–98; financial administration of, 313; first branch office, 79–80; first claim paid, 236; first investments, 203; first million-dollar policy, 284; foundation, principle of, 115; group insurance added, 223–24; highest claim paid, 149; home office expansion, 174–76; home office organization in 1950, 306–15; investment policy, 201–2; investment program, 105, 291–305; Liberty Loan investments, 179; mortgage loans, 203–6, 291; mutualization, 153–55, 162–69, 254–57; new rates, 78; offices, district, 279–81; ordinary insurance added, 106–8; personnel problems, 82–84; personnel research, 309; policies, new types, 123–24, 190–91; policy no. 1,000,000, 98; reconstruction policy, 207; research section, 175; rivalry with Metropolitan Life, 89–98; seventy-fifth anniversary, 307; share of insurance business, 285; symbol chosen for, 119–21; tax problems, 257–60; training program, 286–88; women admitted to staff, 110; World War I, effects of, 178–79; World War II assignments, 264–72

Prudential Old Guard, 111, 339; membership (July 1, 1950), 353

"Prudential Planned Program, The," 287–88
Prudential Weekly Record, 175
Prudential-Fidelity merger plan, 127–28, 138; Dryden's explanation of, 139–40; injunction against, 129
Public Service Corporation of New Jersey, 118
Public utilities, financing of, 298
Pueblo, Colo., 172, 205
Pueblo Opera House, 205
Punched-card equipment, 307–8
Pyne, Moses, 156

Quantico, Va., 179

Railroad Avenue, Newark, 6
Rallies, lunchtime, 54–55
Recession, industrial (1874), 2–5
Recreation program, employees', 309
Red Cross, American, 178
Red Wing, Minn., 172
Regina, Sask., 173
Regional office, first, 319; Ohio Valley, 292–93
Register, Newark, 51
Regular Army retirement board, 243
Rehabilitation, farm, 215
Reilly, Edward A., 284
Remedies, patented, 3
Remington, Mortimer, 119
Republic Life of Chicago, 88
Republic Life Assurance and Trust Company, 45
Republican party, 24
Research, medical, 310; personnel, 309
Research section, Prudential, 175
Retirement plans, 340
Rexall Drugs, Inc., 320
Richards, George, 41, 46, 65
Riots, bread (1877), 76
Rippel, Julius S., 166, 197

Ritz Hotel, London, 151
Robotham, William, 38, 46, 65, 86, 87
Rock of Gibraltar, 120, 284, 324
Rocky Mountains, 120
Rogers, R. R., 213, 262; leader in Prudential's depression fight, 213
Romer, Charles, 46, 65, 86
Roosevelt, Franklin D., 208, 262, 270
Roosevelt, Theodore, 148, 156
Roosevelt, Colonel Theodore, Jr., 249
Root, Clark, Buckner, and Ballantine, 252, 274
Ross, Charley, 3

Saint John, N.B., 173
St. Louis, Mo., 171
St. Louis office, Prudential, 109
St. Valentine's Day massacre, 185
Sales material, prepared, 287–88
Salt Lake City, Utah, 171
Salvage service, World War I, 248
Salvation Army, 178
San Francisco fire and earthquake, 177
San Jose, Calif., 173
Sanford's Healing Lung Balsam, 6
Schlumberger Well Surveying Corporation, 302
Schooley's Mountain, 96
Scott, General Winfield, 113
Secretaries, Prudential, 352
Securities and Exchange Commission, 262
Security investments, 299–300
Security-First National Bank of Los Angeles, 320
Seed grain purchases, 216
Service division, mortgage-loan, 206–7
Sewall, Senator William J., 126

Shanks, Carrol M., 273–75, 282, 289, 300; appearance before Celler Committee, 304–5; belief in common man, 334; education, 273–74; elected president of Prudential, 275; legal experience, 274; letter to a future leader, 324; new concept of welfare state, 342–43; reorganization of ordinary department by, 285–88; statement of Prudential aims and philosophy, 333–43; Stedman calls on, 252; work for decentralization, 318–330; work for tax relief, 259–60
Shanks, Martha Taylor, 274
Sheffield Scientific School, 42
Shelton, James E. (president of Security-First National Bank of Los Angeles), 320
Shepherd, Pearce, 322
Sickness benefits, 70–71, 74
Singer Sewing Machine Company, 144
Slavery, 24
Slogan, Prudential, 120; first use of, 346
Smith, Senator James, Jr., 165
Smith, Joe, 236
Smith, Sylvester C., Jr., 259, 312
Smith's Concert Hall, New Haven, 25
Snake Hill, 120
Snyder-Gray case, 235
Social security, 340
Somerset County, N.J., 142
South Amboy explosion, 238
South Market Street, Newark, 5
Southard, Dr. Lott, 8
Southwestern home office, 329
Spectator, The, 32
Speer, George, 284
S.S. Eastland, capsizing of, 177
S.S. General Slocum, burning of, 176–77
S.S. Idaho, 60

S.S. *Mont Blanc,* explosion of, 177
S.S. *Noronic,* burning of, 238
S.S. *Parthia,* 61
S.S. *Titanic,* sinking of, 177
State Bank, Newark, 36, 45, 53
Statue of Liberty, 99
Stedman, John W.: leader in Prudential's fight against depression, 213; meeting with Shanks, 252; organizer of bond department, 297–98; witness at TNEC investigation, 263
Stewart, Harold M., 287; modernization of agency forces by, 282
Stimson, Henry L. (Secretary of War), 269
Stockholders, demands of, 122, 125–26, 149
Stockholders' suit, 149–50, 254–56
Stokes, Edward Caspar (governor of New Jersey), 198
Stone, Caleb, 298
Stoutenburgh and Company, 55
Strategic Bombing Survey, 269–72; tabulation of information by Prudential, 272
Strikes, 173
Stryker, Josiah, 255
Sunday Mercury, New York, 88
Supreme Court of New Jersey, 166
Supreme Court of the United States, 228
Surplus, problem of, 121–27, 133–35, 149
Surplus capital, flow of, 301–2
Survey Research Center, 309
Sutphen, Henry, 263; head of Prudential field agencies, 282

Taft, William H., 156
Taft-Hartley Act, 229
Tasney, Fred W., 198, 283
Tatlock, H. Woodruff, 313

Taxation, of insurance companies, 257–60; in New Jersey, 257; in other states, 258
Telephone, first Prudential installation of, 109–10; long-distance service, 99
Temple Mills, Me., 18–20
Temporary National Economic Committee investigation, 261–63
Terre Haute, Ind., 172
Testimonials, early use of, 57–58
Texas, industrial expansion of, 302
Textile mills, Southern, 301
Third Presbyterian Church, Newark, 155
Thompson, Rev., Henry P., 143
Thompson Agency, J. Walter, 119
Thornton, George (first New York superintendent), 88
"Tin lizzies," 172, 183
Times, Los Angeles, 320
Times, New York, 50, 276
Tompkins, Judge Henry B., 149
Toronto, Ont., 327
Trade unionism, 100, 228–29
Training, of agents, 52–53, 282, 286–88; of Canadian head office staff, 322; of office personnel, 52, 321–22, 327–28; of Western home office staff, 322
Travelers Insurance Company, 32
Treasurers, Prudential, 352
Treasurer's department, Prudential, 313
Trenton office, Prudential, 80
True American, Trenton, 84
Twenty-fifth anniversary, Prudential, 346
Typewriter, first Prudential use of, 110

Unclaimed equities division, Prudential, 241
Union National Bank of Newark, 117

Unionization, of Prudential agents, 282–83

Unions, effect on group insurance, 228–29

United Office and Professional Workers of America, 283

United States Dispensatory, 10

United States Mutual Benefit Company, organization of, 33–34

United States Steel Corporation, 117, 147, 193

University of Michigan, 309

USO drive, 268

U.S.S. *Maine*, destruction of, 176

Van Syckel, Bennet (Justice of New Jersey Supreme Court), 164

Vice-presidents, Prudential, 351

Vincennes, Ind., 172

Volk, Harry J., 266, 272, 308; as head of Western home office, 319–25; war work with Prudential, 272

Volstead Act, 185

Voting lists, New Jersey absentee, 266

Waco, Texas, 274

Wages (1875), 14

"Walkie-talkie" project, 265

Wall Street, New York, 33, 99

Walnut Street, Newark, 96

Wanamaker, L. Rodman, 284

War Finance Committee of New Jersey, 268

War Loan Drive, Third, 268

War between the States, 8

Ward, Edgar B., 46, 65, 86, 105, 114, 138, 147, 163; investment assistant to Dryden, 104; opposition to ordinary insurance, 107

Ward, Elias, 39

Ward, Jacob E., 139, 296–97

Ward, Josiah, 8

Ward, Dr. Leslie D., 41, 45, 58–

59, 60, 61, 65, 66, 86, 87, 138, 151, 236, 246, 283; death, 155; first investor in Prudential, 39–41; first meeting with Dryden, 10–11; head of agency staff, 104, 281, 283; medical director of Prudential, 56; participation in Fidelity scheme, 127–28

Ward, Marcus, Jr., 46

Ward, Minnie Perry, 8

Ward and Son, A., 4

Ward's Pharmacy, 5–6

Warren Petroleum Company, 302

Waterbury, Conn., 211

Watson's, Newark, 55

Webb City, Mo., 172

Welfare program, employees', 339–40

Welfare state, new concept of, 342

Wells, Fargo Express Company, 22

West, growth of, 24

Western home office, 316–25; autonomy of, 320; formal opening, 324–25; growth of operations in, 325–26; jurisdiction of, 316, 318; laying of cornerstone for, 324; training of staff for, 322

Western home office in Newark, 322

Weston, Edward Payson, 3

Whitehead, John, 36–37

Whittaker, Edmund B., 227

Whitty, William, 45, 65, 86, 87

Widows and Orphans Friendly Society, 36–42, 95; amendment of charter, 41; amalgamation with Prudential Friendly Society, 46; organization of, 36–38

Wilkinson, Elias, 45, 65, 86, 95

Wilkinson, Gaddis and Company, 45

William Street, New York, 33

Williams, George, 93, 129
Wilshire Boulevard, Los Angeles, 316, 319
Wilson, Lee, 296
Winnett, P. G. (chairman of board, Bullock's, Inc.), 320
Winnipeg, Man., 173
Woodruff, Archibald M., 204
Worcester, Mass., 21, 24, 25
World War I, 178–79
World War II, 238–39, 242–43; effects of, 290–91; military service by Prudential employees, 347; Prudential assignments in, 264–67, 272; volunteer work by Prudential employees, 265
Wright, Elizur, 32

Yale College, 22, 25–29, 106, 115; Sheffield Scientific School, 42
Yates, Henry, 41, 46, 65, 86, 87, 107
Young Men's Christian Association, 178